Mark Rothko

Break into the Light

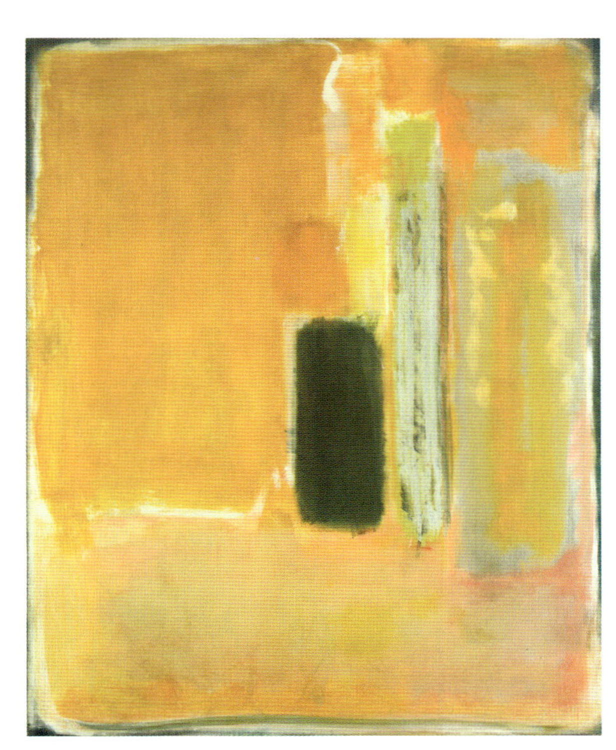

Publisher and Creative Director: Nick Wells
Commissioning Editor: Polly Prior
Senior Project Editor & Picture Research: Catherine Taylor
Art Director: Mike Spender
Copy Editor: Karen Fitzpatrick

FLAME TREE PUBLISHING

6 Melbray Mews
Fulham, London SW6 3NS
United Kingdom

www.flametreepublishing.com

First published 2016

16 18 20 19 17
1 3 5 7 9 10 8 6 4 2

© 2016 Flame Tree Publishing Ltd

ISBN 978-1-78361-999-3

Every effort has been made to contact image copyright holders. We apologize in advance for any omissions and would be pleased to insert the appropriate acknowledgement in subsequent editions of this publication.

A CIP record for this book is available from the British Library upon request.

Printed in China

Mark Rothko
Break into the Light

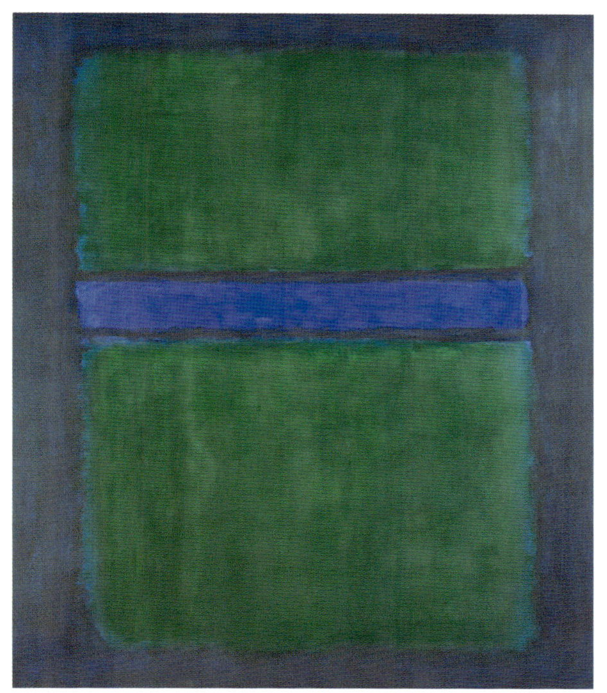

Susan Grange

FLAME TREE
PUBLISHING

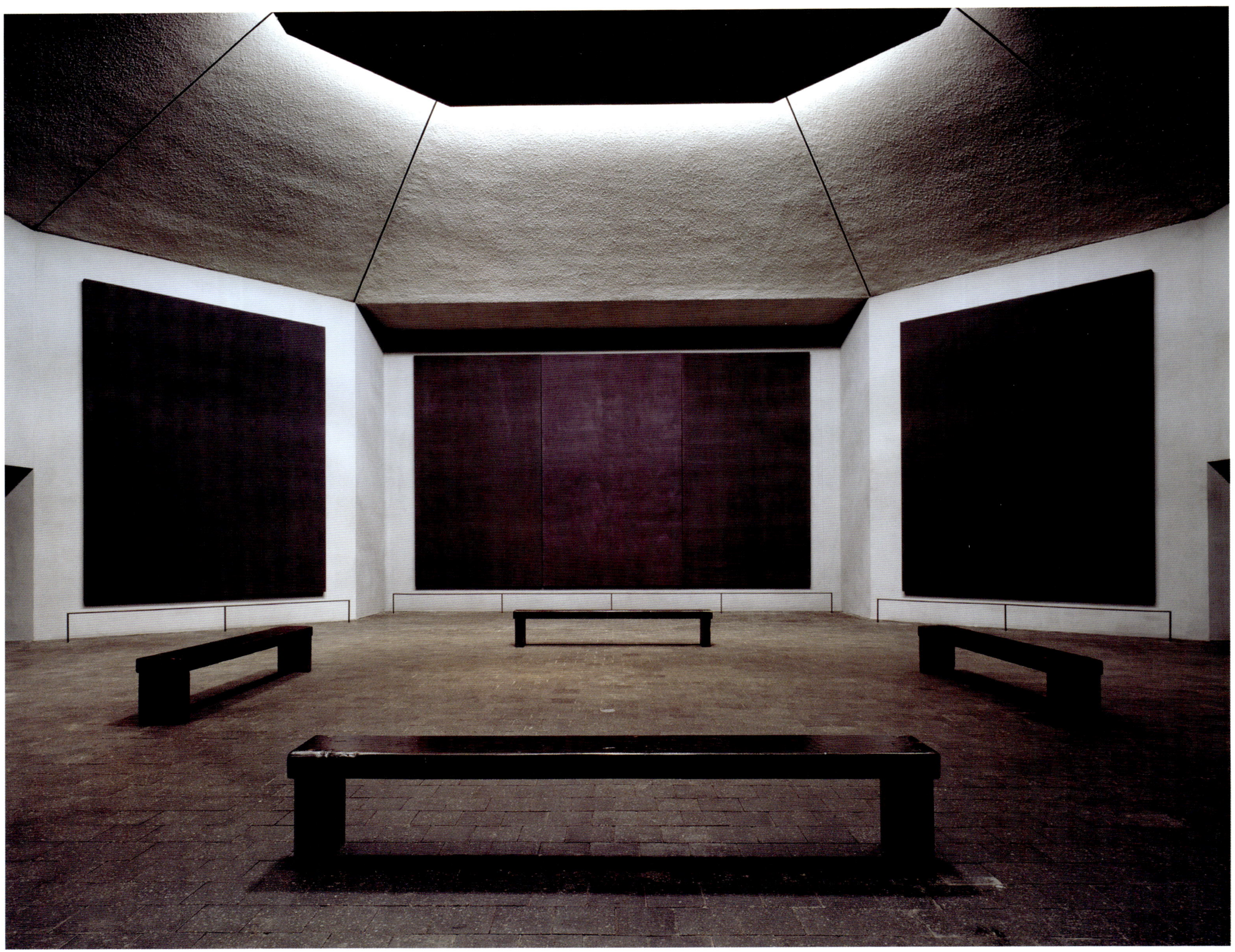

contents

prelude

Mark Rothko (1903–70) was one of a dynamic group of American artists who in the immediate post-Second-World-War era created a new expression of genuine American art. This group of artists rejected what they saw as the conservative nature of the popular scenes of American landscape and the depiction of 'local colour' in scenes of American life. Through experimentation, dynamic intellectual interaction between themselves and confrontation with the prevailing attitudes of the New York galleries, the American Abstract Expressionists, as they came to be called, changed the face of American art.

Abstract expressionism was not so much a style, but more of a general approach shared by a number of artists. This loose grouping of artists did not plan an organized art movement, but rather aimed to express their own feelings in a spontaneous and free way. Scenes of war-torn Europe had shocked the American public; in and around New York in particular, artists were seeking to express their own feelings and the feelings of the nation about the state of the world. This was to be done not by depicting the world as they saw it, but rather by using themes and stories, sometimes using totally abstract means and by harnessing the application of paint and colour to manifest what they felt.

Action and Reflection

Abstract expressionism essentially developed into two main strands, the first of which has been called 'action painting'. The artist would work spontaneously and intuitively, dripping and swirling paint on the canvas without forethought or planning, using large, sweeping energetic movements. Among the artists who became known for this style were Jackson Pollock (1912–56), Willem de Kooning (1904–97) and Franz Kline (1910–62). Rothko was to be in the vanguard and eventually the most important and renowned practitioner of the other main strand of abstract expressionism, which came to be called Colour Field Painting. This was essentially the covering of large areas of a painting with single colour fields, with the aim of inspiring an emotional and even a contemplative response in the viewer. Among other artists known for this approach were Clyfford Still (1904–80) and Barnett Newman (1905–70).

The Human Condition

Whether the artists were action orientated or more passively contemplative in their aims, they were all engaged in fierce intellectual and philosophical debate about the meaning and purpose of art and the essence of human existence. In particular, they drew on the ideas of Carl Jung (1875–1961), in the realms of memory, dreams and the make-up of the human individual, in order to express their inner feelings in a post-war world of turmoil.

With his piercing intellect and philosophical bent, Rothko played a major part in the development of this movement. The classic paintings for which Rothko is best known draw the viewer in by the colourful power of an inner light. Rothko, however, denied being a colourist painter. For him, the most important thing was that there should be a relationship between the viewer and the painting, resulting in an emotional experience. He also insisted he wasn't simply an abstract painter; his works, he said, were about the essence of the human condition, the tragedy and ecstasy of life.

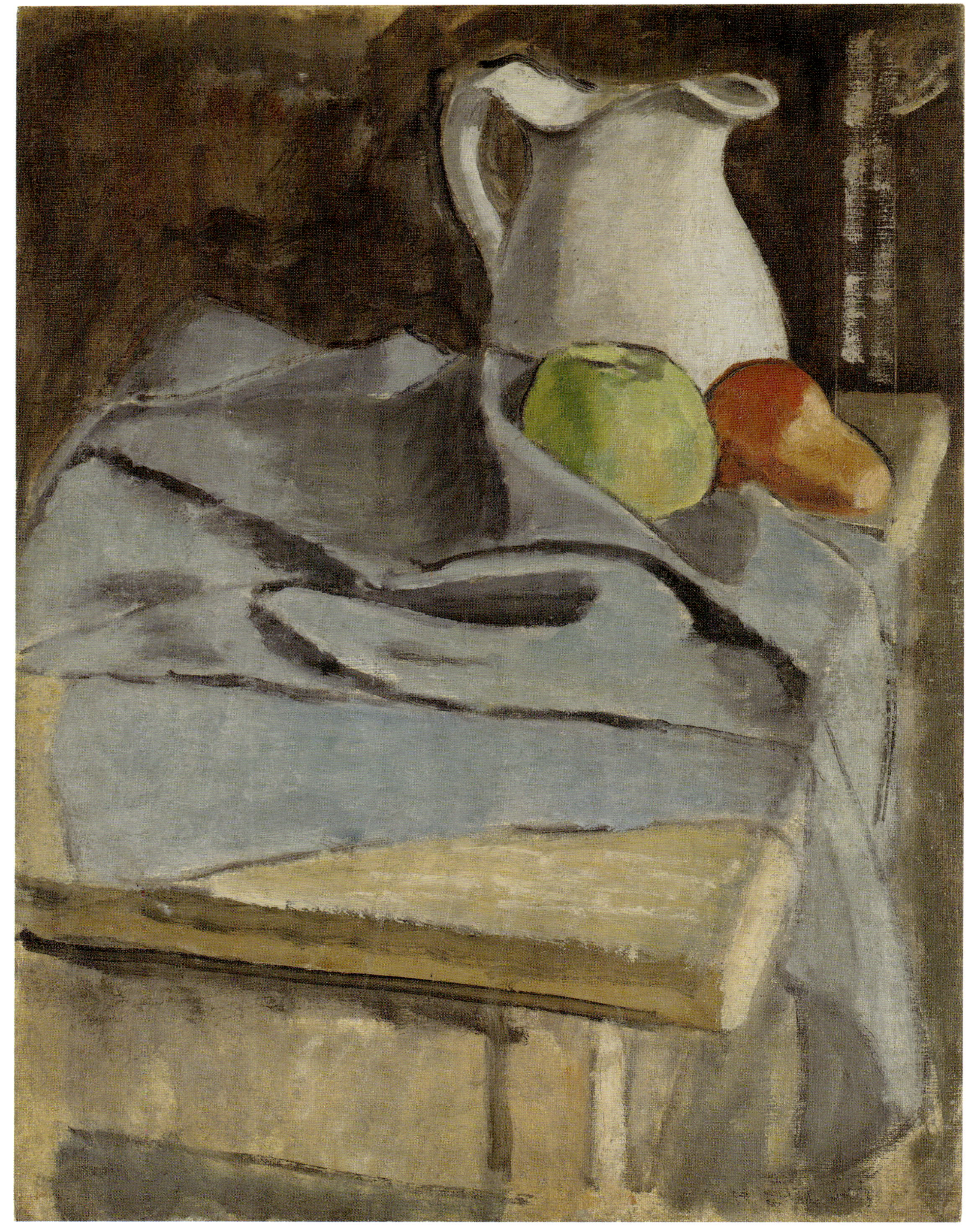

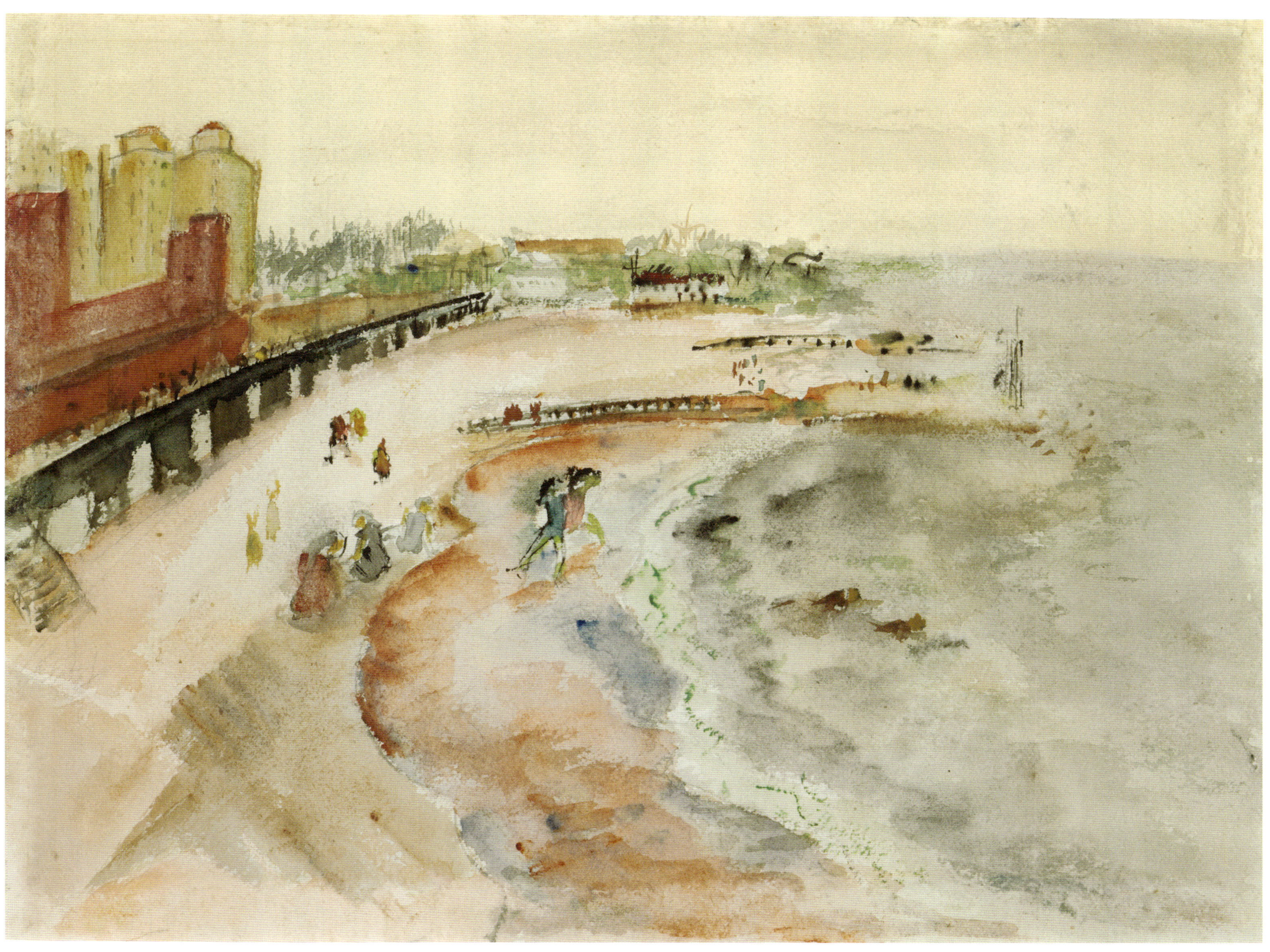

Beginnings

Marcus Rothkowitz was born on 25 September 1903 into a Jewish family in Dvinsk in Tsarist Russia, now Daugavpils in Latvia. Dvinsk was situated in what was known as the Pale of Settlement, the area of the Russian Empire where, from the late eighteenth century to the fall of the Russian Empire in 1917, Jews were required to live and work. Dvinsk was a busy, bustling city where Jews, who were not allowed to own land, were frequently to be found in business and trade.

Rothko's father Jacob (1859–1914) had attended the university in Vilnius and had become a pharmacist; he had married Anna Goldin (1870–1948) in 1896. Marcus was a late addition to the family, with a sister, Sonia, 13 years of age, and two brothers: Moises, 10 and Albert, eight. Jacob provided a steady income for the family, but his interests appeared to have lain not in his religious heritage, but in intellectual and political pursuits. In later life, Rothko would say: 'My father was a militant social democrat. He was profoundly Marxist and violently anti-religious, partly because in Dvinsk ... the Orthodox Jews were a repressive majority.'

It is said that Jacob loved reading, as did the whole family, and that their home contained over 300 books. Liberal and open-minded Jacob ensured that his three older children received a secular education; Sonia attended a Russian school, Moises and Albert a secular Jewish school. But for Marcus things would be different.

The Talmud Torah

After Marcus's birth, his father experienced something of a personal religious revival and began regular attendance at one of the numerous synagogues in the town. This may have been due in part to the spread of violence against Jewish communities in Russia, when pogroms, organized attacks and massacres began to increase in number. As it happened, Dvinsk did not have to bear the onslaught of any pogroms, but the fear of them was real enough. The Cossacks, cavalry groups of warrior-peasants who were loyal to the Tsar, would regularly break up any gatherings thought to be purveying revolutionary thoughts and actions. In this way, Marcus spent his early years in an atmosphere of fear.

Jacob's reconnection with his religious roots led him to send Marcus, from the age of four to the age of 10 to a strict Jewish school – the Talmud Torah. These schools were primary schools for boys where the pupils were given their elementary education in Hebrew, and where they studied the Scriptures, in particular the first five books of the Old Testament, known as the Pentateuch, and the Talmud, the collection of ancient Rabbinic writings which forms the basis of religious authority in Orthodox Judaism. Marcus would be dressed totally in black and, in a strict atmosphere, learned Hebrew and studied prayer books, religious law and commentaries.

The Talmud Torahs prided themselves on their academic discipline and intellectual training. Annie Cohen-Solal, in her biography of Rothko, writes that, 'This complex relationship with the Talmud is in fact a key to understanding the life and work of Mark Rothko.' This early disciplined intellectual training of study and commentary shaped the life and thought processes of its young charges.

The USA

The increase of pogroms and the threat of his two older sons being drafted into the Russian army seem to have spurred Jacob on to consider a change for his family. Other relatives had made a successful move to the United States a number of years earlier, and when Marcus was seven, his father followed their example. When he was nine, his brothers left Russia to join their father and when he was 10, his mother and his sister, now 23 and a qualified dentist, took him to join the rest of the family in America. From their comfortable lifestyle in Russia, they went to an unknown future. Rothko was to say in later life, 'I was never able to forgive this transplantation to a land where I never felt entirely at home.'

On arrival in America, the family stayed briefly with relatives in New Haven and then began their journey to join their father and brothers in Portland, Oregon. This journey took two weeks and around their necks they wore signs that said they spoke no English. The relatives living in Portland had built a wooden house for the family and welcomed them with open arms. Unfortunately, Jacob, who had been working at a clothing shop, which belonged to his brother, was to die seven months after their arriva .

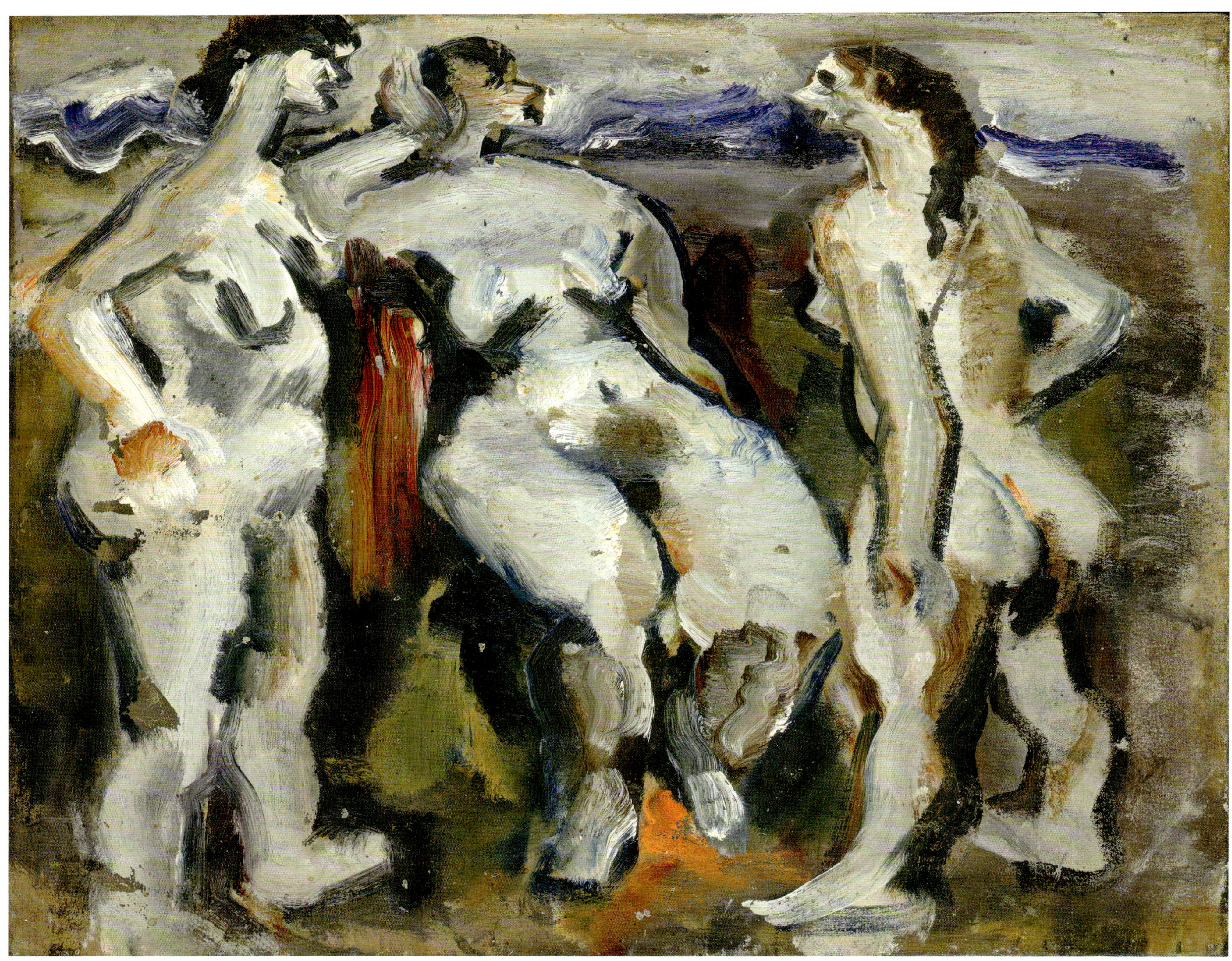

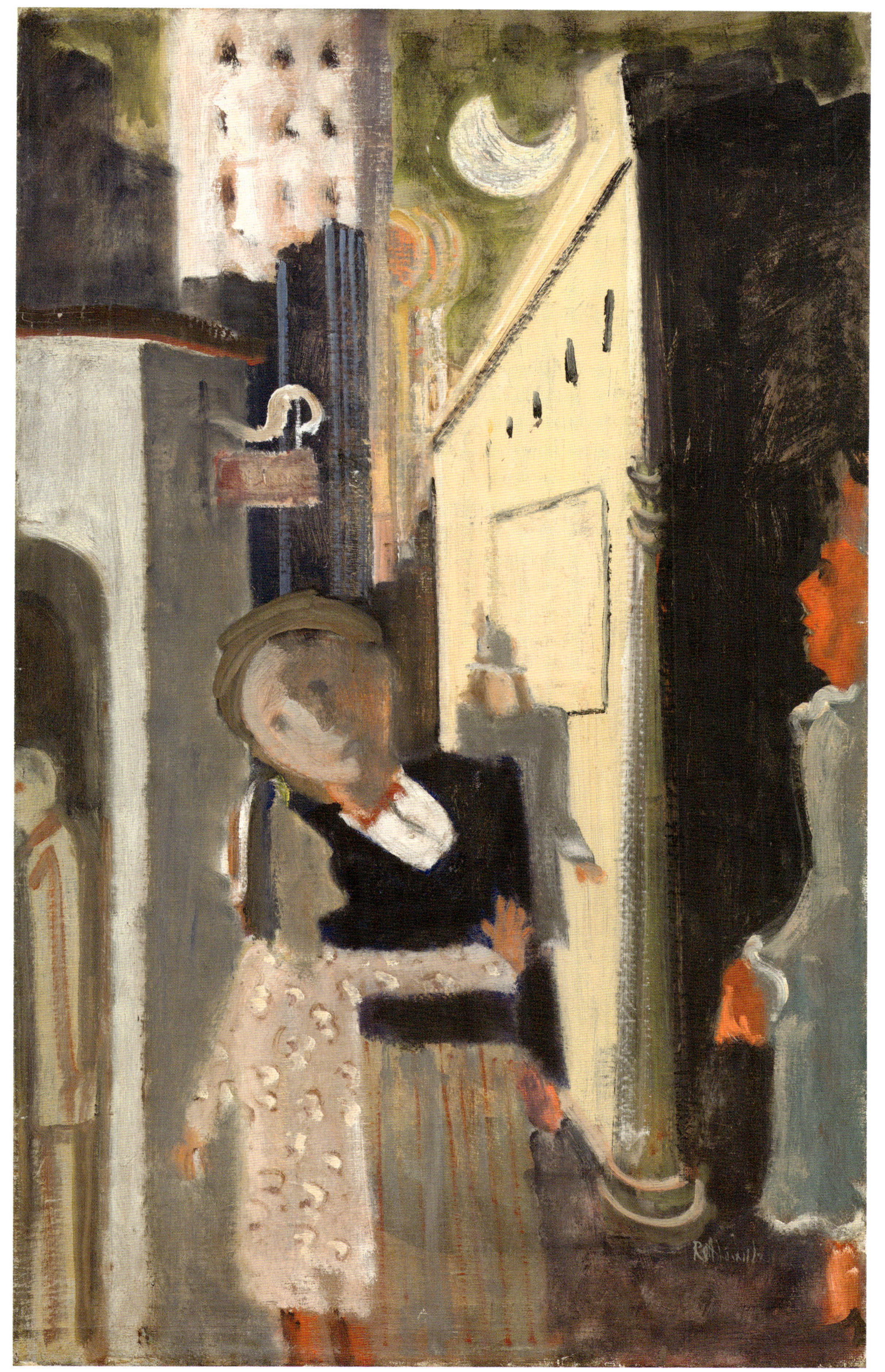

Marcus went to the local elementary school in 1913, where he quickly made progress in learning English. The following year, he skipped a grade and after six months moved up two classes, skipping another grade. He then finished the last four years in three years. The highly intelligent and motivated Marcus then went on to Lincoln High School and at the age of 17, graduated with excellent grades. He does not seem to have been particularly inclined towards art, but developed a love of classical music and also immersed himself in the Greek tragedies, opting to take an elective in drama. His academic talent and prowess was rewarded by winning a scholarship to the prestigious Yale University in New Haven, Connecticut.

Yale: Another World

In 1921, Rothko began his studies at Yale, majoring in the humanities, although it appears that he did not elect to take any courses relating to art. The community at Yale was very different to what he was used to. In Portland, he had been part of a supportive network of Jewish immigrants; at Yale, he was part of a minority among wealthy, upper-class Christians. Anti-Semitism was common and, as a scholarship student, he had to live off campus, which further enforced the sense of being an outsider.

He appears to have had a low estimate of many of his fellow students' abilities and commitment to their studies. These thoughts and feelings were expressed by him and some of his fellows in a newspaper that Rothko founded, called the ***Yale Saturday Evening Pest***. This publication gave him the opportunity, mostly through anonymous articles, to develop his skills in polemical writing and to vent his frustration and resentments. These skills would be useful later when he came to write about his thoughts on the prevailing culture of the New York galleries and museums.

Despite original assurances, for the second year of his studies at Yale, he was told that his scholarship was being changed to a loan. He took a part-time job and ate mostly with his New Haven relatives, but he began to lose interest in his studies and his results were lower than expected. In the autumn of 1923, he decided to leave without graduating.

A Time of Searching

Now Rothko was left without any clear idea of what he wanted to do or where he wanted to go. Drifting between New York and Portland, it seems that his first consideration was a career in the theatre. On one trip back to Portland, in between his forays into the world of art, he enrolled in a theatre group led by Josephine Dillon, the first wife of the actor Clark Gable. In 1925, he applied for, but did not get, a scholarship with the American Laboratory Theater in New York. This seems to have put paid to his idea of an acting career, although in later life he would claim that he was a better actor than Gable.

In between his acting trials, he had been dabbling with the idea of developing his artistic skills. He would say that the idea of becoming an artist first came to him when he visited the Art Students League in New York with a friend who was a student there. He said: 'I knew then that this would be my life.' In January 1924 he enrolled on a course there to study anatomy and drawing. After this, he enrolled at the New York School of Design and took a class taught by Arshile Gorky (1904–48), who lectured on the techniques of the Old Masters, and is frequently considered to be one of the most influential twentieth-century American painters.

Max Weber

Undoubtedly one of Rothko's most formative experiences was when, in October 1925, he enrolled in the still-life class of Max Weber (1881–1961) at the Art Students League. Like Rothko, Weber, although 12 years his senior, was a Russian-born Jew who had emigrated to the States, arriving in 1891, like Rothko at the age of 10.

In 1905, he moved to Paris, where for two years he studied with the French painter Henri Matisse (1869–1954). Matisse focused much of his teaching at this period on the works of Paul Cézanne (1839–1906), the Post-Impressionist painter whose works are frequently considered to have bridged the passage from late-nineteenth-century Impressionism and early-twentieth-century Cubism. Cubism frequently used semi-geometrical forms, showing things from different viewpoints to represent the whole.

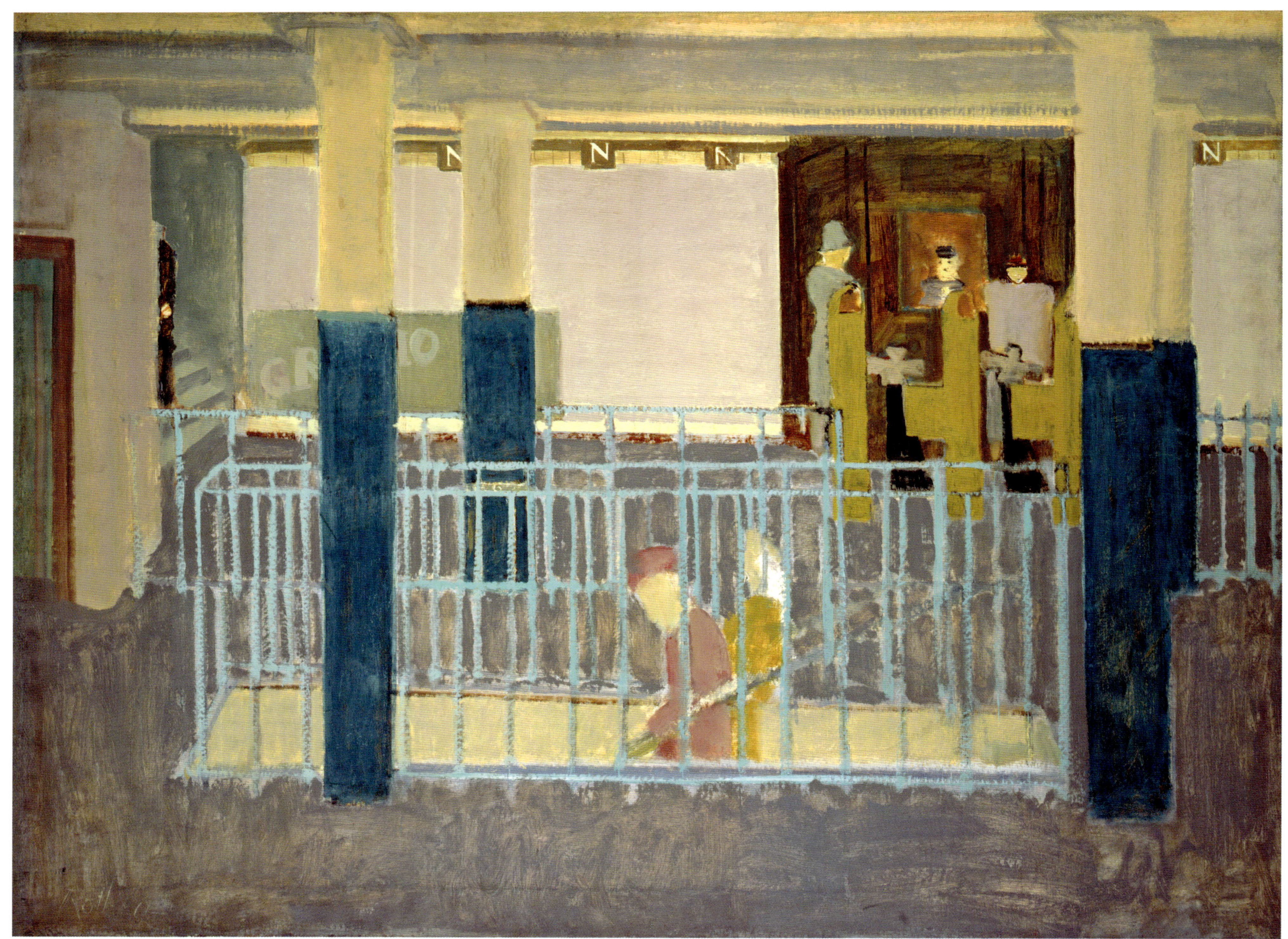

N
N
N
N

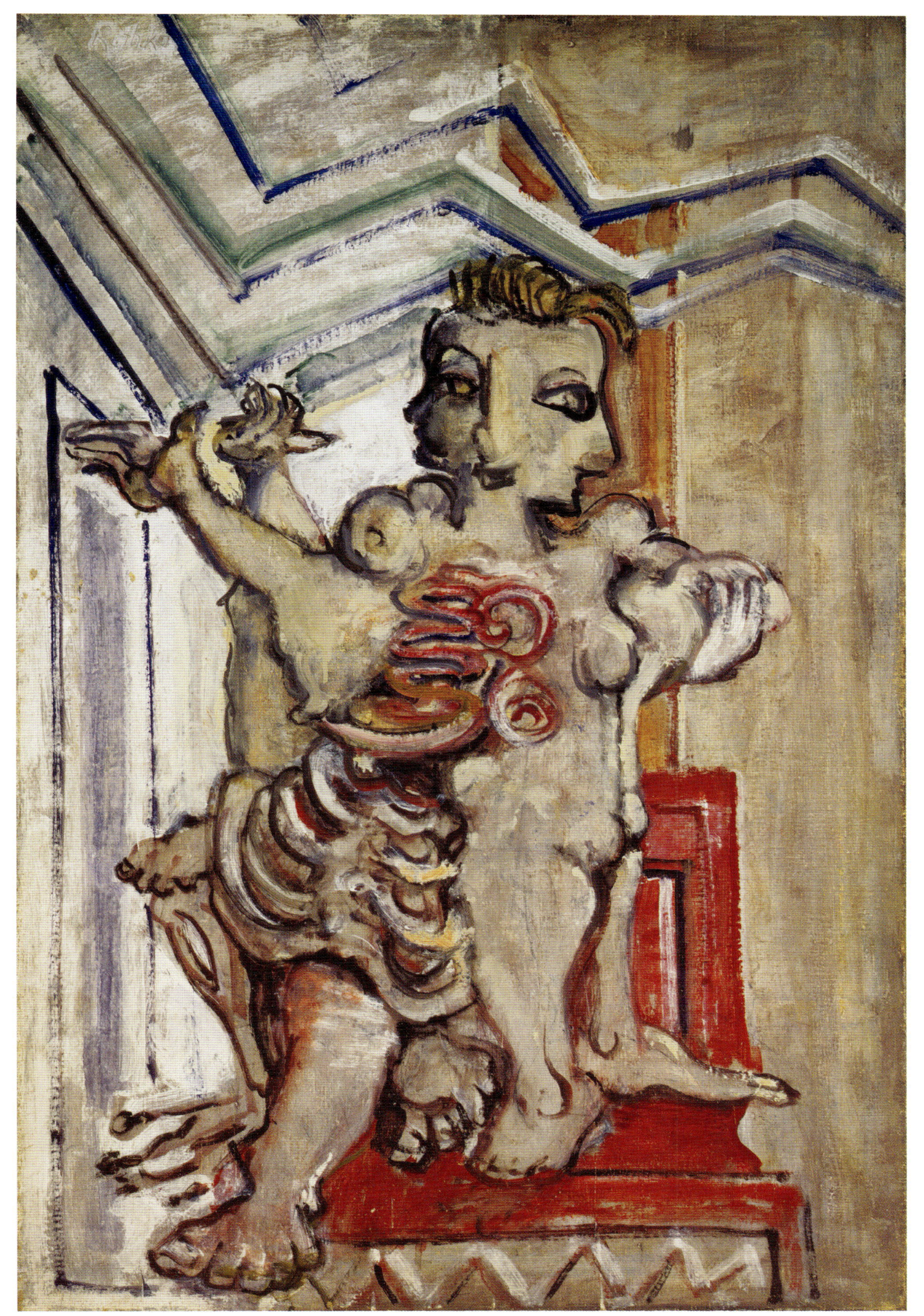

On his return to New York in 1910, Weber was working in a Cubist style, but by the time Rothko began to study with him, while encouraging his students to study Cézanne's works, he had moved on to working in an expressionistic style, attempting to express his own vision, through an interpretation of Cézanne's style. According to Weber's ***Essays on Art***, he stresses that a painting needs to be more than simply an arrangement of form and colour, but that it should have significant meaning and a spiritual dimension. In his teachings, he underlined the emotional power of art, even stating that the artwork was inhabited by the divine spirit; even further, he emphasized the metaphysical nature of art as revelation and also as prophecy.

Although Rothko only studied under Weber for six months, it is likely that these teachings were highly influential on his thinking and philosophy. The intellectual challenge of Weber's approach no doubt resonated with the young intellectual Rothko. The emotional aspect of Weber's teachings, together with his teaching on the transcendental nature of the finished artwork, also appear to have been destined to shape the philosophy of his young student.

Early Work

In 1928, some of Rothko's works were included in a group exhibition at the Opportunity Gallery in New York, a small gallery subsidized by the city authorities to promote the work of young artists. He also did some work in advertising and took on a commission from Lewis Browne, a retired rabbi from Portland who had become an established author, who hired him to illustrate ***The Graphic Bible*** with maps and drawings. Rothko's work for the bible project, studying images of ancient styles of design and ornament, was to be useful in his later mythological works.

In 1929, a new chapter opened for Rothko when he began a teaching career at a Jewish school in Brooklyn, where he was to stay for over 20 years. He was the first art teacher at the school and gave lessons twice a week in painting and working with clay. The school was embracing a more liberal approach, allowing children to develop their natural talents rather than learning facts – quite a contrast to the Talmud Torah.

Rothko appears to have enjoyed this spontaneous approach allied to the simplicity and enthusiasm of his young charges. In 1934, he published an article entitled 'New Training for Future Artists and Art Lovers' in the ***Brooklyn-Jewish Center Review***. He noted the instinctive freedom children have in their art, without feeling the need to keep to any rules or tradition. This helped to focus more on the basic elements of art and created a more accessible emotional impact.

Elsewhere, he noted the freedom children had to dispense with perspective and sense of space, and in some of his earlier works, Rothko did the same by placing large figures in cramped and confined spaces. He even shared his first solo exhibition in 1933 at the Portland Museum of Art with some works produced by the children. Most of his works on display were watercolours of the landscape of woods and mountains around Portland, many inspired by Cézanne.

Avery and Edith

Around 1932, Rothko got to know the American artist Milton Avery (1885–1965), who was known as 'the American Matisse'. Avery was of a steady, calm nature, in contrast to the restless and searching Rothko, and worked regular long hours in his studio. Avery's works were 'full of poetry and light', Rothko was to say in later life.

Rothko was a frequent visitor at Avery's apartment in New York, where they arranged literary gatherings. A circle of like-minded artists, including Adolph Gottlieb (1903–74), who became a close friend of Rothko, gathered round Avery. Rothko, Gottlieb and Avery spent a number of summers together at Lake George in New York State, painting during the day and in discussions at night.

In 1932 at the Lake George campsite, Rothko met the 19-year-old Edith Sacher, a creative young jewellery maker. It seems that Edith was somewhat reluctant to begin with, but the couple married in November that year. Their bohemian lifestyle in New York led to financial difficulties, which was to cause problems later on. Marcus was not materialistic or looking to make large sums of money; Edith was a hard worker and her jewellery business eventually became very successful and prospered. This seems to

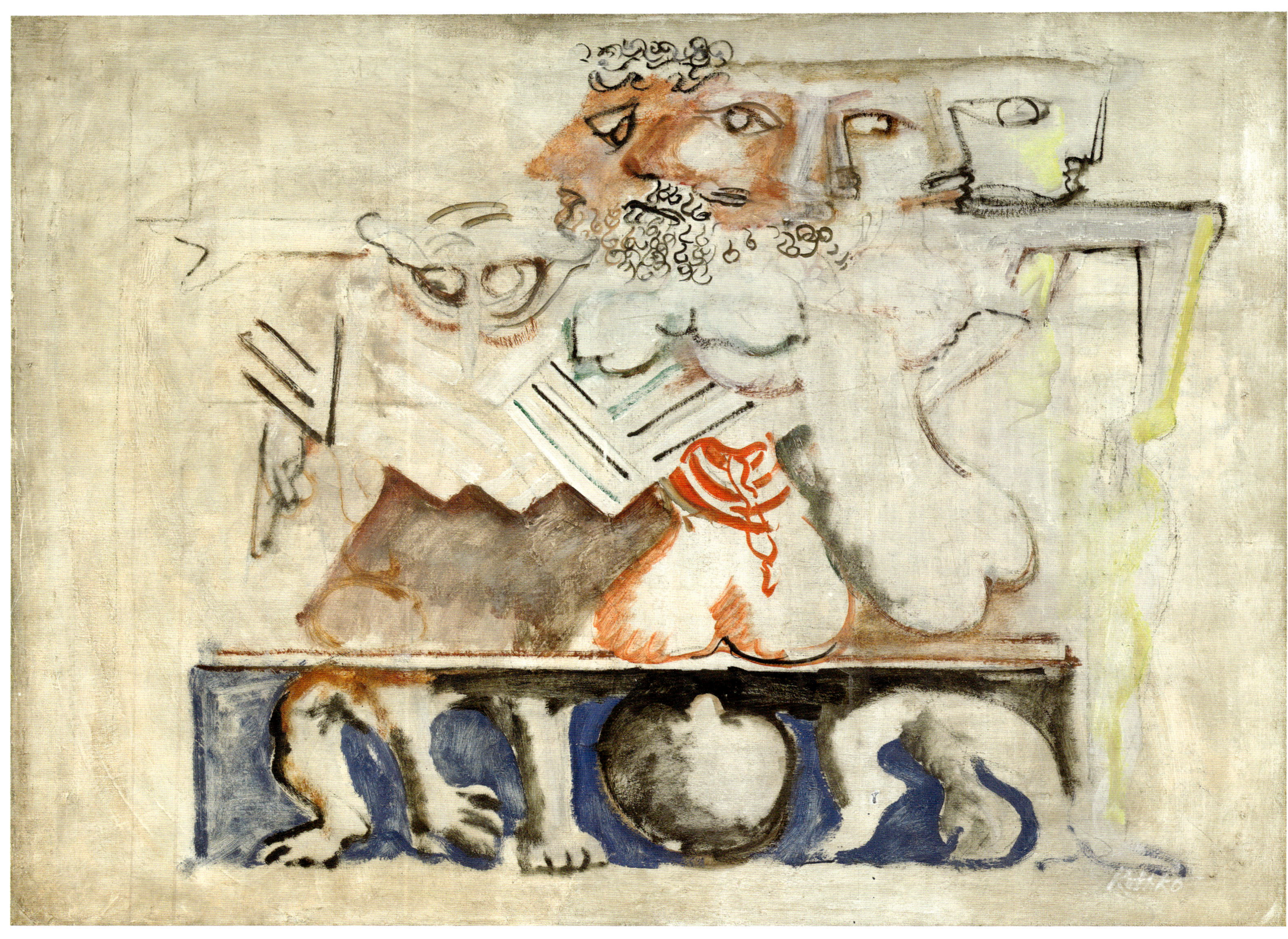

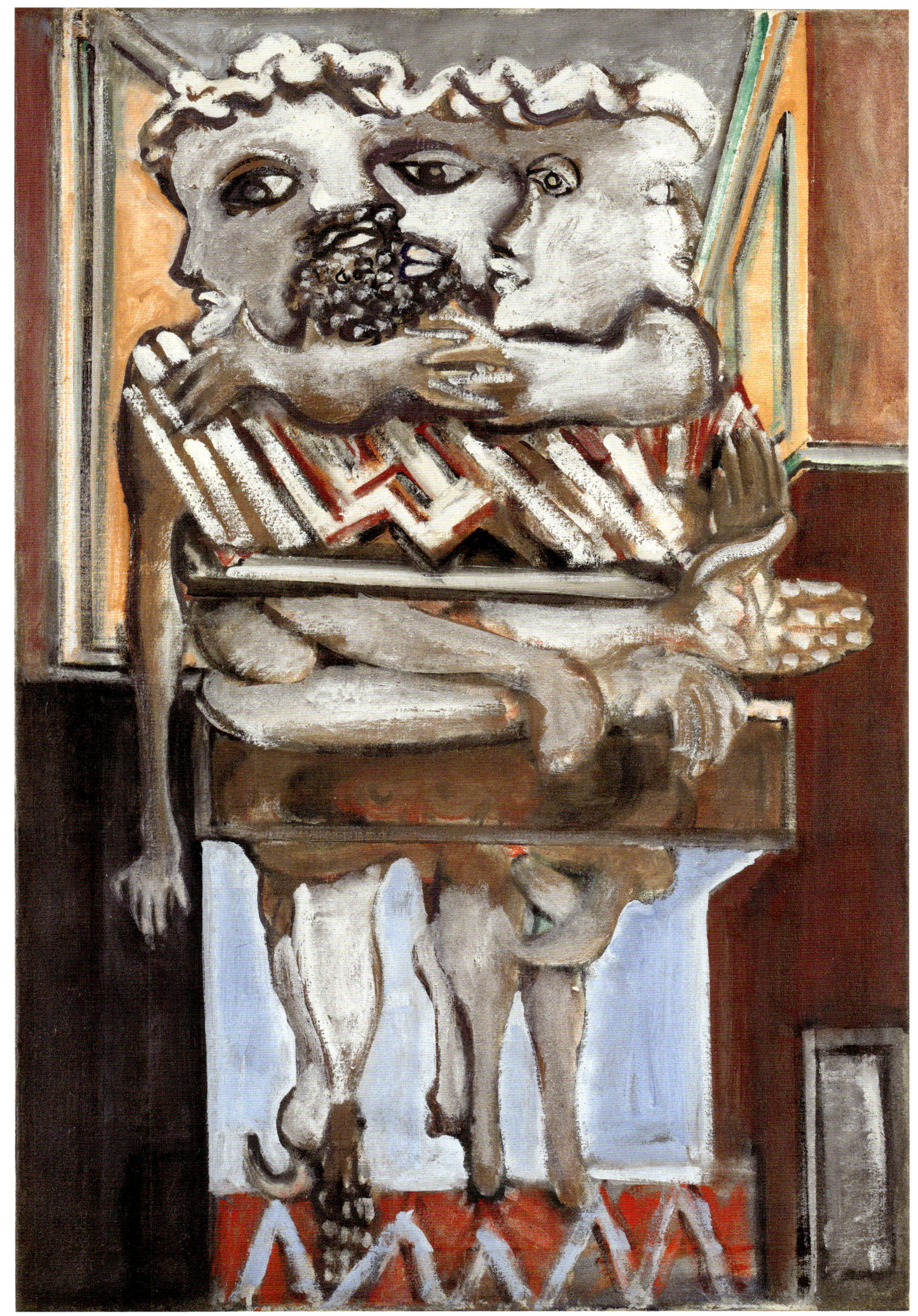

have caused difficulties between the couple, seemingly highlighting Rothko's ambivalent approach to money and material goods and Edith's desire to succeed.

The Ten

In 1935, a group of artists, including Rothko and Gottlieb, formed 'The Ten'. The group aimed to promote the work of more avant-garde artists, such as themselves, as opposed to the artists of American regional and scene painting, which were displayed by the major galleries. One of their aims was to open a new gallery with more progressive ideas, where they could organize the exhibitions themselves. They achieved this aim and the Municipal Art Gallery opened in 1936.

The Ten worked in a variety of styles from expressionism to geometric abstraction, but they were bound together in their fight against what they saw as American provincialism. In 1936, the group was invited to hold an exhibition in Paris. Already Rothko was attracting attention for his use of colour; a French review noted that his works displayed 'an authentic coloristic value.'

In 1938, they mounted an exhibition titled ***The Ten: Whitney Dissenters*** in a reference to the type of provincial works shown at the Whitney Gallery. This exhibition caught the attention of the press and initiated discussions in the newspapers about what constituted American art, challenging the viewpoint that it was simply about American local landscape and scenes of American life.

By 1939, the individual members of the group were beginning to branch out in different directions and the group was disbanded. Throughout this period, Rothko had continued to study in detail the great collections of the Old Masters in the New York galleries and museums. He was also to benefit from the exhibitions of modern art from abroad that were mounted by the galleries. In 1936, the Museum of Modern Art in New York put on two shows, ***Cubism and Abstract Art*** and ***Fantastic Art, Dada and Surrealism***, meaning that striving young artists were able to see some of the best examples of modern art without having to travel, and were able to study the style and approach of their European contemporaries.

Early Style

During the years from 1924 to 1940 Rothko's work was figurative, depicting landscapes, interiors, city scenes, still lifes and a series of subway scenes. His admiration for Cézanne was notable and he used a technique that Cézanne favoured to create depth in a painting, by creating overlapping layers without the need for the use of perspective. He used the same overlapping technique in his city scenes to create depth. From the late 1920s, his works were in an expressionistic style, urban scenes or dark interiors. People seem to be isolated and lonely, with echoes of the work that Edward Hopper (1882–1967) was doing at the time, depicting the alienation of the individual in the city. The atmosphere is heavy with anxiety and a sense of foreboding.

In his series of subway paintings from 1936–38, Rothko is clearly relishing the interplay of vertical and horizontal lines and the use of geometric design (*see* fig. 6, page 18). People become part of the architectural arrangement, losing their identity, cramped underground without fresh air. In his work, the subway becomes an underworld of homeless individuals alienated from each other. Rothko experimented with the theme of windows in some of his works, allowing him to experiment with issues of depth and projection. Paintings of huge distorted nudes, cramped in spaces that are too small for them, echo Picasso's work and form part of this early period (*see* fig. 4, page 14).

The influence of Avery can be discerned in paintings of the era, with single colour areas taking up more space, and forms becoming simpler. Under Avery's influence, Rothko's colour palette became noticeably lighter. A series of beach scenes in watercolour (*see* fig. 3, page 11) use large areas of a single colour and simplified forms. The use of colour to create spatial effects clearly interested the artists of Avery's circle, and Rothko experimented with the use of colour to make things appear to come nearer or to recede. He also painted a number of works on coloured construction paper, experimenting with the effects he could create. There are a few still lifes (*see* fig. 2 page 10) in his early work, but, even then, it seems that Rothko was showing a preference for living things that breathe and feel, and with which he could explore the inner life.

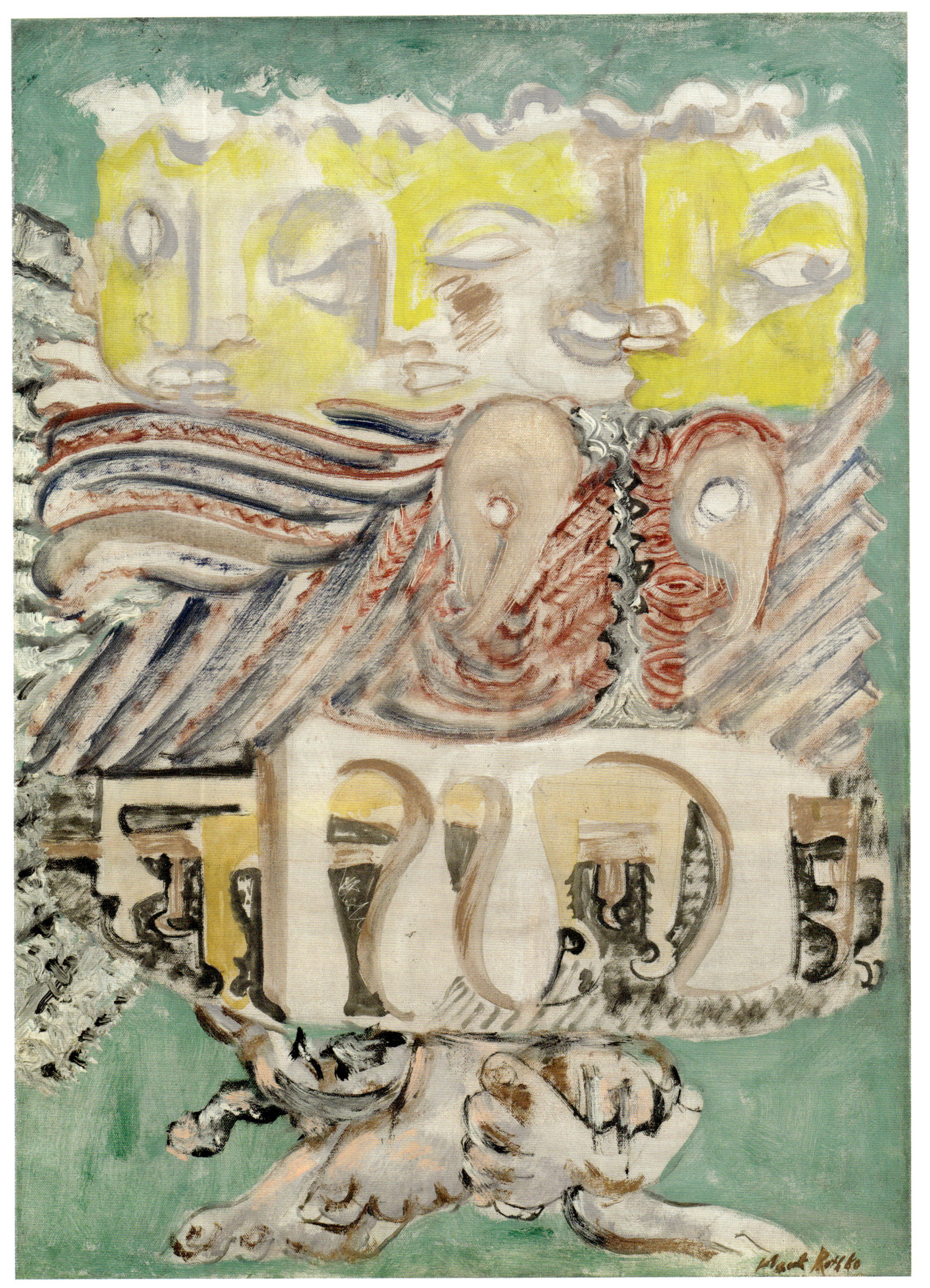

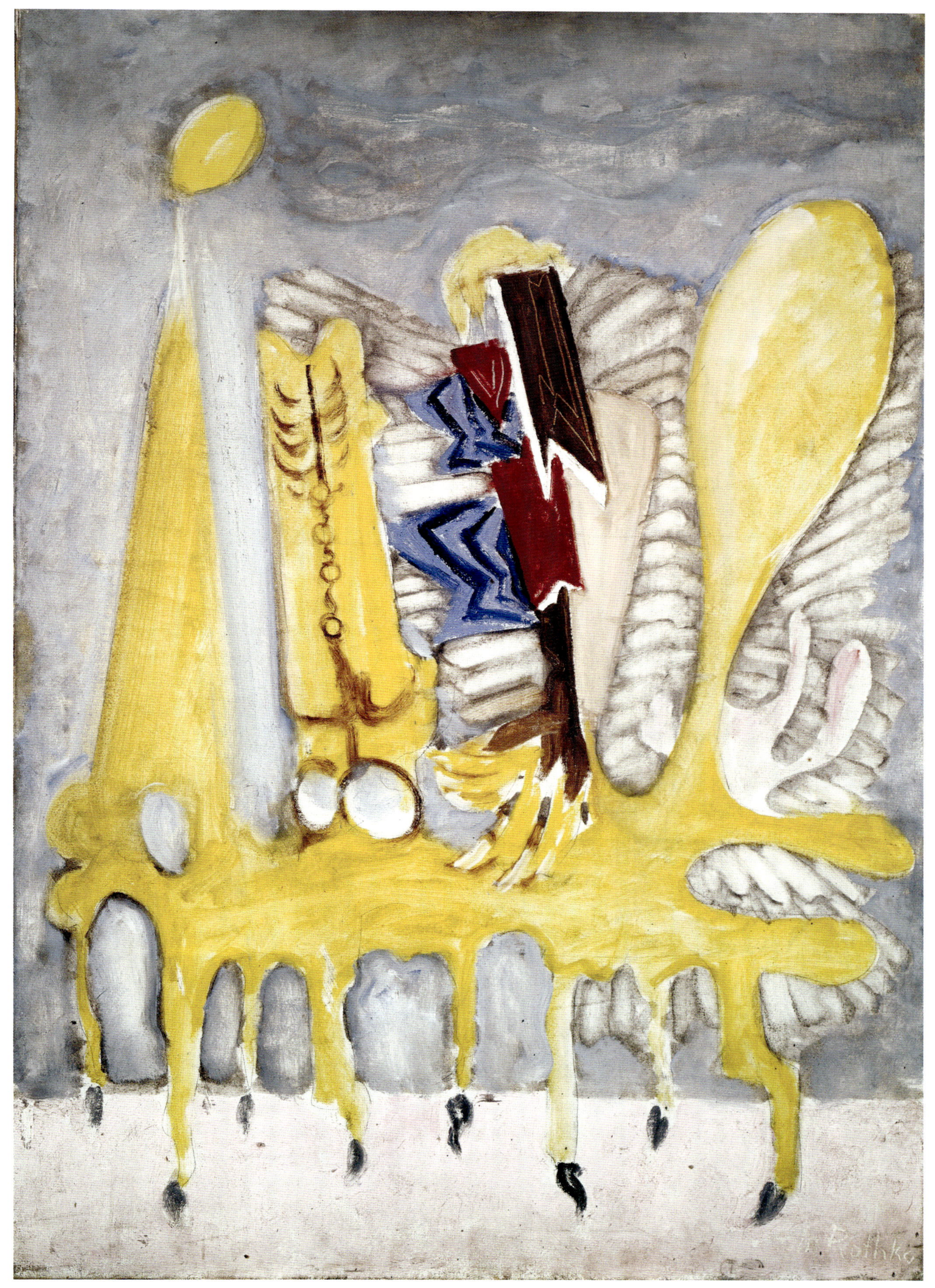

seeking expression

The turmoil of the Second World War created upheavals in society and stimulated questioning and heart-searching regarding the inner motivations and actions of man. Many artists felt that it was not possible to continue painting in the same vein as before the war. Speaking from an artist's perspective, Barnett Newman summed up the situation by saying: 'We felt the moral crisis of a world that was a battlefield … It was impossible to just keep painting like before – flowers, reclining nudes, or musicians playing the cello.'

Rothko, Gottlieb and others were involved in deep discussions as to what the subjects of art should be. Looking back beyond the history of the Renaissance and the Middle Ages, they found subject matter and primeval expression of man and his attempts to make sense of the world in legends and myths. This exploration of the ancient myths offered the opportunity to grapple with universal issues that face humankind. In a defence of his use of myth, Rothko wrote: 'Those who believe that the world today is less brutal and ungrateful than in these myths with their overwhelming primeval passions, are either unaware of the reality or they do not want to see it in art.'

This journey back in time, seeking answers to issues of the present, was not only experienced by artists: Cohen-Solal notes that at around the same time, Colombia University was offering a seminar on myth in the increasingly complex modern society, and also that a study of Jungian archetypes through Western literature by Joseph Campbell was published. A return to the roots of European civilization, and an exploration of its foundations through myth, was sought as enlightenment by historians, cultural commentators and writers, as well as by artists.

The Artist's Reality

Leading up to this period of searching for a new expression in his work, Rothko had felt that he needed to move on from realism (that is resembling the world of appearances), but appears to have been uncertain as to how best to express visually the stream of his thoughts and ideas. It seems that for a period of around a year, he painted little, if at all. This was a difficult time for him; disillusionment with the New York galleries, difficulties in his marriage and the seriousness of the unfolding events in Europe may all have contributed to the seemingly low ebb of his artistic creativity.

However, he took up his pen and wrote down his thoughts instead, probably around 1940–41. With his background of strict intellectual training at the Talmud Torah, followed by his education in the American system, up to and including his time at Yale, it was second nature for him to write essays and articles to put forward his ideas and to argue his points of view. At this time, he mentioned to his friends that he was writing a book, but his notes and essays were lost and hidden for years until, in 2004, they were found among papers in storage. These writings, left unrevised by the artist himself, give us a view of Rothko's philosophical ideas and beliefs at a pivotal time in his development and career. His son, Christopher, took on the task of editing them and arranging them in an order, and they were published under the title ***The Artist's Reality.***

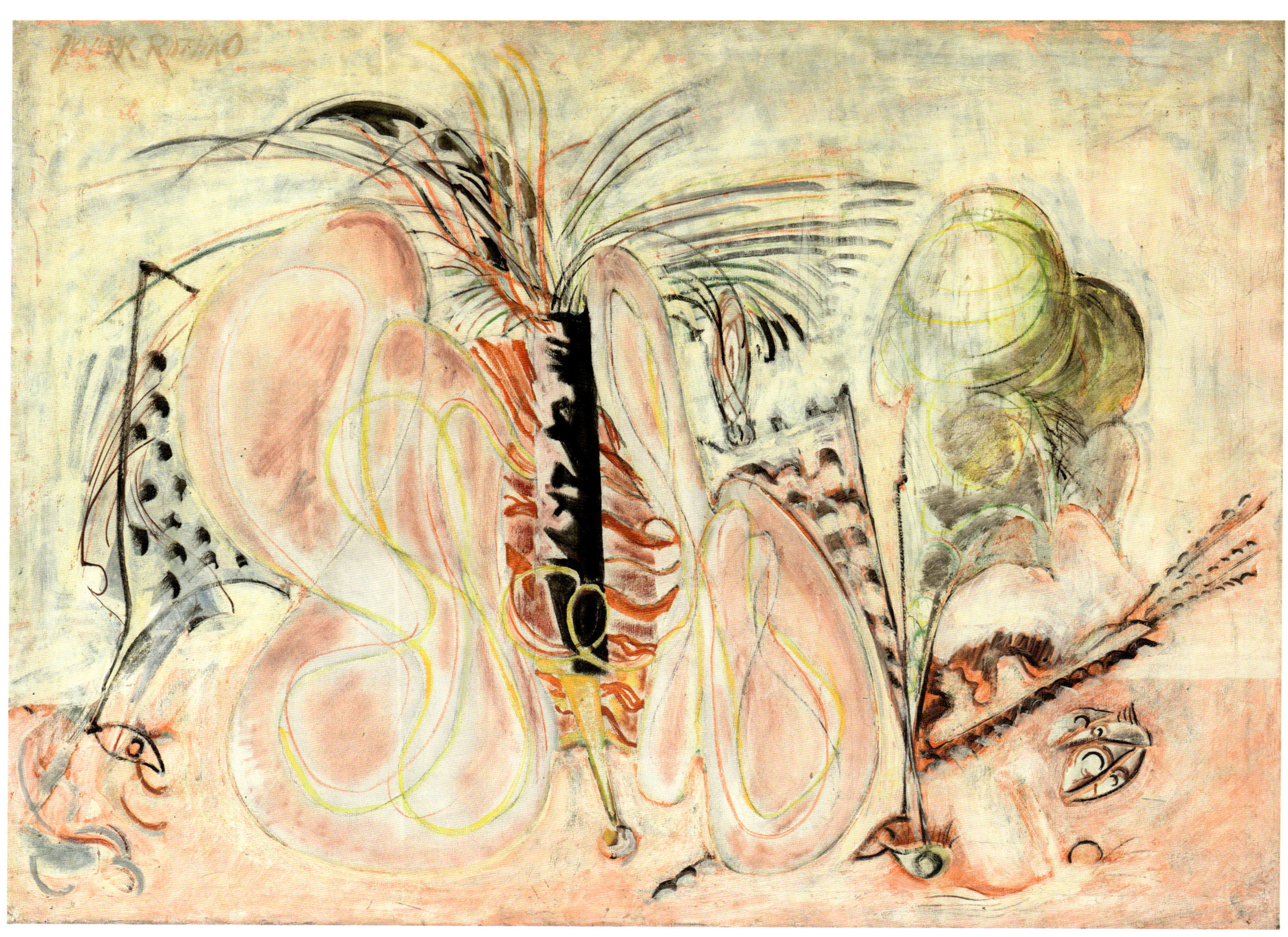

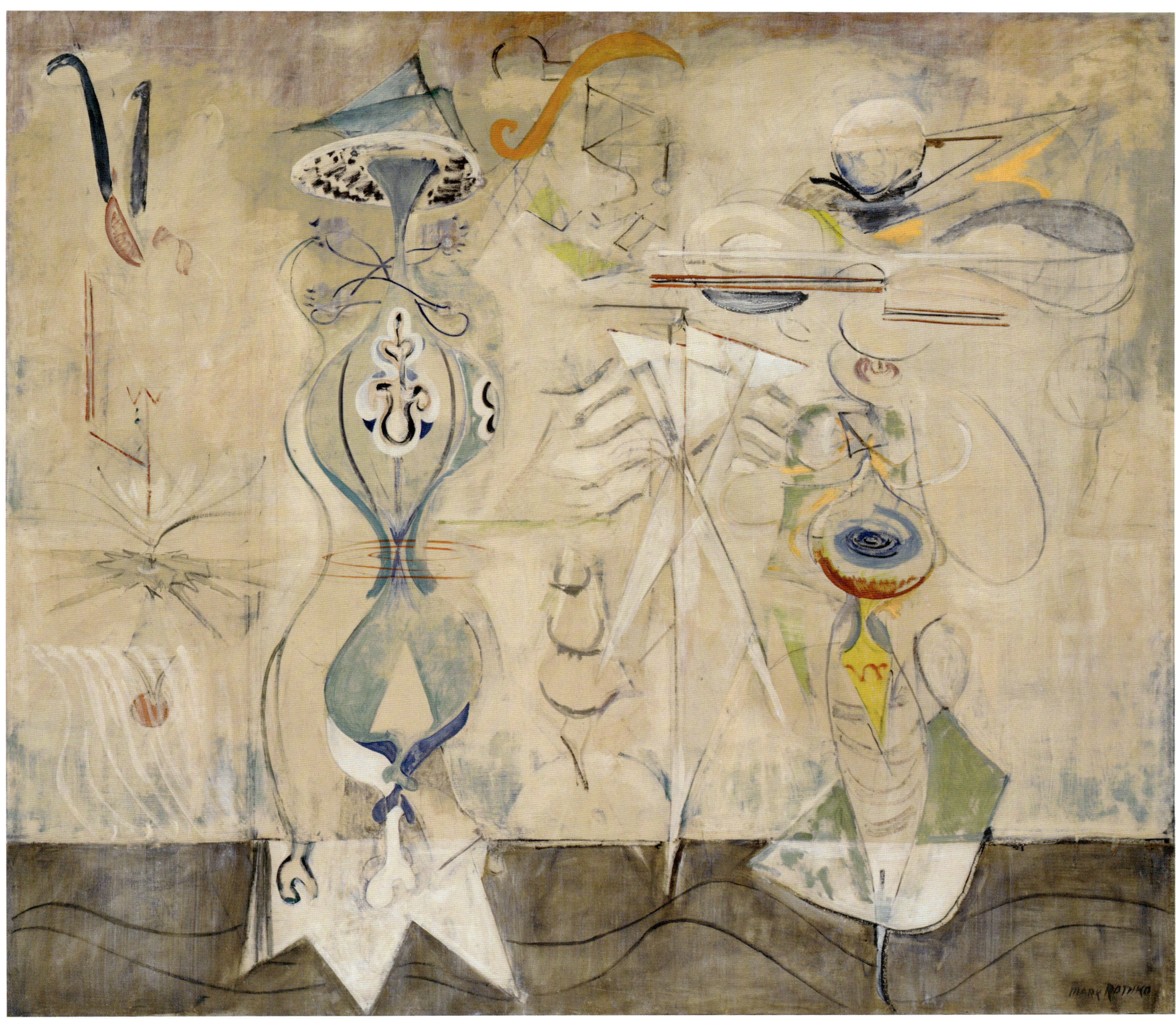
MARK ROTHKO

History of Art

Reading and working fervently, Rothko expresses in these writings his despair at the social status of the artist in America at that time. He looks enviously back to the past at the careers of such artists as Leonardo da Vinci (1452–1519) and Giotto (*c.* 1266/7–1337) who, he considers, were respected by the commissioners of their works and were sought after for their artistic creations and gifts.

Comparing this situation to the America of his time, he finds that business people and pioneers are venerated, but the arts are not. On the other hand, he portrays many of the great artists of the past as being at odds with the prevailing view of their society, 'who have for the most part, preferred hunger to compliance' – this possibly provided some consolation to him in the position in which he found himself. Considering the art of Byzantium, Egypt, the Dutch Golden Age and Renaissance Florence, he draws together an art-historical scheme across a wide sweep of time and geography. Although Rothko does not mention the German philosopher Hegel (1770–1831) by name, he appears to put forward a thesis in his writings about art history that is very similar to that of Hegel, who proposed that the 'universal spirit' (*geist*) was gradually realized through art over the centuries. Rothko writes: 'A study of the history of art is ... a demonstration of the inevitable logic of each step as art progresses on its way from point to point.' Rothko considers that the 'work of each artist is a different facet of each stage and functions as an accretion that serves as a corollary to the preceding stage'.

The Artist as Intellectual

Aiming to evaluate the basis of Western culture, Rothko set himself the task of discussing the ideas of great cultural leaders of the past. Cohen-Solal considers that to do this, he took up the tools he learned to use at the Talmud, discussing the ideas and works of such writers and philosophers as Plato (*c.* 424 BC–*c.* 347 BC), Shakespeare (1564–1616), Michelangelo (1475–1564), Sigmund Freud (1856–1939) and Carl Jung (1875–1961).

In doing this, Rothko could be considered to have been setting himself apart, not simply as an artist, but as an intellectual. Was he positioning himself as part of this long line of philosophers and intellectuals down through the ages? If that is so, Rothko was actually writing himself into the continuity of the cultural line from the past to the present. In effect he was lining himself up with the achievements and developments of the whole history of the European continent. Christopher Rothko points out that for someone who was breaking with tradition at the time of writing, he saw 'himself not in the vanguard of the new, but as someone carrying forth the torch of the great Western tradition'.

Ultimately, in these texts, Rothko considers the artist of his day as socially responsible, committed to being a positive force in society, but who voices his opinions and holds to his principles despite opposition. He writes that art 'is not only a form of action, but of social action ... For art is a type of communication, and when it enters the environment it produces its effects just as any other form of action does'.

The Vulnerability of the Artist

His tone in these writings is sometimes bitter, which could possibly indicate his feelings about what he considered to be the lack of recognition and respect he was receiving for his work. As an artist, he had plenty to say, aiming to crystallize his concept of reality and truth in each work he produced, but few were listening; he aimed for the highest of ideals, but society was more impressed with the cartoonist and the superficial.

This distrustful attitude to the viewing public was something that Rothko would continue to carry even when he was successful and recognized. In the introduction to *The Artist's Reality*, Christopher Rothko points out that Rothko constantly feared that the viewing public would misunderstand his work. The artist's act of sending his work out into the world is one full of trepidation and vulnerability. In a later article of 1947, Rothko was to clarify this by saying, **'A painting lives by companionship, expanding and quickening in the eyes of the sensitive observer. It dies by the same token. It is therefore a risky and unfeeling act to send it out into the world.'**

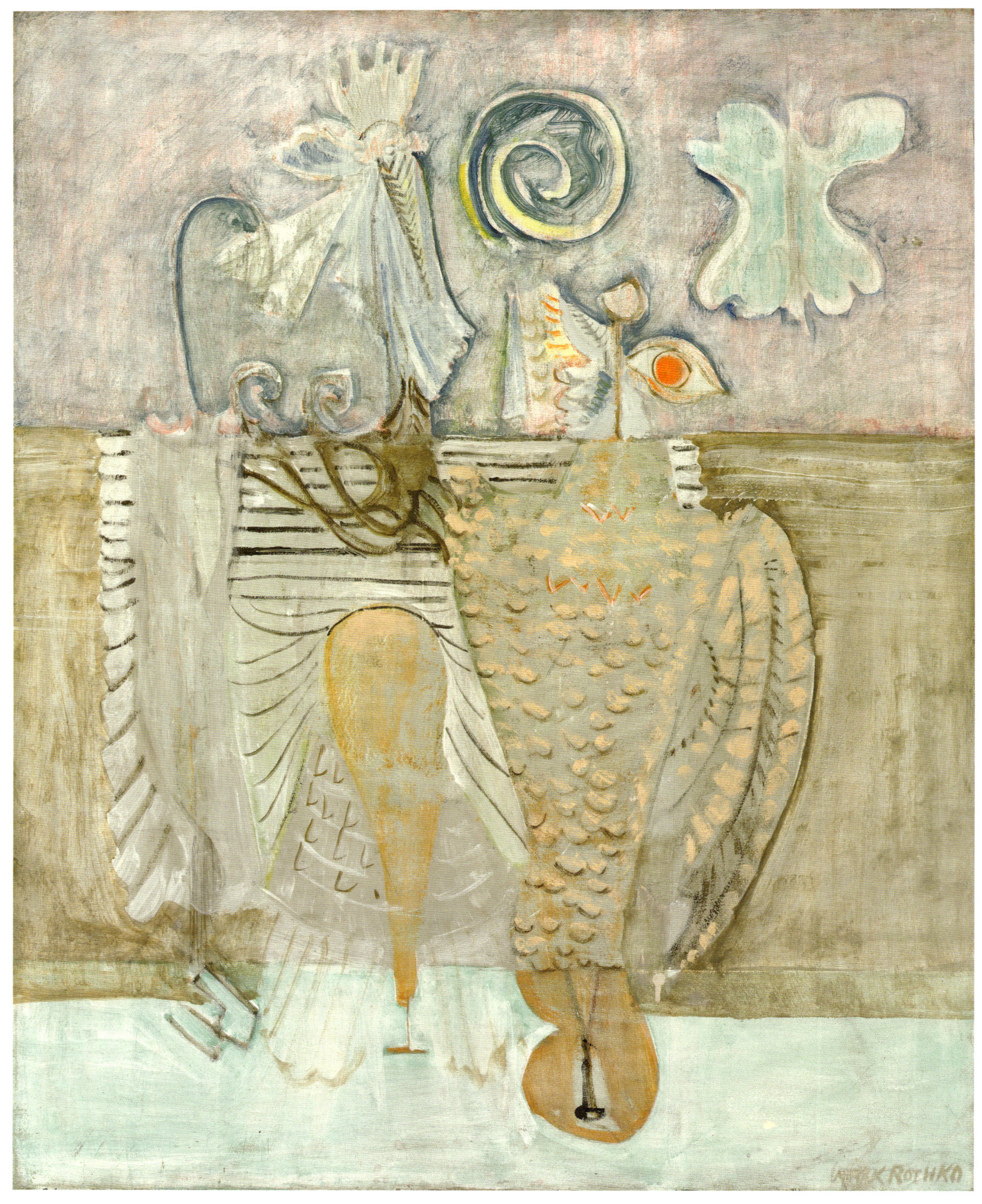

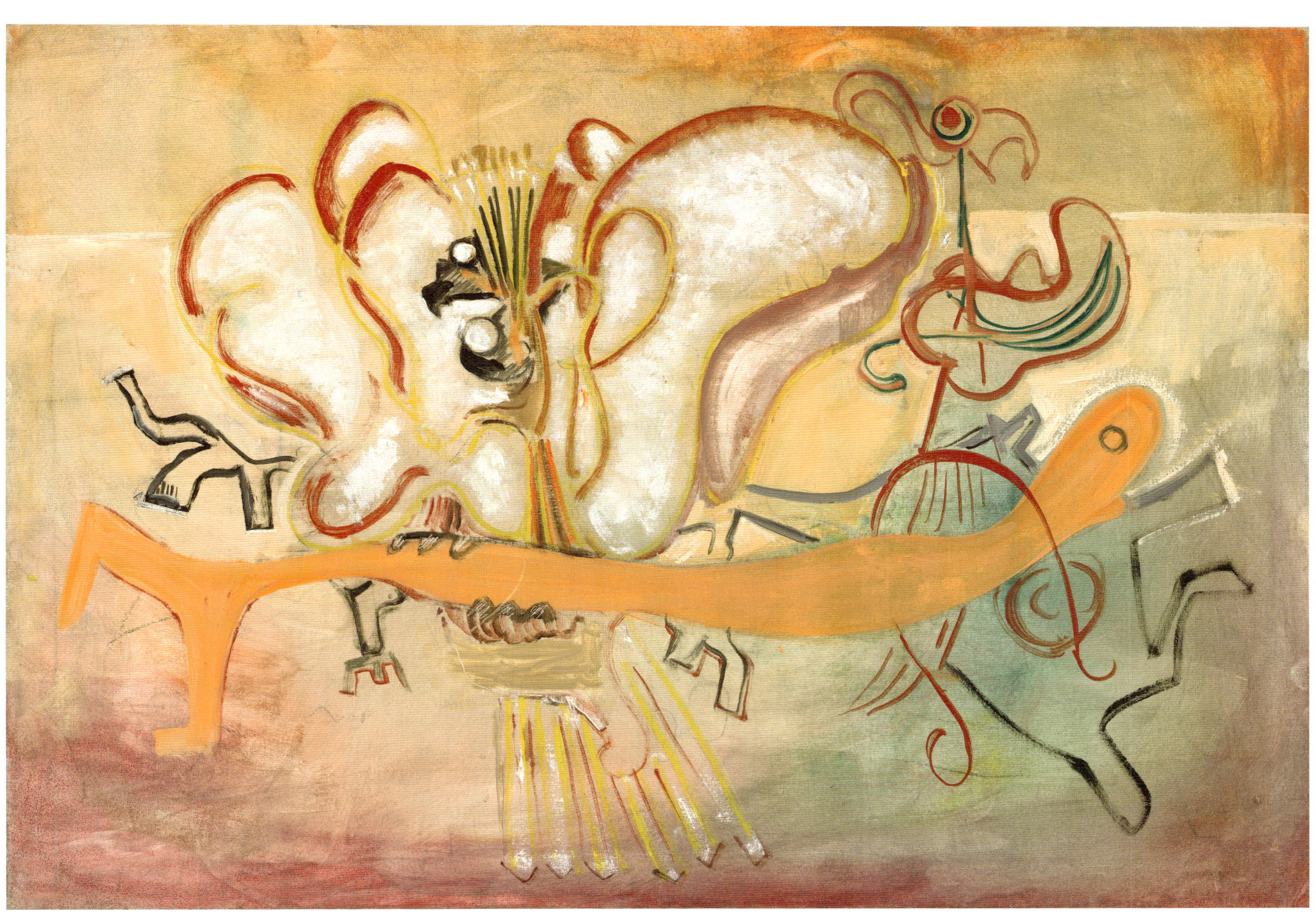

An Artist's World-view

Rothko's wrath also falls, in these writings, on those who merely illustrate or design. For him the true artist does not use form, design and colour simply to create a visual display, but in order to communicate something profound and meaningful. Perhaps his marriage to a successful jewellery maker coloured his view here, as he castigates those who are in his mind superficial. Edith, it seems, may not have respected Rothko as an artist as much as he would have wished; when he was earning very little from his work, she had him help her out in her workshop, which he seems to have strongly resented and found demeaning.

Those looking for any commentary by Rothko on his own paintings in *The Artist's Reality* will be disappointed. He does not mention his work once, nor does he refer to the fact that he is an artist. He writes about what artists do, discusses their ideas and how they express them and considers their cultural, social and geographical milieux. At the time of writing, he had still been working within realism, depicting forms and objects, albeit often distorted and convoluted, and had not yet begun painting the colourist classic works that were ultimately to make him famous, which were almost a decade in the future. Even if he had, though, he would not have mentioned them, as Rothko, in fact, throughout his life spoke little of his work and what it meant, perhaps not wishing to create any misunderstandings but rather allowing his paintings to speak for themselves. As Christopher Rothko says, in *The Artist's Reality*: 'we get a rare glimpse of an artist's worldview, expressed in the written word and in considerable detail.'

Identity

As noted before, there was little in Rothko's education and training to suggest him for a career as an artist. It did, however, have certain attractions, as it fulfilled his criteria for a career that offered the opportunity to create a role for himself as a social activist in an area where his ethnic and religious origins would not limit his progress. Free from materialistic aspirations, art offered him a pathway to communicate his developing philosophy and provided a platform for social commentary on the essence of what it is to be human.

This period of seeking a new way to express himself in art was preceded with the significant step of becoming a citizen of the United States in February 1938. Rothko may be considered to have been ambivalent in his approach to finalizing American citizenship, particularly in view of his later comment, already quoted on page 13, that he never got over leaving Russia. He had first begun the process towards citizenship around 14 years earlier, but had not pursued it with any consistent intention, only pulling everything together for his application in 1935. The whole process was only fully legalized, however, when he obtained his passport in 1959.

A New Name

Perhaps the worsening situation towards Jews, with the rise of the Nazis in Germany, and concern about a personal situation arising, regarding a possible rise in Anti-Semitism, spurred him on to complete the citizenship application. Many American Jews at this time were changing their names to sound less Jewish; Rothko's own brothers many years earlier had changed their name to Roth.

In the end, Marcus Rothkowitz decided upon Mark Rothko as the most fitting choice for him personally and professionally as an American artist. Rothko sounded unlike any European name, it was unusual but caught attention. Along with the change of name and the writing of his book, all happening around this period, Rothko was further developing his involvement in social action through his membership of societies for artists. In 1940, he left the American Artists' Congress and with others founded the Federation of Modern Painters and Sculptors, which declared itself to be 'fighting for the welfare of free and progressive artists.' The aim was to keep art free from politics and economics, but to support freedom of expression and independence for artists. Annual shows were held to provide a gallery for the works of members to communicate their vision to the wider society.

Subject and Style

Throughout this period of change and rethinking, Rothko had been involved in discussions with fellow artists, in particular with Gottlieb, as to what subjects for art would be suited to this new age of turmoil and uncertainty. Around 1940–41, it seems that he left

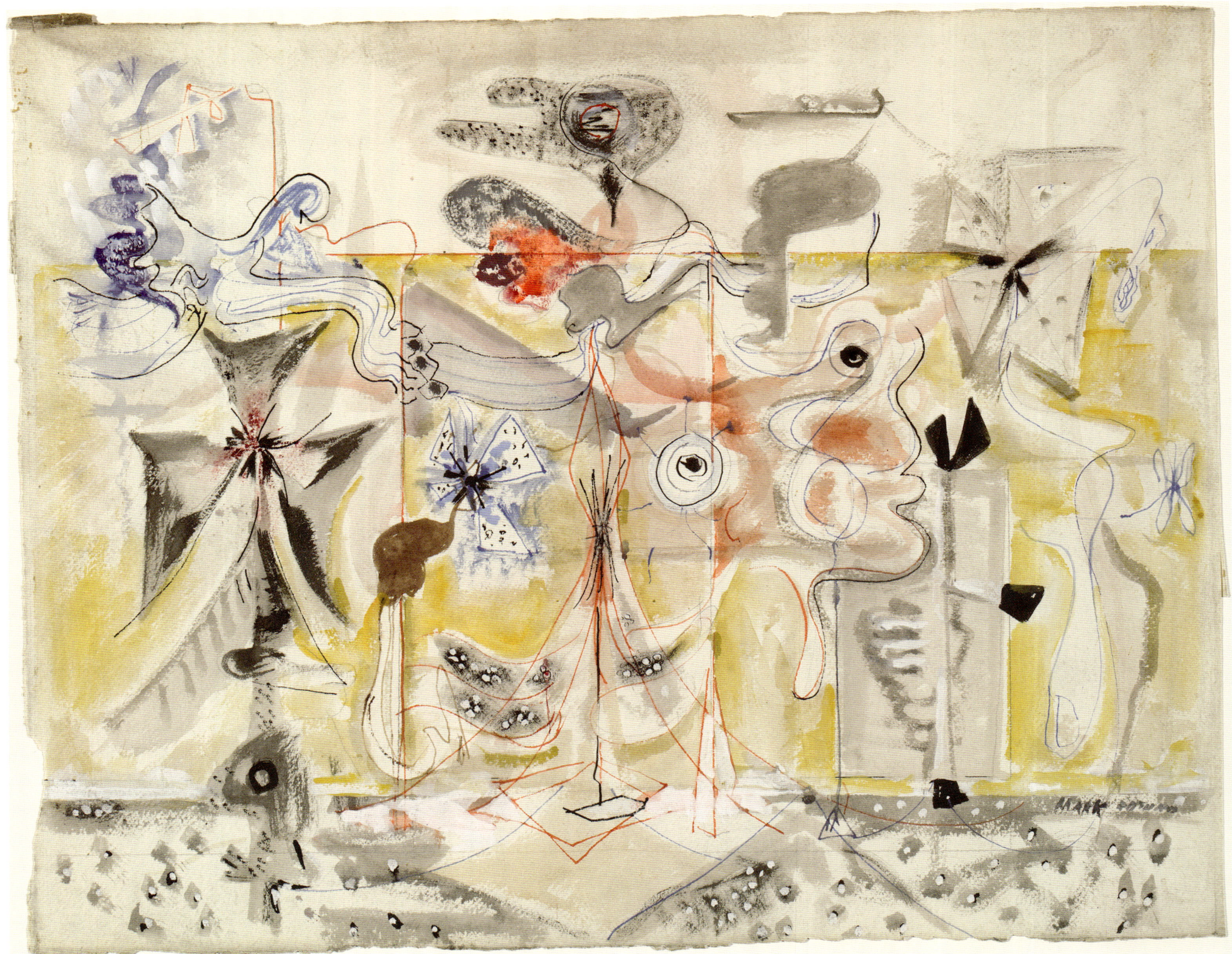

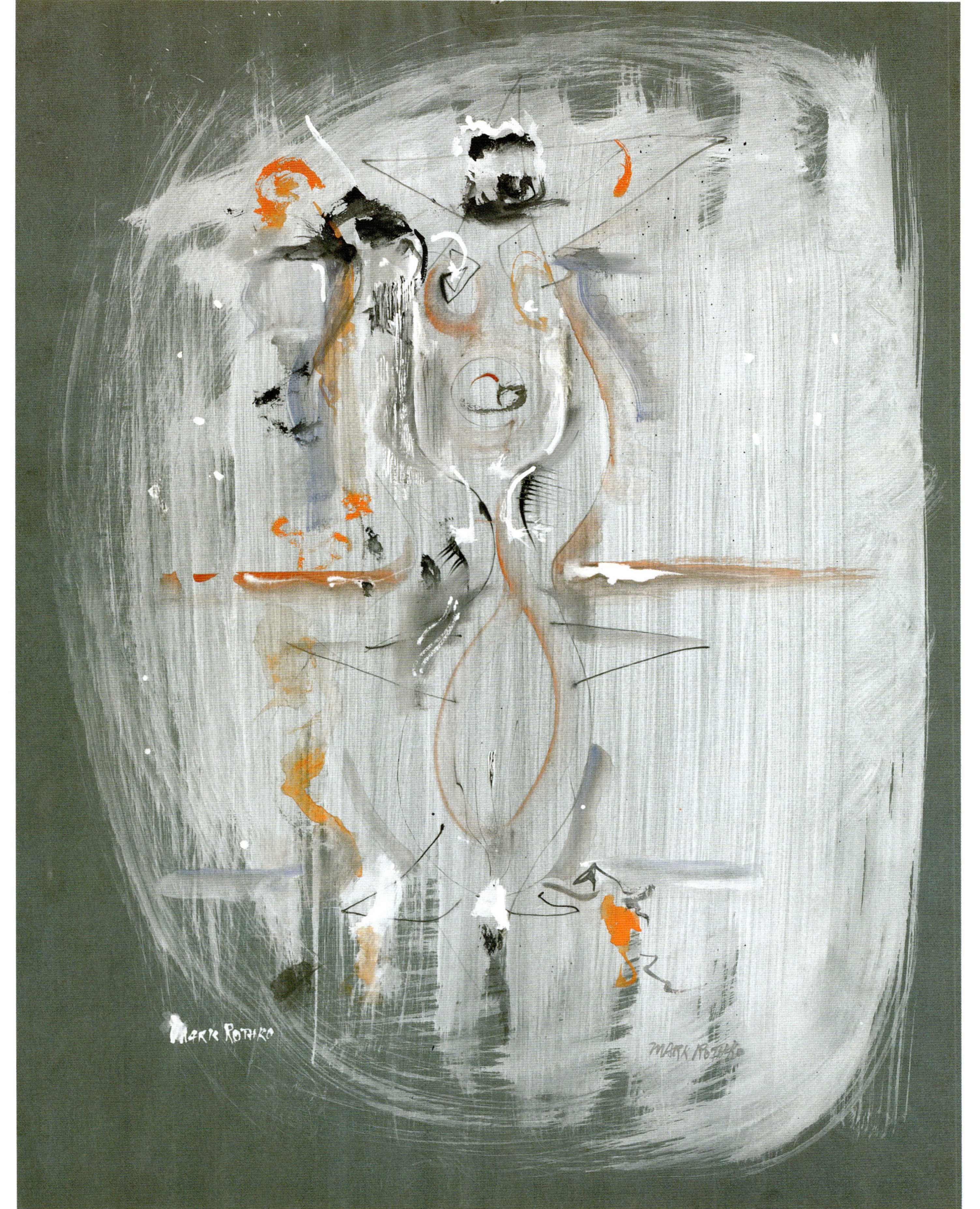

behind his time of intense writing and began to paint in a new style, embracing themes from mythology, in particular myths of the ancient Greeks. Ancient Greece, the cradle of European civilization, not the contemporary Europe of war and chaos, became his main source of themes, although he also drew from the ancient stories of Egypt and Mesopotamia, and even painted one work entitled *Crucifix*, thus expanding into the Christian tradition, an usual foray for a Jewish artist. While myth became the subject, Rothko also developed his style to become increasingly surrealistic.

New York in the late 1930s and 1940s had increasingly become the haven for many artists and intellectuals fleeing the situation in Europe, which included such men as André Breton (1896–1966), Piet Mondrian (1872–1944) and Max Ernst (1891–1976). Many of these artists could speak little English, so their personal links with the New York artists were limited, but their presence was felt as part of an international element in the New York art scene. This influx also included the presence of foreign art dealers, critics and collectors. Pierre Matisse, the son of Henri Matisse, opened a gallery that sold a variety of works by these incoming European artists and also works of other Europeans, including some by his father. By 1942, there were so many displaced artists from Europe in New York that Pierre mounted an exhibition of their work, which he entitled *Artists in Exile*.

The Art of This Century Gallery

Another factor, which developed links between the New York artists and the Europeans, was the arrival in New York, in 1941, of Peggy Guggenheim (1898–1979), wealthy heiress, wife of Max Ernst and avid collector of contemporary art. Looking for a way to display such works, she enlisted the Romanian architect Fred Kiesler (1890–1965), who had spent most of his life in Vienna, and created the Art of This Century Gallery.

The gallery was divided into four clearly defined spaces. The Abstract Gallery functioned as gallery and entrance hall with undulating walls of blue canvas; the Kinetic Gallery was a darkened space where viewers could interact with the displays; the Daylight Gallery where all the temporary exhibitions were held, had large windows fronting on to 57th Street and was rectangular in shape with white walls. The fourth gallery was the Surrealist Gallery, painted black with wall units, on to which the surrealist works were fitted and accessed by adjustable arms. The lighting of the gallery was randomly timed and occasionally the room plunged into darkness, accompanied by the sound of an oncoming train. In 1942, André Breton, who was helping Guggenheim develop her collection, and Marcel Duchamp (1887–1968) organized an exhibition at the gallery entitled *First Papers of Surrealism*. Although surrealism was a major part of this European effect on the New York art scene, other aspects of modern art such as pure abstraction and even early installation art were also exhibited.

Surrealism

Surrealism had emerged in Paris in the 1920s and, based on the psychoanalytical theories of Freud, aimed to free the unconscious mind so that people's deepest thoughts could be accessed. There were three main surrealist approaches to painting: scrapping and rubbing surfaces to create random patterns; the creation of realistic and dreamlike works, such as those by Salvador Dalí (1904–1989) or René Magritte (1898–1967); or works created by the artist simply taking up the brush and painting randomly, without stopping to think, often resulting in completely abstract works such as those by Joan Miró (1893–1983) or André Masson (1896–1987).

The aim was that through these techniques, the artists would tap into their hidden feelings and desires; the deep world of emotions and fantasy would then be linked with the known world of logic and reason. Surrealist works are full of strange juxtapositions, odd placements of objects and people together with disturbing, unsettling random events. The overall aim of the works was to challenge the viewer to look deep into the inner recesses of their own minds and feelings in order to develop more profound personal awareness and understanding. In this context, one can see why this approach would appeal to Rothko, whose development as an artist took him to a place where, through his art, he wanted to explore the essence of being human and to reach and affect the emotional and inner world of his viewers.

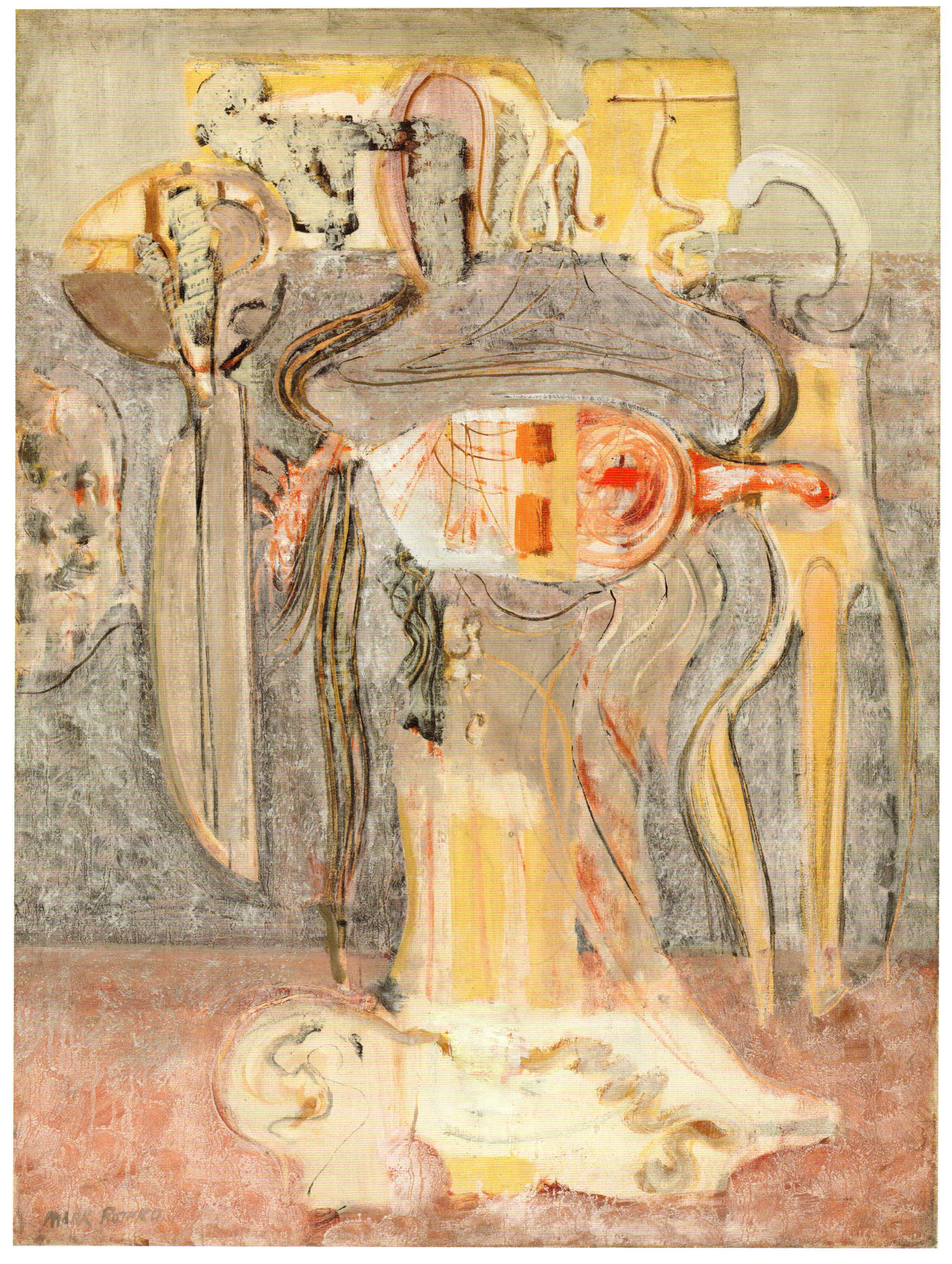

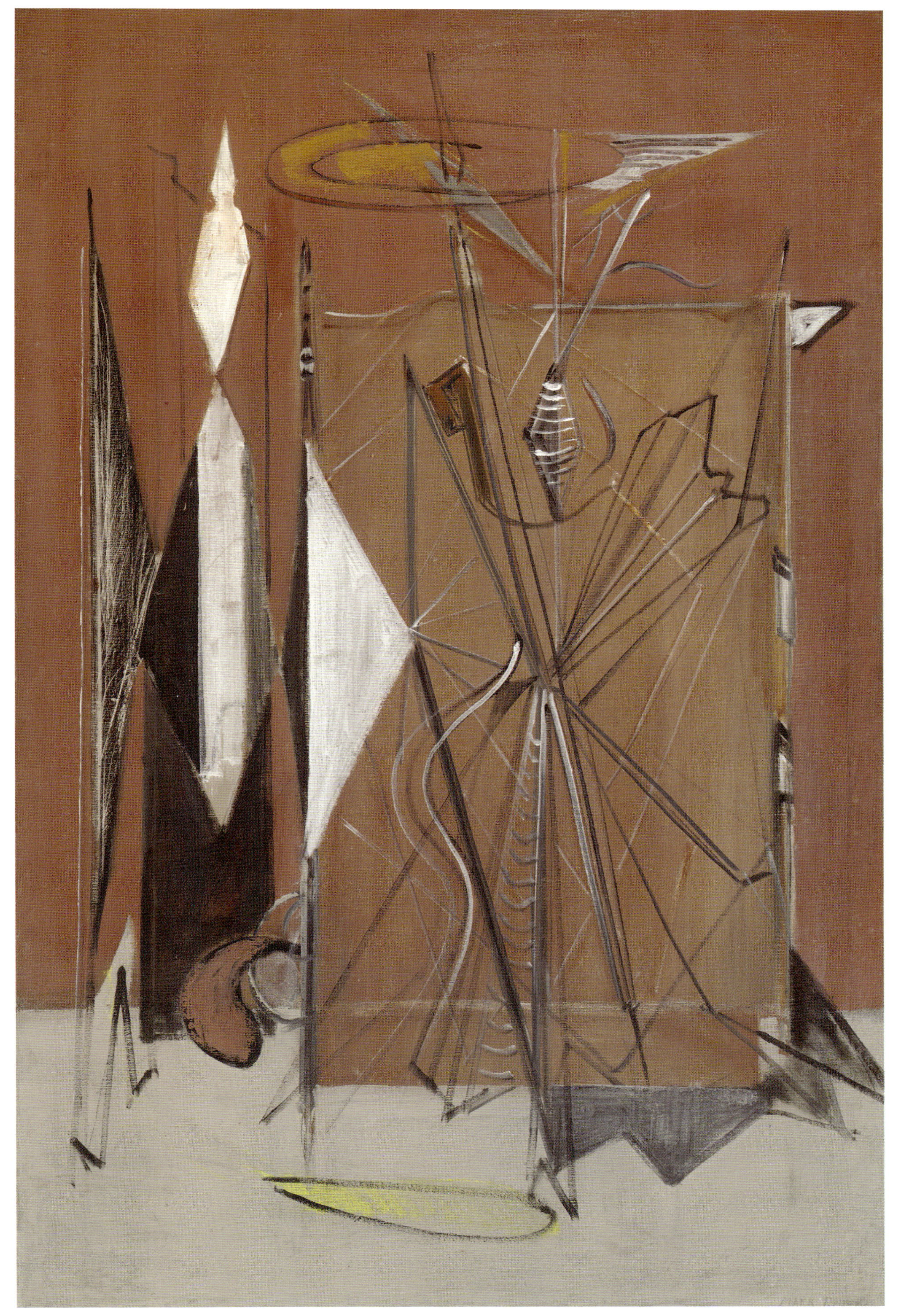

The Collective Unconscious

As well as the influence of surrealist painting and theories, Rothko and others were particularly interested in the theories of Carl Jung on the collective unconscious. This theory explained that people were not simply individuals with their own bank of experience that they had built up through their personal life experience, but that humans, as Jung described in 1936 in a lecture at St. Bartholomew's Hospital in London, 'have a collective universal and impersonal nature which is identical in all individuals. This collective unconscious does not develop individually but is inherited.' He explains that: 'It is the mind of our unknown ancestors, their way of thinking and feeling, their way of experiencing life and the world, gods and men.'

The collective unconscious also consists of what Jung calls 'pre-existent forms, the archetypes.' According to Jung, these archetypes, imprints of momentous or frequently recurring situations in the human past, such as the Great Mother or the Wise Old Man, act as universal symbols that live in the deep layers of the unconscious. Linking this theory with legends of ancient civilizations was to provide a way forward for Rothko in his search for ways of expressing universal truths of human experience.

Rothko and Music

Since childhood, Rothko had enjoyed music, although he seems to have had little opportunity to follow a course of musical or instrumental study. Christopher Rothko states of his father: 'Had he received the training and been blessed with the acumen, I have little doubt that music would have been my father's expressive medium.'

Christopher's childhood memories of his father are that he filled his world with music, playing record after record, typically Mozart, Haydn or Schubert, his favourite always being Mozart. During the 1950s and 1960s, he would play music, mostly opera, as he worked in his studio. Christopher attributes his father's love of Mozart to the fact that Rothko was inspired by Mozart's clarity of form and expression, as well as the economy of means by which he expressed his ideas. The idea that music is an expression of an elemental human need and a universal language that plumbs the depths of emotion, and can be transformational in its power and effect, has been expressed by a number of commentators. The German philosopher Nietzsche (1844–1900) proposed that painting and music had mutual affinities and could be considered to be different forms of expression of the same fundamental needs. For Nietzsche, music was the true language of emotion. Certainly the power of music to affect the emotions is a power that Rothko looked to harness in his works. He himself said: 'I became a painter because I wanted to raise painting to the level of poignancy of music and poetry.'

Drama

Throughout the course of his career, Rothko would regularly refer to his paintings as 'dramas'. Rothko's love of acting and his attempts to break into a theatrical career have already been mentioned. The desires that spurred him to express himself as an actor found their expression in a different form in his art work.

Drama, as used here, is in the sense of the drama of the ancient Greeks as they dealt with existential issues through the means of theatrical productions. Rothko also credited Shakespeare with challenging him on the subject of drama, in particular tragedy. In an interview in 1960, he said: **'Shakespeare's tragic concept embodies for me the full range of life from which the artist draws all his tragic materials.'**

Rothko's paintings become the platform for a dialogue about human concerns and interaction, creating the human drama in paint and at the same time initiating a dialogue between the painter and the viewer, as well as facilitating this discussion and the processing of human reactions to the drama of life and how it is lived. In his later works, Rothko was to pare this down to the economy of means, which he so admired in Mozart's music, using the bare elements of colour and form. As a visit to the theatre takes the audience on a voyage as they journey through the drama played out on stage; as listening to a work of music is an experience frequently full of the changing hues of human life; so responding to a work of art is an experience which takes the viewer on a personal journey of discovery.

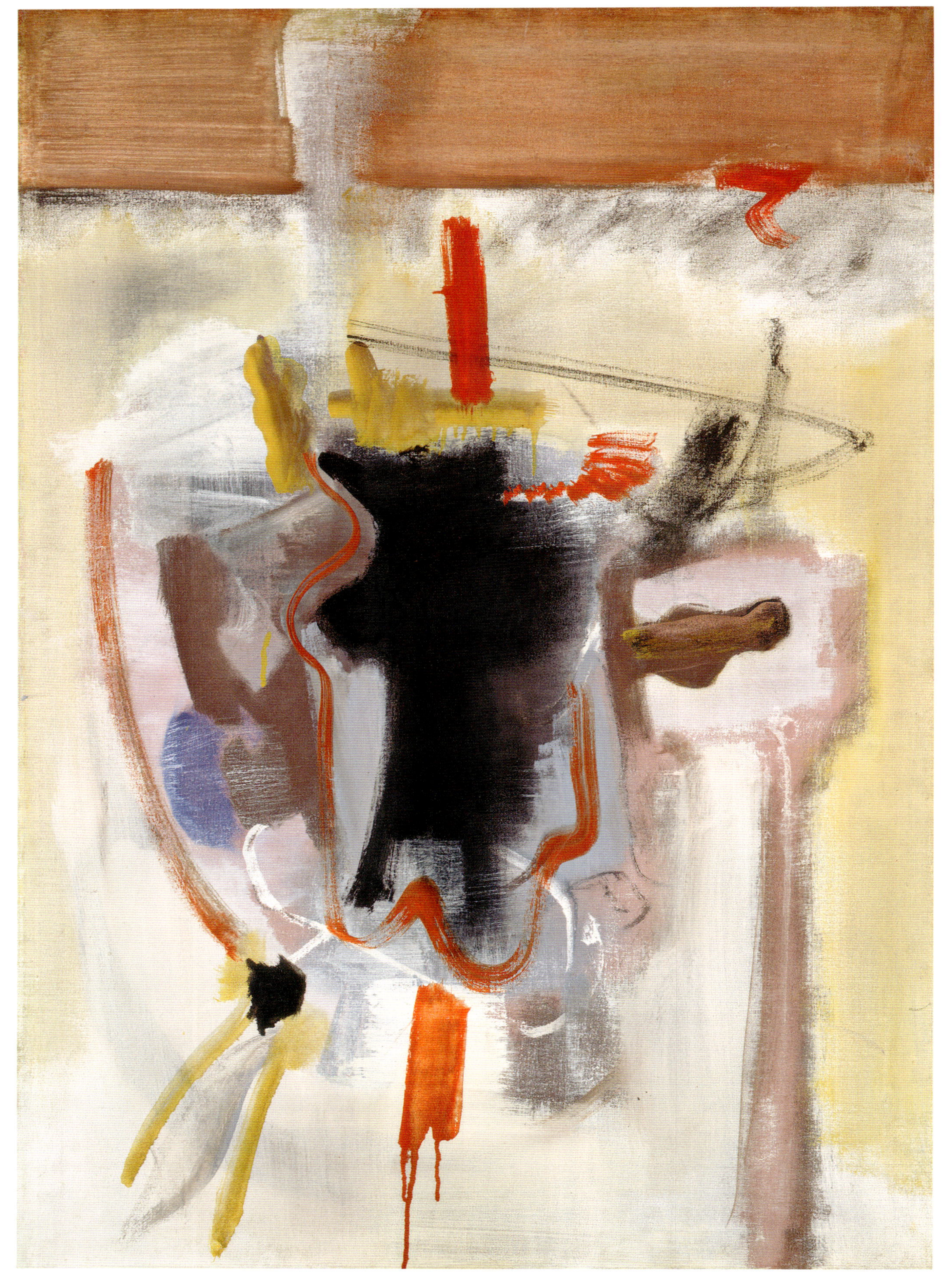

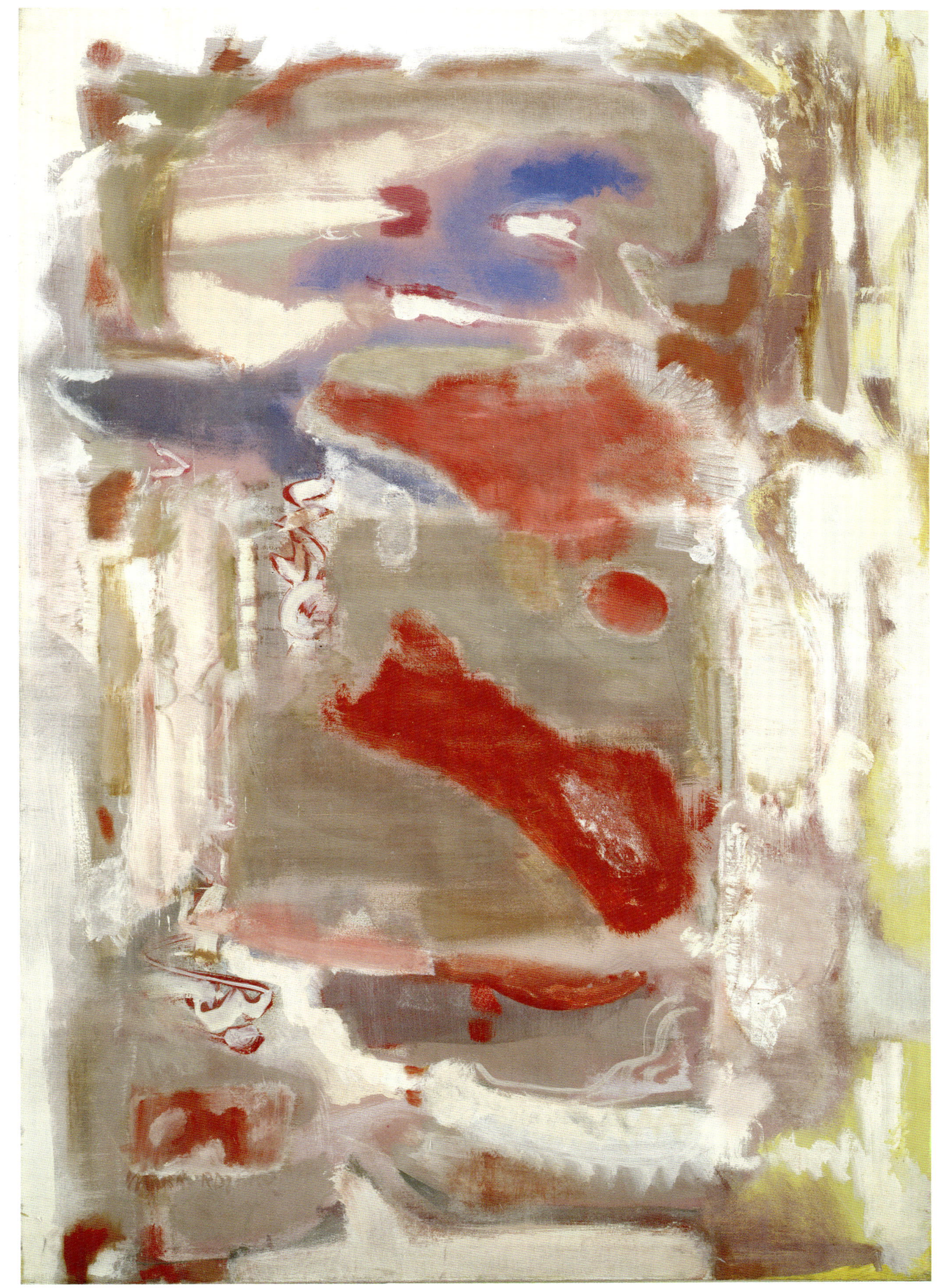

The Tragic

Rothko's reading of *Birth of Tragedy* by Nietzsche combines both the philosophical rationale for the emotional power of music and a theme that Rothko was to make his own, the tragic. On a number of occasions, Rothko was to refer to what he considered to be one of the overriding preoccupations in his art: that of the tragic or, put another way, the tragedy of the human condition.

According to Nietzsche, tragedy occurs when the Dionysian force and the Apollonian force come together. The Greek god Dionysus frees those oppressed by self-conscious fear and care through his wine, music and dance. Apollo, for Nietzsche, represents the art of the sculptor who desires to create form by making his material conform to his will. Nietzsche proposes that when the primal desires of Dionysus meet the force of Apollo to mould and control, the result is tragedy. In Greek theatre, the audience are saddened by the tragic consequences of the characters' acts, but through them experience a catharsis, a purification or cleansing of emotions, so that at the conclusion of the drama, they feel lightened and uplifted. Greek tragedy thus has the effect of inspiring both sadness and emotional uplift, so making life more understandable and endurable. According to his daughter Kate, one of Rothko's favourite phrases was 'smiling through the tears', which can convey to us some of the tragic drama and yet the emotional uplift that can coexist in the individual's experience of life and art.

From his reading of Nietzsche, Rothko evolved his goal of developing his art to be a means of addressing what he considered to be the spiritual emptiness of modern man, in part created by the fragmentation of modern life; mythology, according to Nietzsche could aim at least partly to address this emptiness. For Rothko, the use of mythology became a means, for a time, through which he could aim to do that.

A New Freedom

Although Rothko was not fully committed to the philosophy of surrealism, it gave him freedom to range across subjects, time and space, the visible and the invisible, the conscious and the unconscious. Without any need to represent the visible world, he was free to invent shapes, forms and symbols, a number of which became part of a repertoire that he drew on with regularity.

Representing the anxieties of the modern world using a surrealist-inspired style, yet paradoxically, certainly in the earlier mythological works, with archaic forms and references, he was liberated to do something totally different in his work. These features are not strictly speaking confined to Rothko alone, but a number of the New York artists of the day moved into a surrealistic phase around this time, many of them like Rothko, ultimately en route to another destination. Although Abstract Expressionism styled itself as a rejection of surrealism, it was in many ways a direct result of it.

Antigone

One of Rothko's first mythological paintings in this new period in a surrealist-inspired style was *Antigone* (1939–40; *see* fig. 8, page 22), based on the story by Sophocles (*c.* 497–406 BC). Antigone is the tragic heroine who tries to provide an honourable burial for her brother Polynices. Polynices and his brother Eteocles have been sharing the throne, but Eteocles exiles Polynices, who raises an army and fights back. Both brothers are killed in the ensuing battle. The new king Creon decrees Polynices is not to be mourned or buried on pain of death. Antigone defies his decree and is found out. Brought before Creon, she gives an impassioned speech in her own defence in which she says she put the will of the gods before man-made laws. The result is she is imprisoned in a tomb and hangs herself. The son of Creon, Haemon, who was engaged to Antigone, kills himself, at which his mother, the Queen, wife of Creon, kills herself. Creon is left alone to ponder this scene of death and devastation due to his refusal to listen to the opposition from his subjects and the prophet Tiresias.

In the painting, five heads merge as one on top of a classical style frieze-like base. Their style is reminiscent of some of the illustrations Rothko used in *The Graphic Bible,* which drew from Assyrian sources of the depiction of humans and beasts. Perhaps the five heads represent the five people who die in the story, or possibly refer to Antigone's complicated line of descent, being the daughter as well as half-sister of her father Oedipus and the daughter and granddaughter of her mother. They could be taken to represent fragmentation in the family and society, but in the painting are unified into the one figure, possibly an indication of Rothko's aim to unify through his art. In the centre, underneath the frieze, is a globe, which may suggest the universal significance of the tragic.

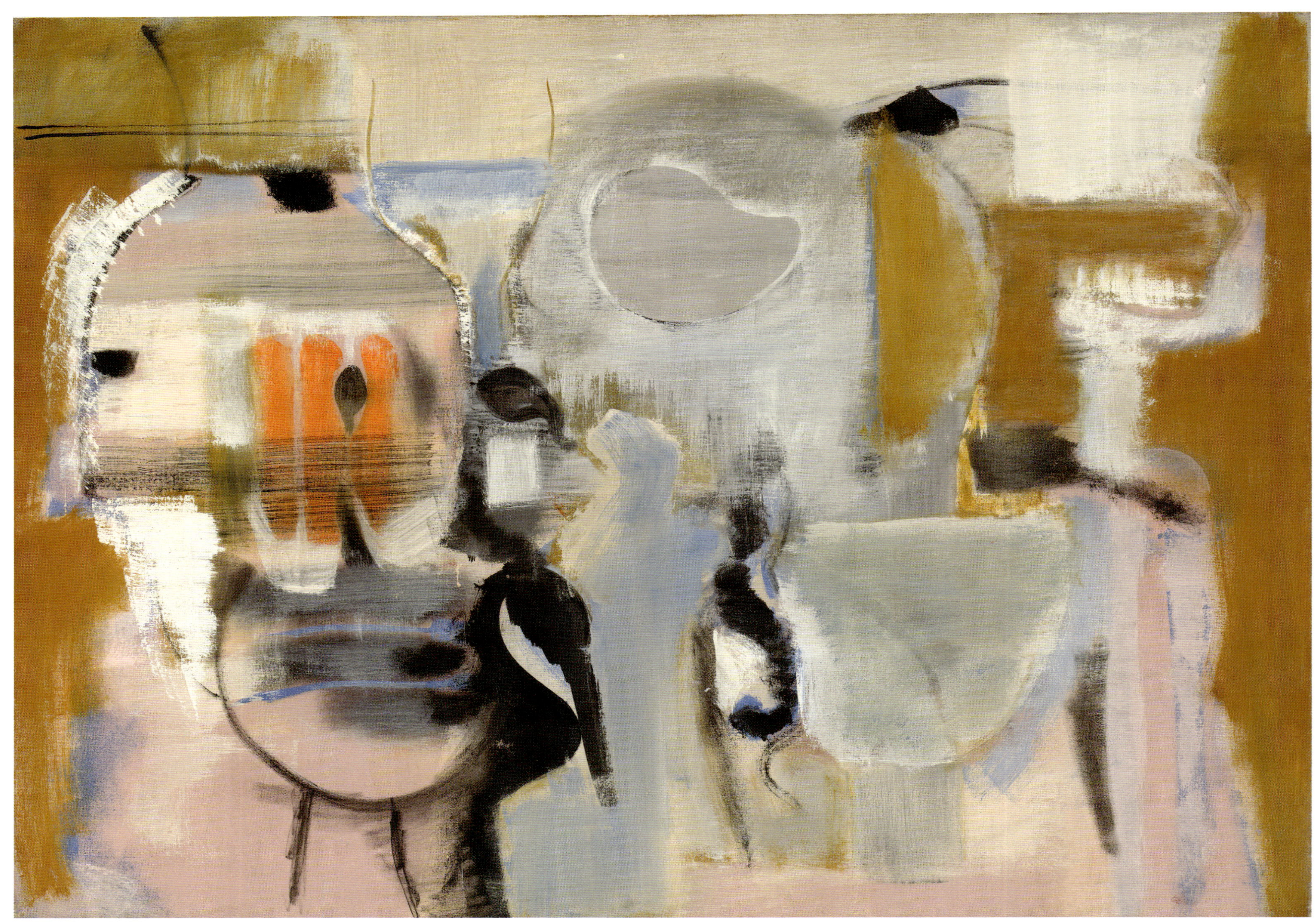

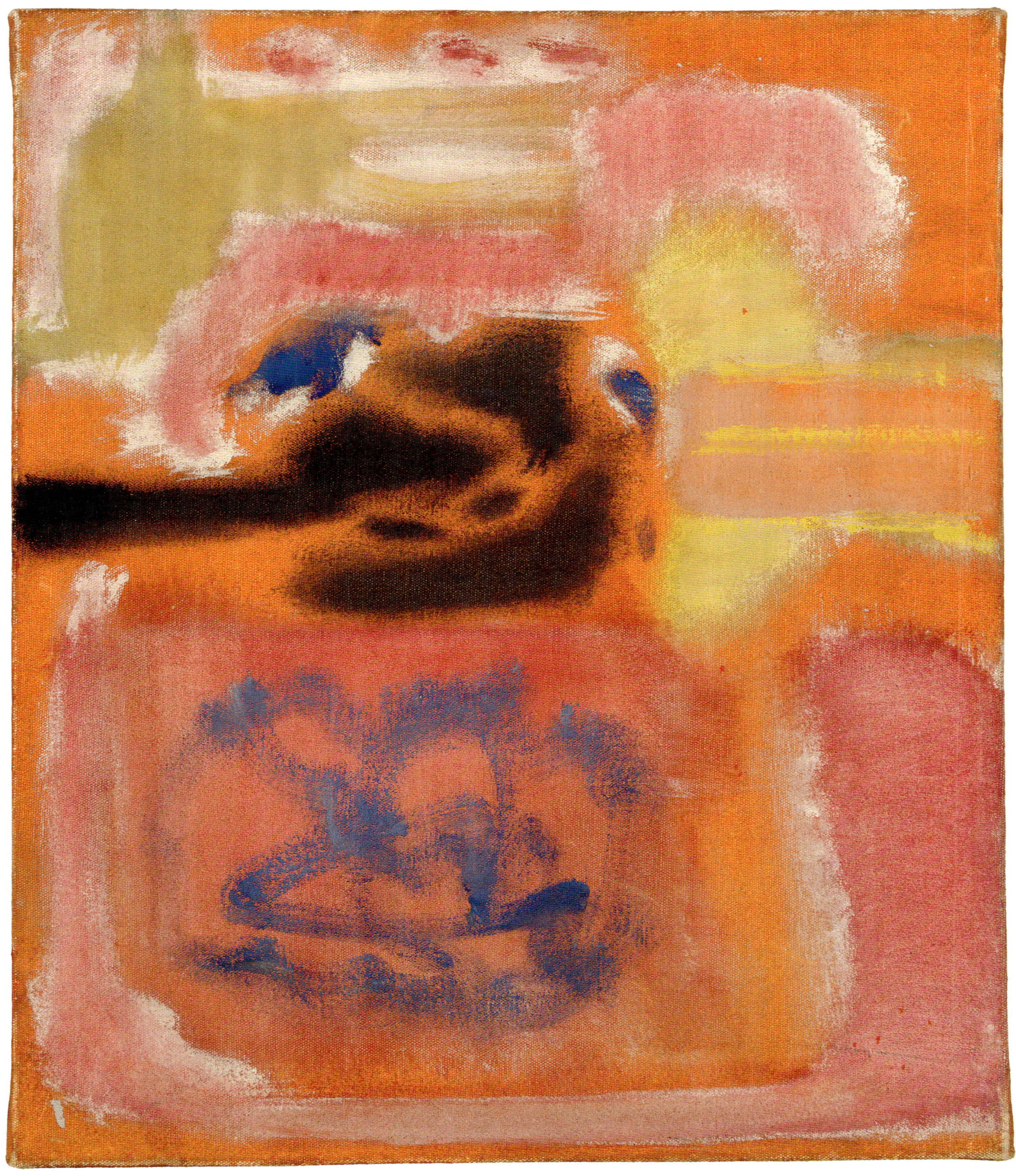

Oedipus

Oedipus (*c.*1940; *see* fig. 7, page 19) also displays a multi-headed figure, this time consisting of three heads. A number of suggestions have been made as to the significance and meaning of this trinity. Nietzsche in ***Birth of Tragedy*** attributes three titles to Oedipus, 'murderer of his father, the husband of his mother, the solver of the riddle of the Sphinx'. It has also been suggested that it may be a reference to the Christian doctrine of the Trinity, with the central figure representing the suffering of Christ.

Rothko in his own writings talks of the human body as: 'the embodiment of mechanical perfection, spiritual perfection, and the beauty to the senses unified within a single form … the unison of the three must remain the ideal of perfection of any age.' The character of Oedipus is a form of the embodiment of pride and passion, part of the destructive elements of man's nature. The central figure has been dismantled and recombined to form a human mass. Perhaps Rothko is suggesting that all humankind is bound together by tragedy. The context of the tragedies by the classical Greek playwright Aeschylus (*c.* 523 BC–*c.* 456 BC) of which Oedipus is one, provided Rothko with themes that powerfully express the influence of fate. The unfolding devastation of the Second World War underlines a practical application of Rothko's preoccupation with fate and the cruelty of human nature; the expression of violence and suffering in this painting is forcefully conveyed by Rothko. Rothko's representation of the figure of Oedipus brings us to a confrontation with the passions and contradictions, the cruelties and selfishness of our own personal nature.

The Omen of the Eagle

The Omen of the Eagle (1942; *see* fig. 10, page 26) is a painting of strong forms and bold colours based on ***Agamemnon***, the first play in the trilogy of the ***Oresteia***, by Aeschylus, about the Trojan War, whose overall subject is the human condition in many of its multiple manifestations. Rothko's unsettling and disturbing painting conveys some idea of the doom-laden recitation of the Chorus which, telling of King Agamemnon's return from his victory in the Trojan War, recites the omen at the beginning of the play predicting the destruction of Troy by the Greeks. The Chorus warns that two eagles will devour a pregnant hare, seemingly a symbol of the people of Troy who, together with their descendants, will be destroyed by forces more powerful than themselves. Clytemnestra, the King's wife, is angry at her husband's order to sacrifice their daughter Iphigenia to the gods to calm a storm at sea, and also at his relationship with the prophetess Cassandra, and ultimately kills him. At the end, the Chorus predicts that Agamemnon's son, Orestes, will return to avenge his father's death. Clytemnestra is considered to be one of the most powerful and effective characters in Greek tragedy, vengeful and cruel, but underneath this nursing a deep, powerful and inconsolable grief for the death of her daughter; this wound fuels the remorseless killing of her husband.

The blue-green background of *The Omen of the Eagle* provides a constant, calm and fresh colour base for the ferocious and cruel depictions of the central painting. At the top is a bright yellow three-headed creature, possibly representing multiheaded gods; in the central panel, bold lines of strong red and black represent the two wings of the eagles whose heads peer out at the viewer; a layer of archways, with possible phallic symbols hanging from them, provides another layer of forms; at the bottom of this whole edifice is a jumble of human feet. One of the important themes of this whole trilogy of plays is the recurring cycle of blood crimes; blood must be paid for by blood down the generations as a self-perpetuating cycle of violence. There is, however, some indication by Aeschylus that this cycle of vengeance could be stopped, as the Greek society of the time moves from a Dionysian approach of primitive and spontaneous emotions to a more Apollonian approach of democracy based on reason.

The Spirit of Myth

That *The Omen of the Eagle* was painted during the war and it references the origins of military conflict has not been lost on the critics of Rothko's work. The eagle can have multiple layers of meaning; it was the imperial emblem of Caesar; it is found in Mesopotamian art; it can represent the sun; it was the symbol of both Germany and America; and as author Jacob Baal-Teshuva points out, in America the war was cast as the battle of barbarism against civilization. He proposes that Rothko has 'united that savagery and civilization into a single barbaric figure that embodied aggression and vulnerability in one, the figure of the eagle.'

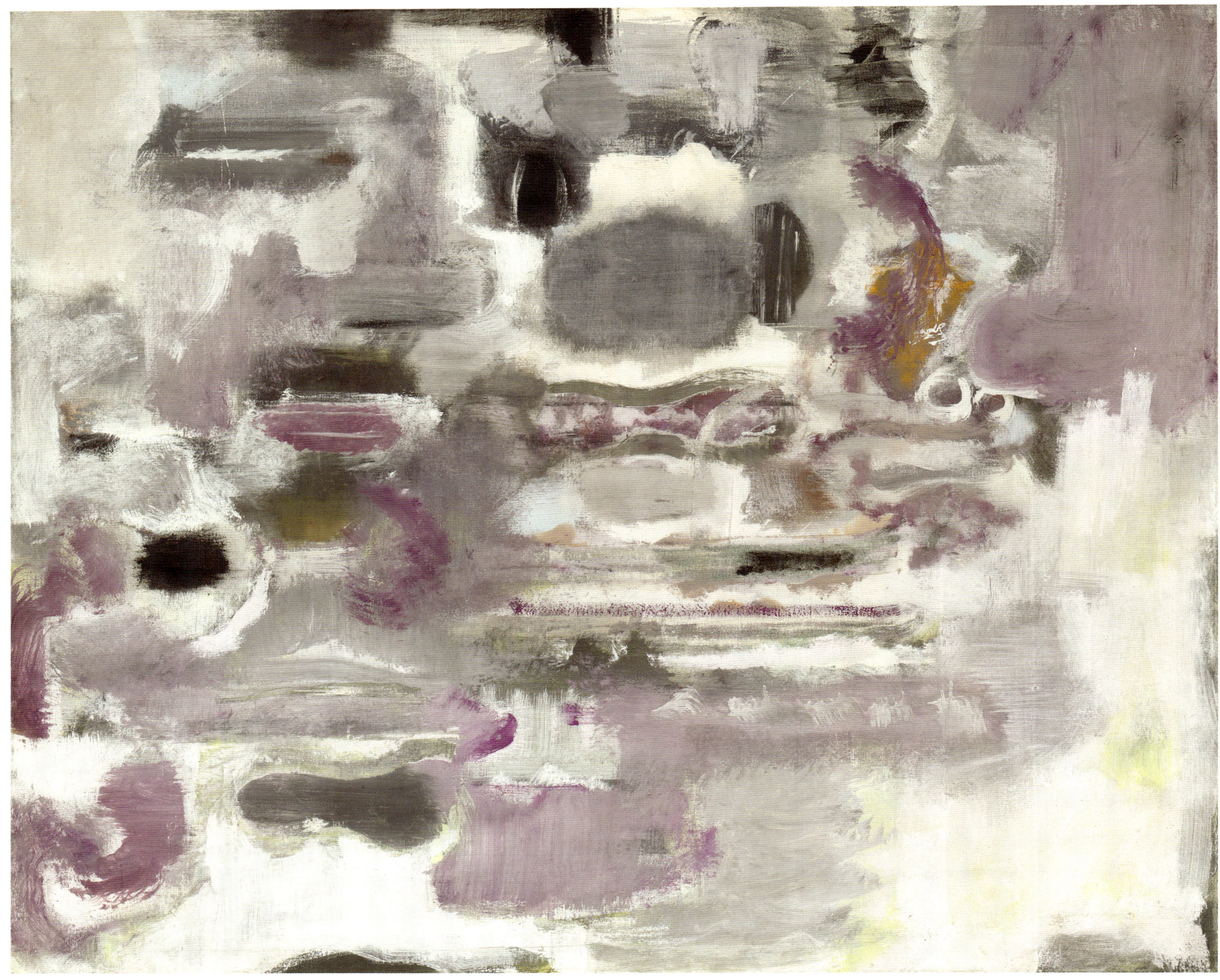

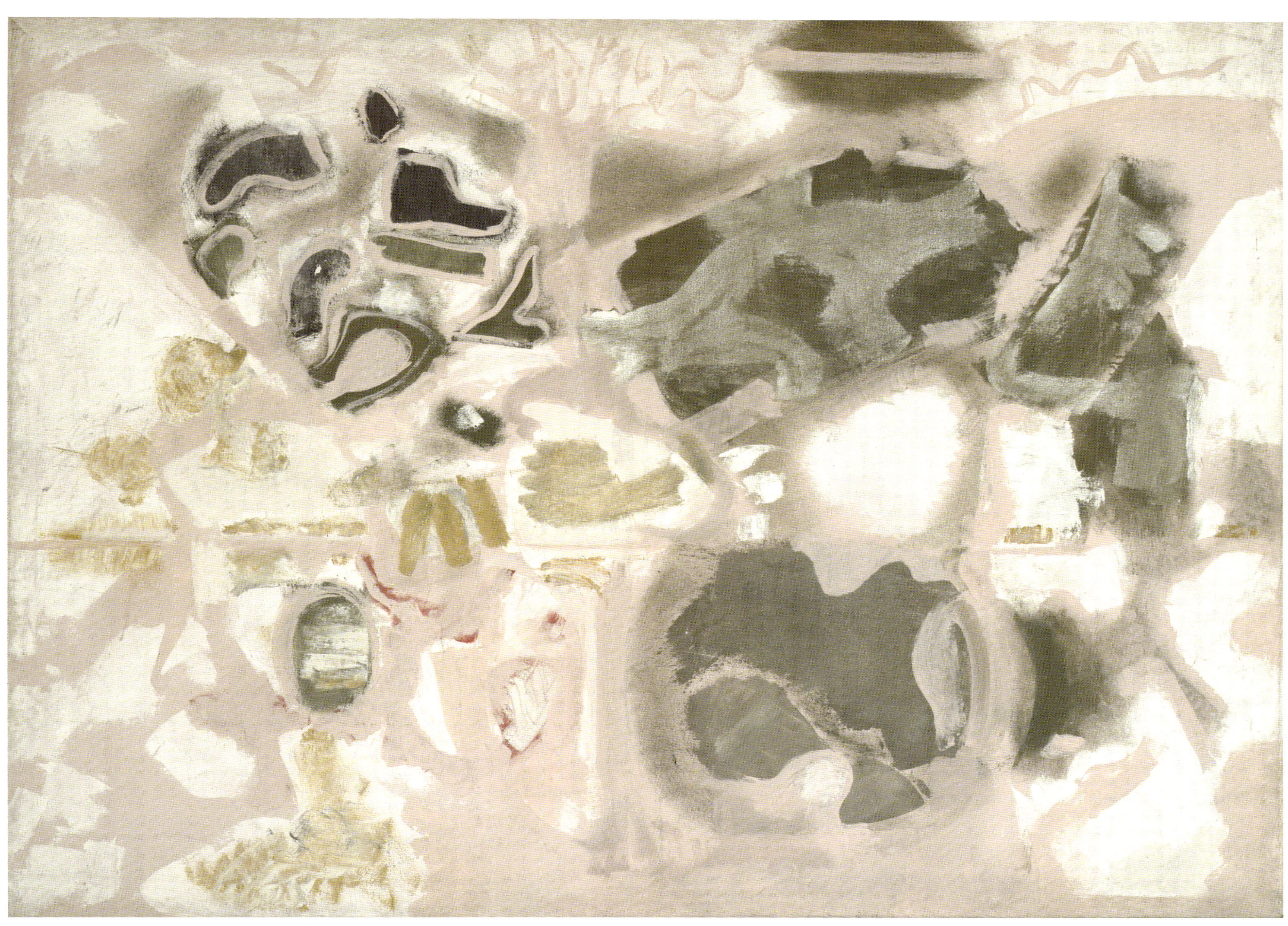

Rothko himself made a number of comments on the work, noting 'the human tendency to slaughter each other, something that we all know about today.' The eagle is a symbol of power but also of cruelty, representing threats overhead, hovering above mankind, the randomness of the power of nature and the gods. Rothko also stated that the picture does not deal with the story of Agamemnon in particular, 'but rather with the Spirit of Myth, which is generic to all myths at all times. It involves a pantheism in which man, bird, beast and tree – the known as well as the knowable – merge into a single tragic idea.' Rothko's biographer James Breslin has added to the discussion by saying that Rothko wanted to depict 'not the Greek or Christian subject matter, but the emotional roots, the essence of myth that is effective across cultures'.

Phalanx of the Mind

A work from 1944, *Phalanx of the Mind* (*see* fig. 19, page 45), indicates that Rothko considers we have the capacity to understand and take control of the life of our mind. Spears and arrows fly out of a quiver. On top of one of the spears a disc revolves; black and white diamond shapes could possibly represent shields; and in the centre of the work is a snakelike creature. The mind may be represented by the phalanx of shields, indicating that strife and the resulting violence can be used to fight the seeming absurdity of fate and our own, at times, contradictory nature. What we could call Rothko's archetypes in his mythological works depict the elemental, primal forces of savagery and violence, pain and aggression, with reference not primarily to the situation that was unfolding in Europe, but to events in the long-distant past that nonetheless resonated with the contemporary world. It is likely that Rothko meant his representations to show that myth has impact, it is a powerful force which modern man, shorn of symbols and stories, needs to rediscover in order to understand and interpret his life, to reconnect himself to the past and so give meaning to his existence.

The Syrian Bull

In 1942, Rothko exhibited examples of his mythic paintings, including *Antigone* and *Oedipus*, at an exhibition that was held at the New York department store Macy's. For the third exhibition of the Federation of Modern Painters and Sculptors, held in June 1943, Rothko showed another of his mythic works *The Syrian Bull* (1943; *see* fig. 11, page 27).

This work shows a yellow form with eight legs silhouetted for the most part against a blue-grey background, while the lower level strip of background is of a pale pink mottled effect, which has the hoofs of the yellow legs dangling in it, possibly indicating an aquatic pool. Above the yellow form hover areas of red, brown and blue, while white, feather-like fronds cluster behind it; the painting thus references flesh, birds and water. Rothko indicated that this painting referred to the legend of Mithra, the Zoroastrian god who, by slaying a bull, created the world. In Rothko's painting, bull and god appear entwined, merging in this depiction of the creative event.

The exhibition catalogue was combative, calling for a new American art in response to the Second World War, which embraced a global perspective. The exhibition was significant in another way, for it resulted in a written statement by Rothko and Gottlieb shedding light on their ntentions and motivations for their art. The art critic of the ***New York Times***, Edward Alden Jewell, had written a review of the show, declaring, in an ironic manner, how puzzled and perplexed he was by some of the works, singling out for special mention Rothko's ***The Syrian Bull*** and Gottlieb's ***Rape of Persephone***. Gottlieb telephoned Jewell, offering to provide him with a statement about the paintings, and Jewell accepted. Eleven days later, on 13 June 1943, Jewell's column contained excerpts from the statement written jointly by Rothko and Gottlieb, which had been edited by Barnett Newman, although he did not sign it.

Rothko's Draft Letters

Rothko and Gottlieb shared the writing of the letter, and to some extent it was a compromise, with each supporting the other's statements. Rothko wrote a number of drafts of a letter of his own, in which he attempted to clarify his personal views. The author Bonnie Clearwater considers that these drafts of Rothko's own letter are 'more conciliatory than the adversarial joint letter sent for publication.'

Rothko puts forward his own case, challenging Jewell, who had commented largely on the form of the works and on the artists' techniques, that concentrating on the form of a work is limiting in that 'any serious artist or thinker will know that a form is

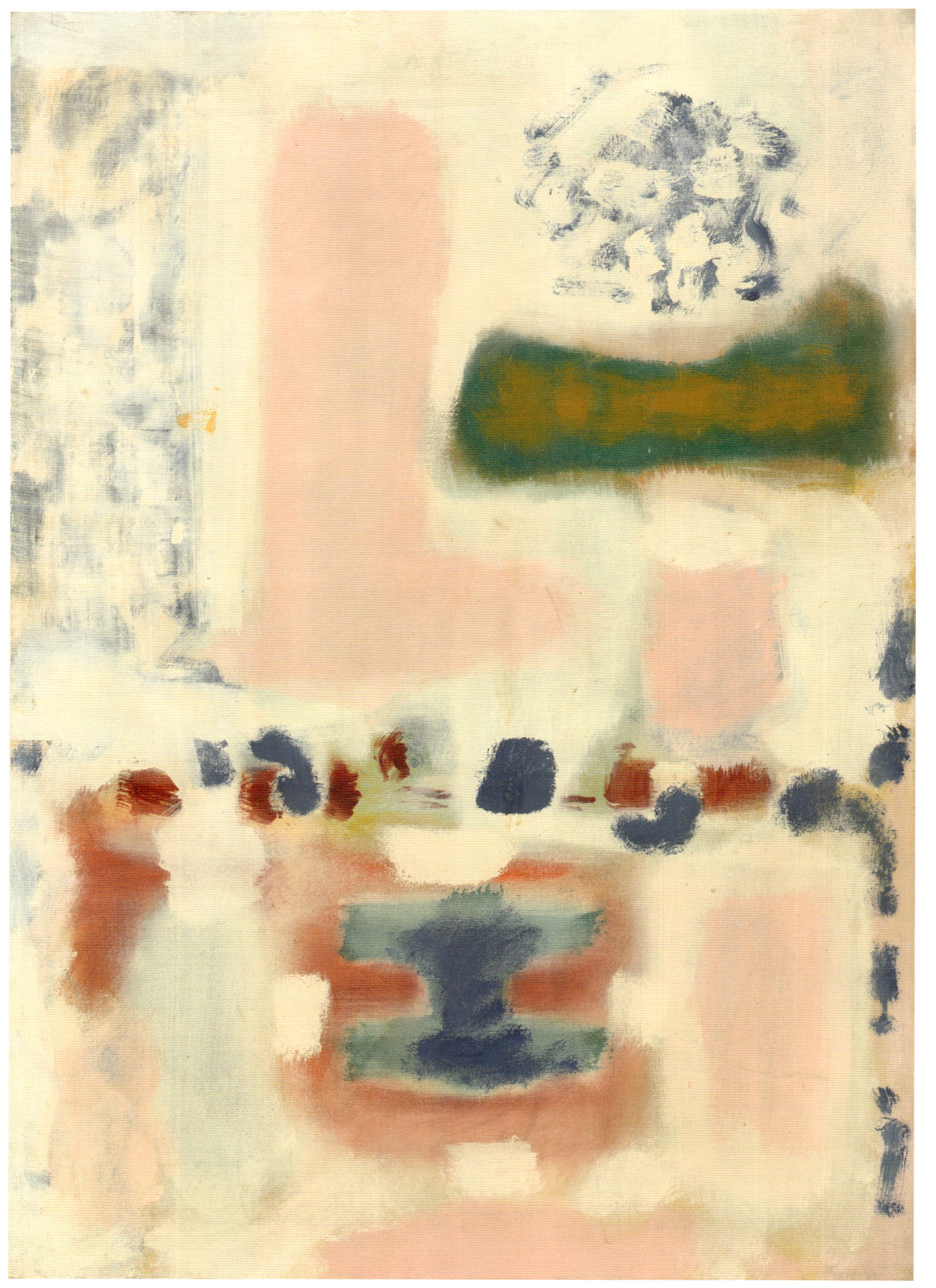

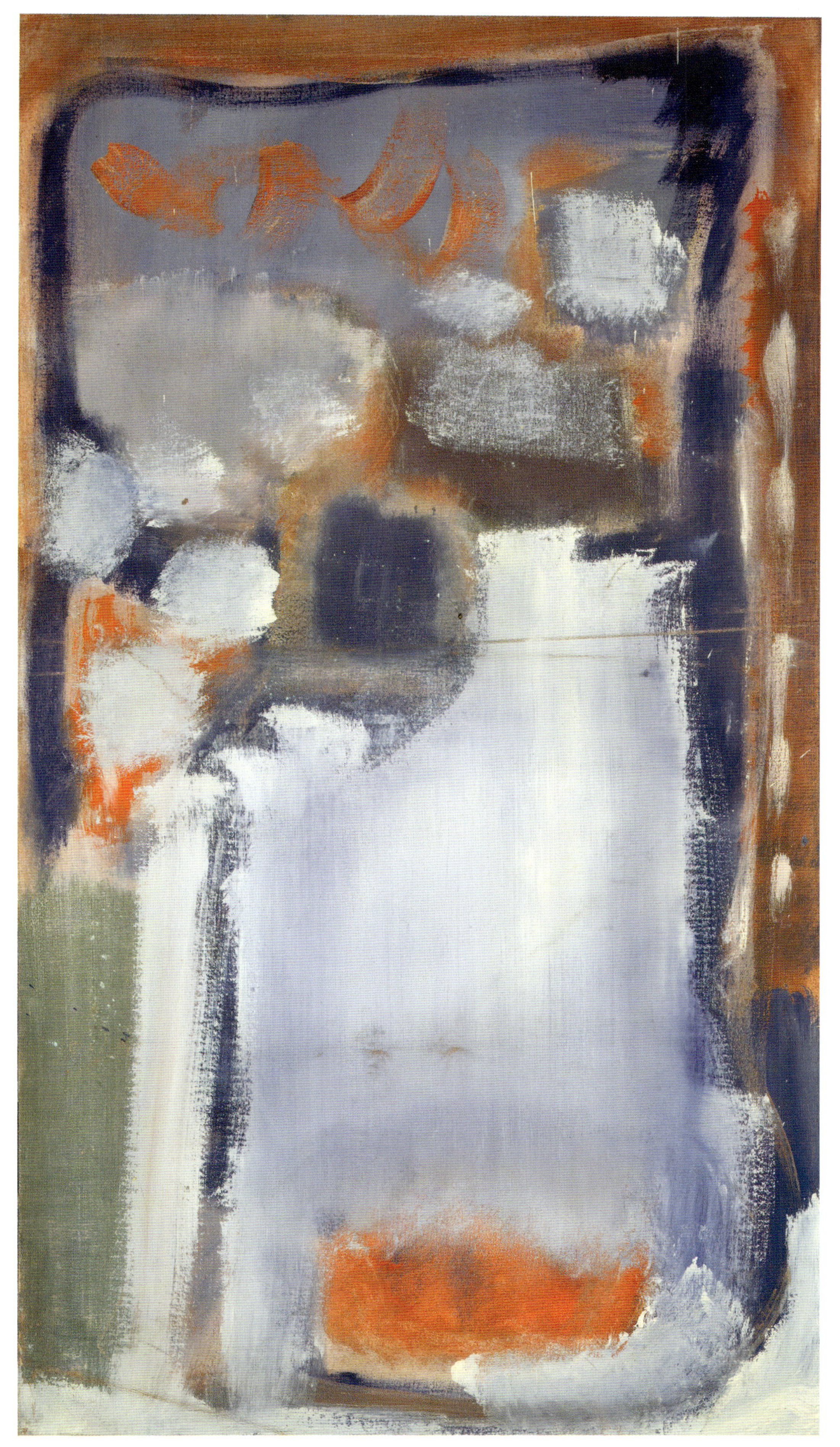

significant only in so far as it expresses the inherent idea.' He puts forward that 'the truth is therefore that the modern artist has a spiritual kinship with the emotions which these archaic forms imprison and the myths which they represent.' He ends by acknowledging that other artists and colleagues are working on similar mythological themes and modestly declares that his art is 'simply a new aspect of the eternally archaic myth and I am neither the first nor will be the last compelled to evolve these chimera of our time.'

The Joint Manifesto

Two major areas of importance, which were to continue to be reflected and developed in Rothko's work, are reflected in the joint letter that was eventually sent to Jewell. One was the relationship between the viewer and the art work, the other that the work of art conveys what Baal-Teshuva calls 'prophetic and ethical messages'.

In this joint letter, Rothko and Gottlieb claimed that 'no possible set of notes can explain our paintings. Their explanation must come out of a consummated experience between picture and onlooker. The appreciation of art is a true marriage of minds.' Having stated this, they decline to provide any indication of the content of the works, other than underlining the view that the use of mythological subjects to shed light on contemporary events was valid: 'Since art is timeless, the significant rendition of a symbol, no matter how archaic, has as full validity today as the archaic symbol had then.'

Instead, they provide a list revealing some of the goals and intentions they were seeking to fulfil through their art. They round this off with a somewhat amusing flourish, describing what their work is definitely not: 'as it must insult anyone who is spiritually attuned to interior decoration; pictures for the home; pictures for over the mantle; pictures of the American scene; social pictures; purity in art; prize-winning potboilers; the National Academy; the Whitney Academy; the Corn Belt Academy; buckeyes; trite tripe; etc.' They preface the main list of their goals and aims by stressing that: 'The point at issue it seems to us, is not an "explanation" of the paintings but whether the intrinsic ideas carried within the frames of these pictures have significance.'

Five Aesthetic Beliefs

Rothko and Gottlieb continue by stating that they feel their pictures demonstrate their aesthetic beliefs, five of which they go on to list. As these beliefs are fundamental to Rothko and his work, they are listed in full.

'1. To us art is an adventure into an unknown world, which can be explored only by those willing to take the risks.

2. This world of the imagination is fancy-free and violently opposed to common sense.

3. It is our function as artists to make the spectator see the world our way – not his way.

4. We favour the simple expression of the complex thought. We are for the large shape because it has the impact of the unequivocal. We wish to reassert the picture plane. We are for flat forms because they destroy illusion and reveal truth.

5. It is a widely accepted notion among painters that it does not matter what one paints as long as it is well painted. This is the essence of academicism. There is no such thing as good painting about nothing. We assert that the subject is crucial and only that subject matter is valid which is tragic and timeless. That is why we profess spiritual kinship with primitive and archaic art.'

This manifesto, as Baal-Teshuva notes, clearly shows the influence of surrealism in its championing of violent opposition to common sense, a free-ranging imagination and taking risks, as well as the ideas of the abstract in its rejection of a realistic, representational art.

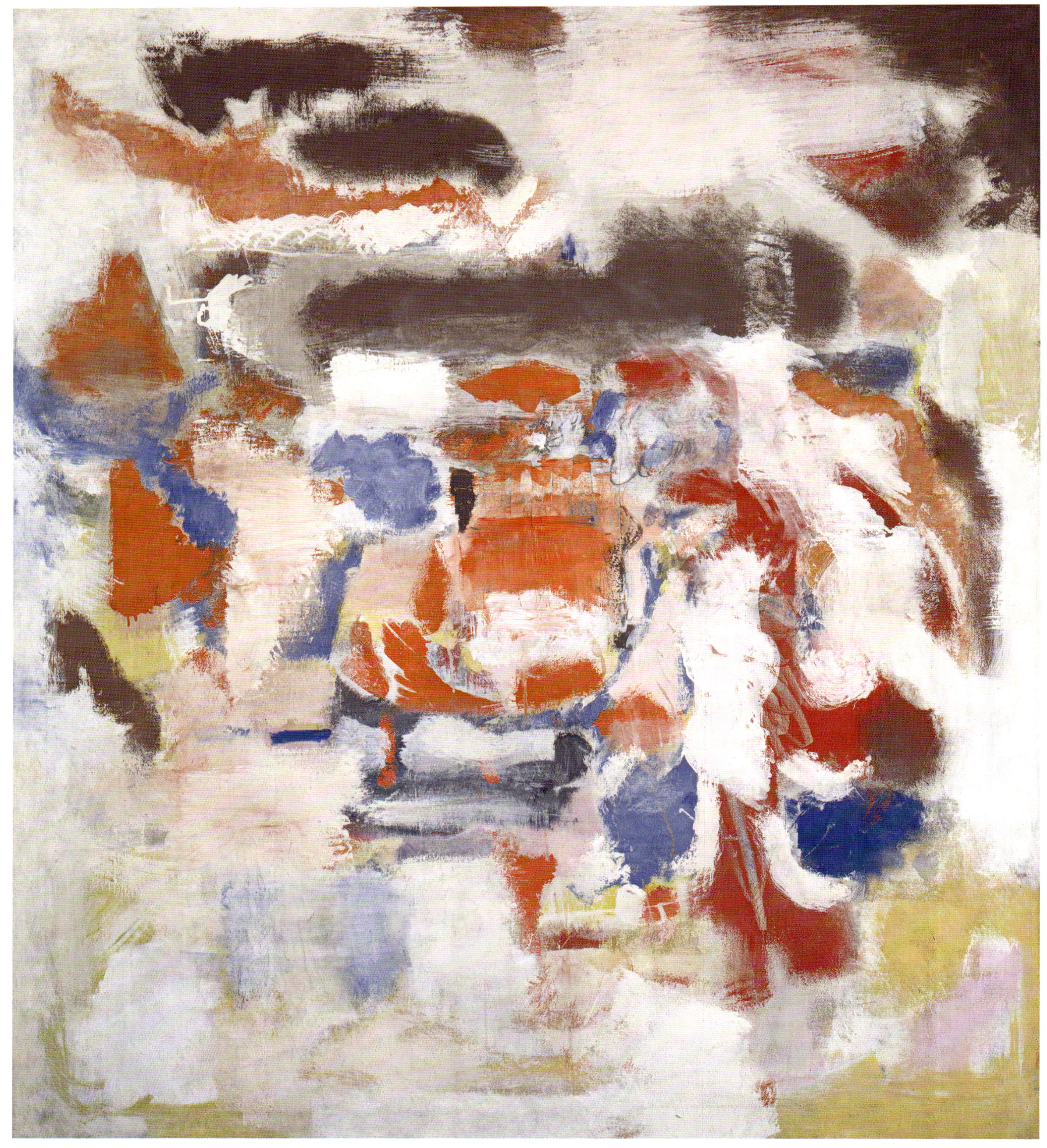

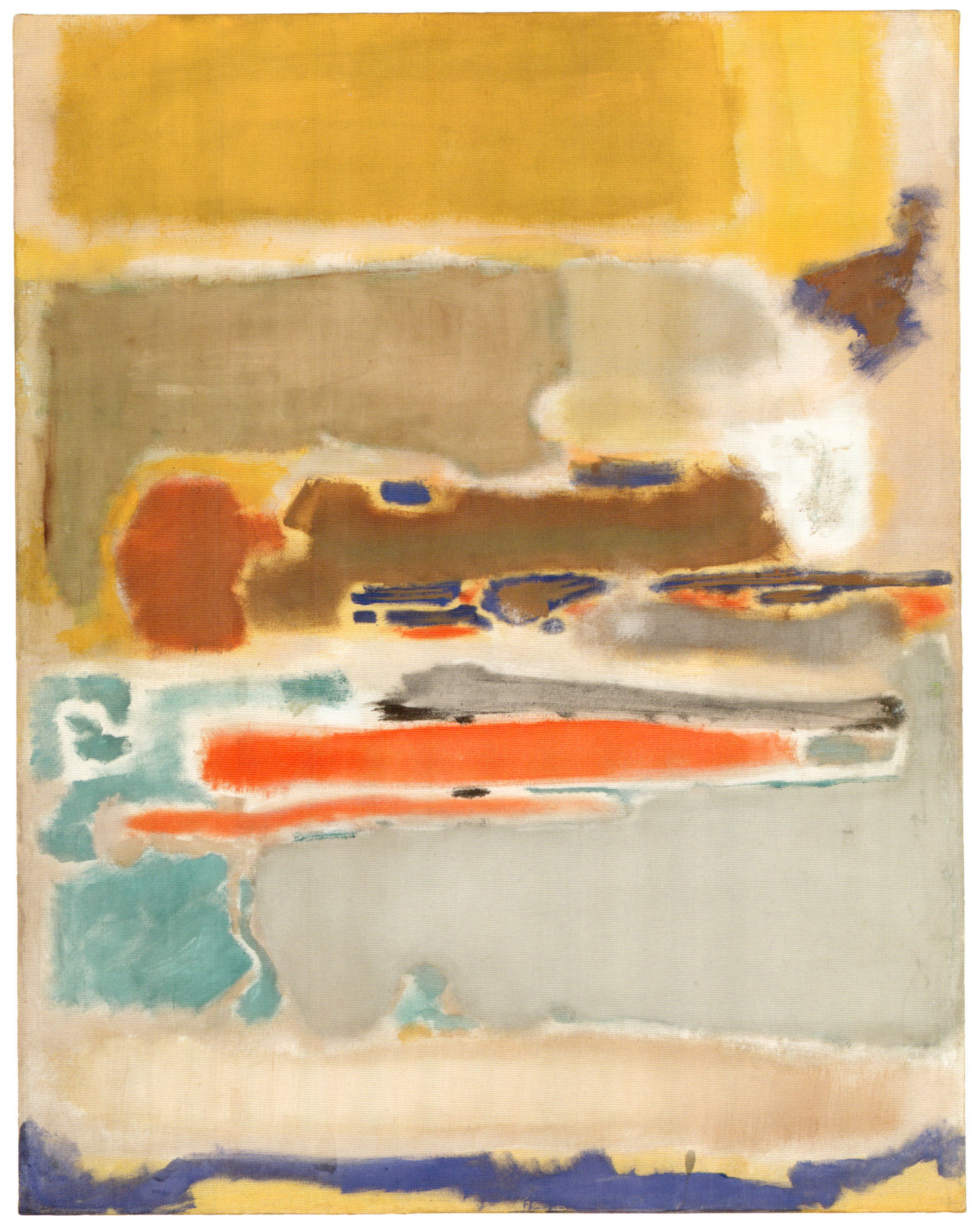

Divorce, Duchamp and Miró

Up to around 1946, Rothko continued to work in a surrealist-inspired style, while at the same time experimenting with further developments in a more abstract style on his journey to his own ultimate personal stylistic expression. Swirling figures made their entrance in his work around 1942, and in one review he was called a 'Mythomorphic Abstractionist'.

The year 1943 was to be significant for Rothko as he and Edith separated for the last time; Rothko took it very badly and seems to have had some sort of breakdown and spent some time in hospital. Depressed and badly shaken by the events, he travelled to Portland to visit relatives and spend time with some friends, the Kaufmans in Los Angeles. They took him to visit the Louise (1879–1953) and Walter Arensberg (1878–1954) collection of modern art, which was on display in the Arensbergs' home and which contained a number of works from the New York Dada era of art.

Dada was an anti-art movement (*c.*1916-22) that was intentionally irrational as a protest against accepted artistic standards. Members of the Dada movement considered society to be oppressive and inflexible, and proposed that this had led to the First World War and man's inhumanity to man. The Arensbergs had become very close to Marcel Duchamp, a leading proponent of Dada, even lending him their New York apartment while they were on vacation in 1915; they became his lifelong patrons and developed the most important collection of his works.

Clearwater suggests that viewing some of Duchamp's works in the Arensberg collection, in particular those containing floating figures that appear to be part-human, part-machine, may well have been a catalyst for Rothko to abandon the frieze-like layers of a number of his mythological works and to experiment in a new, more abstract style, with gyrating spirals and elements of design based on patterns and shapes occurring in nature and living organisms; a technique known as biomorphism. Joan Miró (1893–1983), some of whose works had been exhibited in New York at the Pierre Matisse Gallery and elsewhere, which Rothko may well have studied, also painted lighthearted depictions of playful biomorphs.

Guggenheim and Remarriage

Rothko had been recommended to Peggy Guggenheim by a contact who knew her from a period of time spent living in Paris. Guggenheim initially appeared to have little interest in his works, but eventually agreed to include him in a 1944 exhibition at her gallery, entitled *First Exhibition in America of Twenty Paintings*. In 1945, she went on to give him a solo show, which attracted favourable reviews and was instrumental in furthering his reputation.

During this period, Rothko met his future second wife at a party in December 1944. Mary Alice Beistel, known as Mel, had moved to New York earlier that year and was working as a commercial artist. She had recently graduated from Skidmore College in Saratoga Springs in upstate New York and at 22 years of age was 19 years younger than Rothko. From a financially comfortable middle-class family in Cleveland, Ohio, she had been illustrating, from the age of 16, the children's books that her mother wrote and published. Impressed by the older Rothko, who was already establishing himself as a significant presence on the New York art scene, she was soon involved in a relationship with him.

For his part, he was delighted with this young, beautiful, talented woman and the couple married in March 1945, a year after his divorce from Edith. His new marriage appeared to have a positive effect on Rothko. This change for the better in his personal life also corresponded with positive events pointing towards the end of the war in Europe, and his restless, unsettled temperament became calmer and more settled with a resulting beneficial effect on his career.

Slow Swirl

As the relationship with Mel was developing, Rothko painted one of his most delicate and pleasing works, which he entitled *Slow Swirl at the Edge of the Sea* (1944; *see* fig. 13, page 33). This was exhibited at his solo show at Peggy Guggenheim's gallery in January 1945 and was the one work which Guggenheim herself bought for her own collection when the show closed.

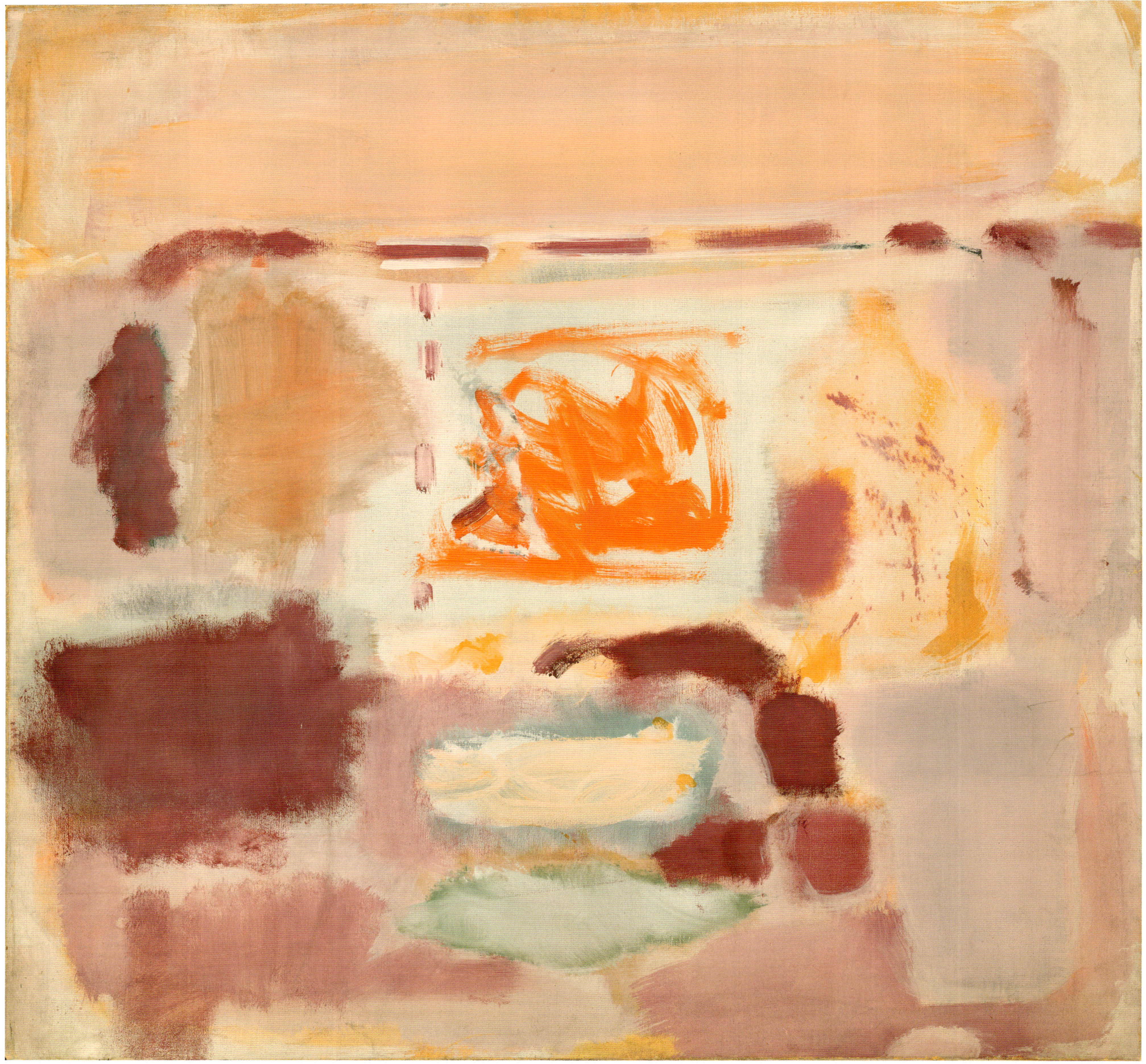

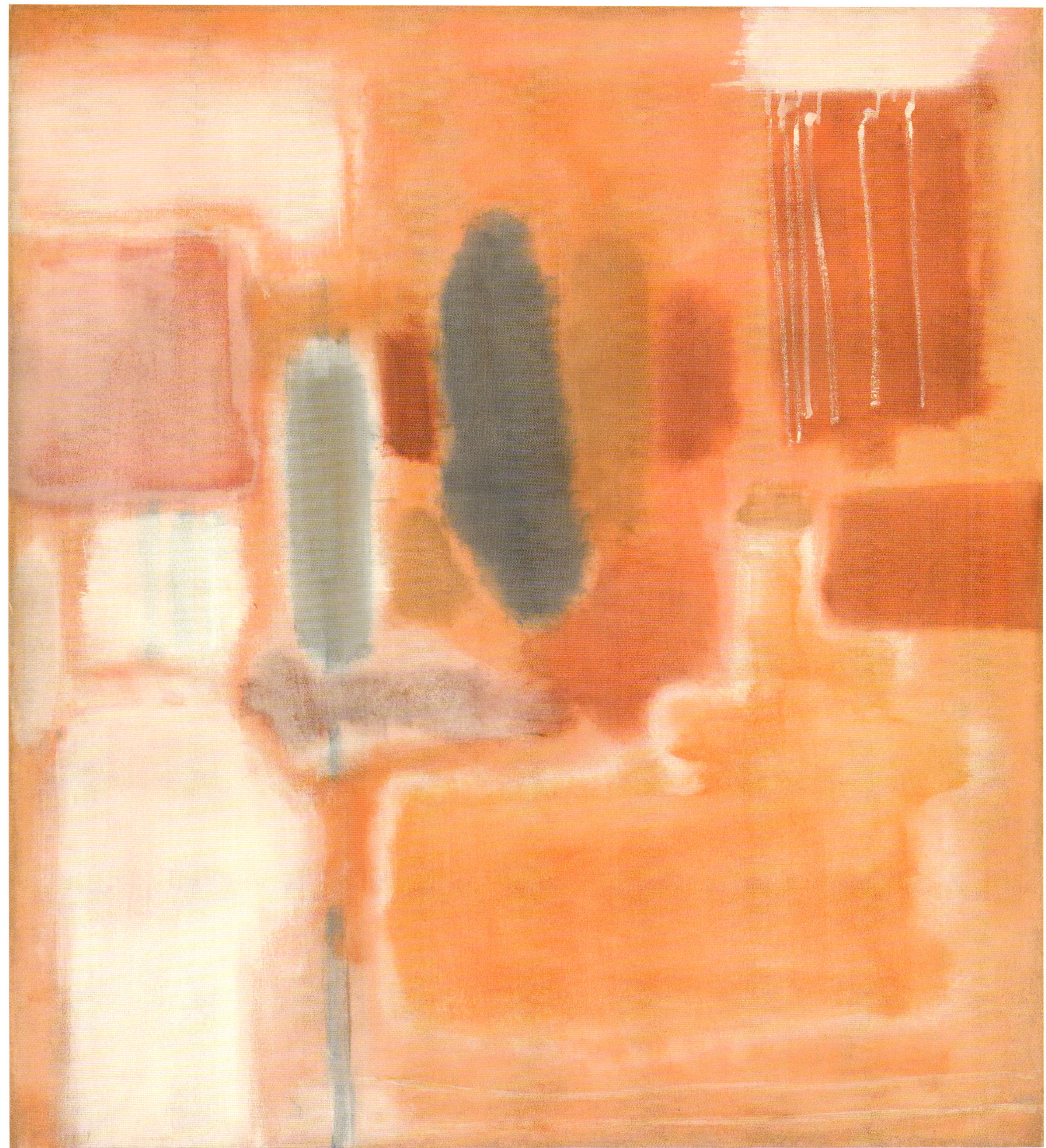

All of Rothko's other works in the exhibition were mythological paintings, but ***Slow Swirl at the Edge of the Sea*** was in his newly developing style using biomorphic forms. The 'edge of the sea', the only division in the painting, is suggested by a darker band of colour at the bottom of the work, the rest of which has a pinkish glow as background, suggestive of dawn. Two graceful abstract figures emerging from the sea dance towards the viewer in a spiral of organic forms, suggesting vegetation, primeval amoebas and a constant life force of creation and recreation.

Possibly inspired by ***Birth of Venus*** (*c*. 1485) by Botticelli (*c*.1444/5–1510), which had been exhibited at the Museum of Modern Art in New York in 1940, the figure on the left is curvaceous and feminine. Rothko did not clarify the meaning of the painting, but clearly regarded it as significant in his body of work. When Guggenheim was organizing a show at the San Francisco Museum of Modern Art, she wrote that Rothko wanted to show this work in particular 'since he considers it his most important.' In 1946, when Guggenheim donated it to the museum, he said: 'It is my favourite of all those I have painted.' A codicil to these events is that in 1962, he gave a later, dark painting of 1960 to the museum in return for receiving back ***Slow Swirl***, which he then gave to Mel who displayed it at their home.

Biomorphism

Rothko had experimented with the surrealist technique of automatic drawing, that is taking up the brush or pencil and letting it roam freely on the paper or canvas, probably as early as the late 1930s. This had freed him from the heavy lines and confined spaces of his works from his earlier realistic phase. With the incorporation of the free-floating biomorphs, he appears to have been able to enjoy this creation of new, transforming and transformative forms. This fluid process also enabled him to create more ethereal atmospheres and use a lighter palette of colours as he combined symbols and dreams in a melange of objects and forms within a sense of movement.

The appeal is to the senses, inviting the viewer to participate in the free-flowing movement on the paper or the canvas. Using a theatrical allusion, he said that within his pictures, 'the shapes ... are the performers.' For Rothko, the shapes in his work were types of life forms. Biomorphs are not always positive elements in his works as they are in ***Slow Swirl at the Edge of the Sea***. They can often be disturbing and threatening, leading the viewer to a place where they perhaps would prefer not to be.

In ***Birth of Cephalopods*** (1944; *see* fig. 12, page 32), the black, feathered line slightly to the left of centre appears as a threatening gash amid the swirling aquatic forms, which are thus rendered more unsettling. The dualist aspect of Rothko's mythological works, with their more overtly surrealist style, and the freer, less stratified, more biomorphic works exist side by side for a time. Although a new, lighter freedom can be identified in some works, the sense of the tragic is never far away. Examples of titles such as ***Gethsemane*** (1944), ***Entombment*** (1946) and a number of paintings dealing with human sacrifice, which date from this time of burgeoning success and greater personal happiness, bear witness to his continuing preoccupation with the tragic. In 1945, he was to state 'tragic experience ... is the only sourcebook for art.'

Clyfford Still

Rothko had first met Clyfford Still (1904–80) on his trip to California in 1943. Still was from North Dakota and had seemingly developed his art without recourse to any noticeable influence of European art, which he regarded as extremely decadent. He was known as difficult to get along with, very self-confident, steadfastly refusing any theories to do with the intellectualization of art and working in a totally abstract style. He emphasized working by intuition through flowing energy to create his abstract works, which consisted of large areas of a single colour punctuated by patches of contrasting colours.

Rothko appears to have been very impressed with Still's confident assertions, particularly his rejection of European art, which almost by default emphasized a new American art, a subject close to Rothko's own ideals. Still's distrust of and disdain for the art business also resonated with Rothko's moral code and his lack of materialistic ambitions. Still's uncompromising stand seems to have inspired

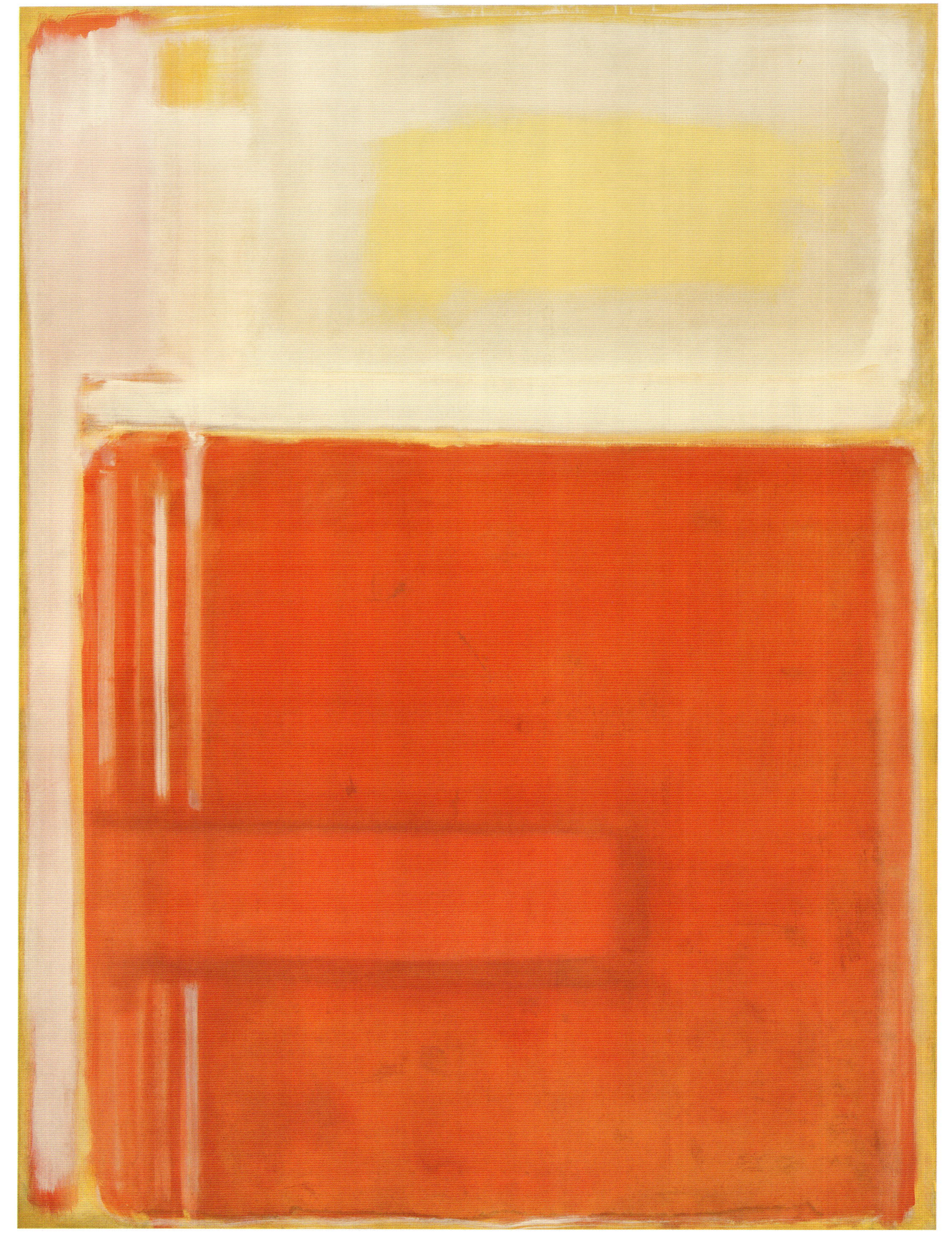

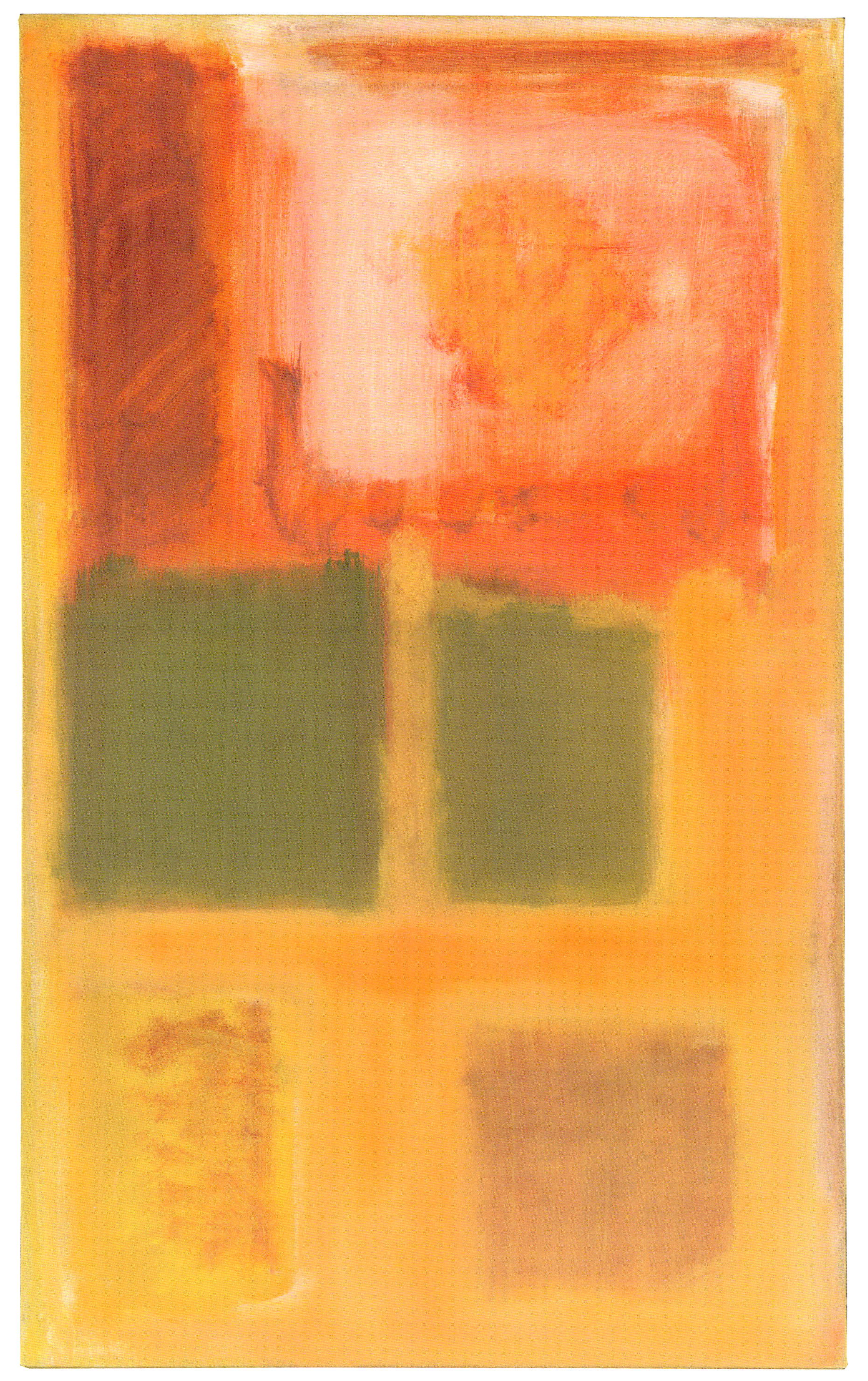

Rothko to a new freedom to stand up for what he believed in art. In 1945, Still left San Francisco and moved to New York, settling in Greenwich Village. Here Rothko and Still were able to meet frequently and discuss their ideas and aims. Still recalled later that they were complete opposites who came from different sides of the world. He said of Rothko: 'He was thoroughly immersed in Jewish culture.' Ironically, they had grown up only a few hundred miles apart and had read many of the same things. 'And we could walk through the park together and talk about anything.'

Exhibitions and Sales

Still's canvases were very big, with a raw, unpolished finish, totally abstract with large dark areas with rough edges impinging on to occasional patches of bright colour. Baal-Teshuva writes that Still once referred to his works as 'life-lines', which for him recalled the plains of North Dakota, saying 'these are living forms climbing out of the earth'. Rothko was so taken with Still's works that he persuaded Guggenheim to give him a solo exhibition, for which Rothko himself wrote the catalogue. In it, he wrote that Still's works were 'of the earth, the damned and of the recreated'. At the same time, he highlighted 'their unprecedented forms and completely personal methods'.

Rothko was at this time in a phase of experimentation with new ways of painting, and felt encouraged by Still's example of independence from European and surrealist influences to free himself to move into new areas. Still was to promote Rothko for his first solo show in a national institution by helping to arrange an exhibition at the San Francisco Museum of Modern Art in 1946. The show was made up of 19 oil paintings and 10 watercolours. Writing to New York gallery owner Betty Parsons, Still states: 'It was without question the best show I have ever seen in the gallery for years and it commanded the highest respect from those who know good work when they see it.' The museum bought one of the paintings, *Tentacles of Memory* (1945–46), which was the first acquisition of a Rothko work by an American institution. Encouraged by this act, the Whitney Gallery bought *Entombment I* (1946) and the Brooklyn Museum bought *Vessels of Magic* (1946).

Burgeoning Success

In 1947, Rothko began to exhibit his works in Betty Parsons' gallery. Three other big names to exhibit there were Newman, Still and Pollock. As Cohen-Solal notes, Parsons referred to the group as 'The Four Men of the Apocalypse'. They were very supportive of each other to begin with, and helped each other hang their works. Parsons said: 'I give them walls. They do the rest.'

The year 1947 was also one of the years when Rothko was invited to be a guest teacher at the California School of Fine Arts in San Francisco, along with Still. Rothko seems to have enjoyed this experience, finding it supportive and encouraging. His lecture once a week was well attended by people from other classes. One of his students there, Ernest Briggs, describes Rothko as 'the epitome of the New York intellectual artist/painter .... urbane, deep intent.' His lecture, the student recalls, 'was more like a conversational thing, responding to a few questions and then going on ... he would be quoting Herodotus or something … in answer to some inquiry on the part of a student.'

Although Rothko enjoyed his time in California, he found that his creativity was at a low ebb. It was only when he returned to New York that he began to find inspiration once more to actually paint. Reflecting on his stay in San Francisco, he realized that it had stimulated his work. 'Elements occurred there which I shall develop, and which are new in my work.'

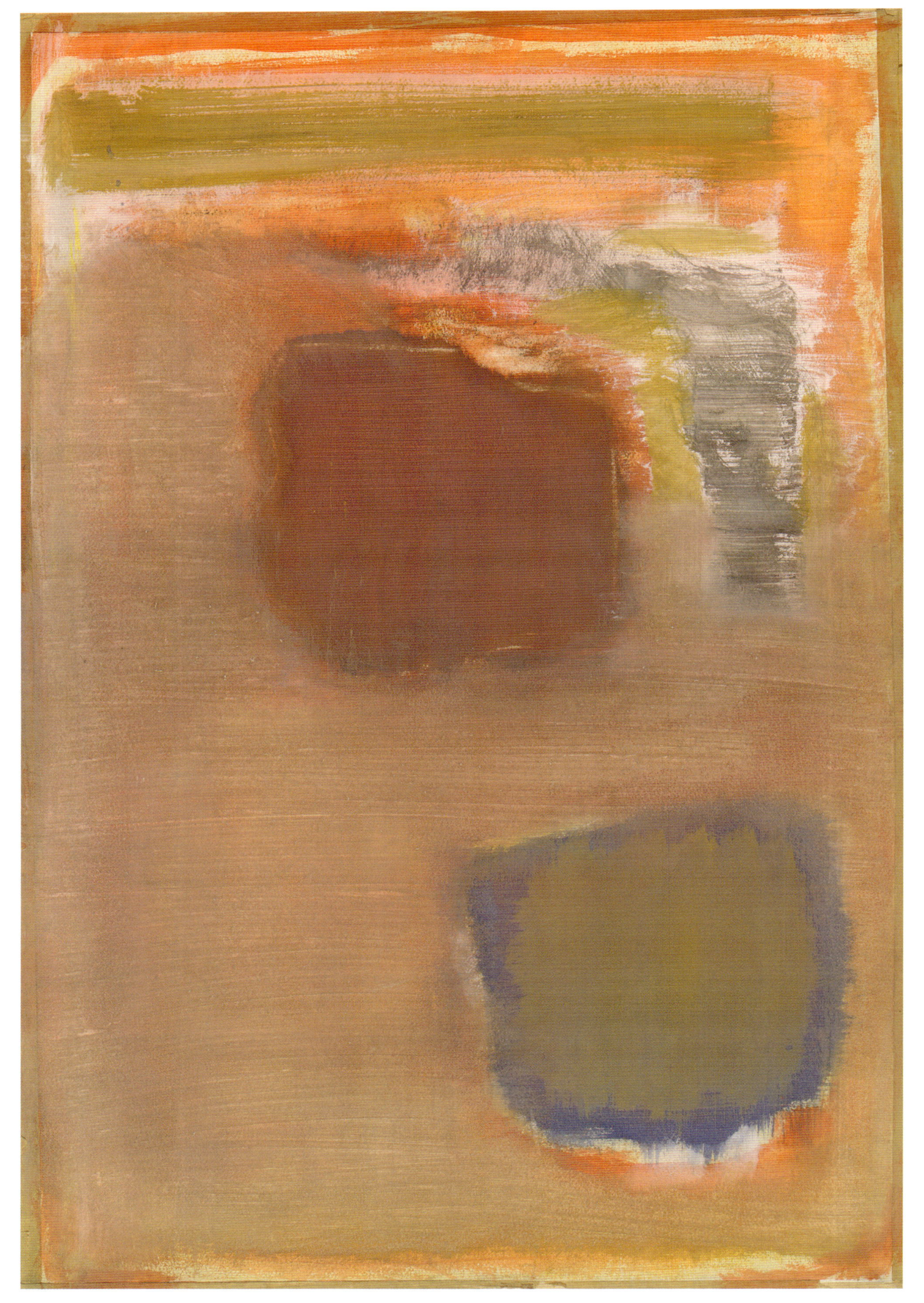

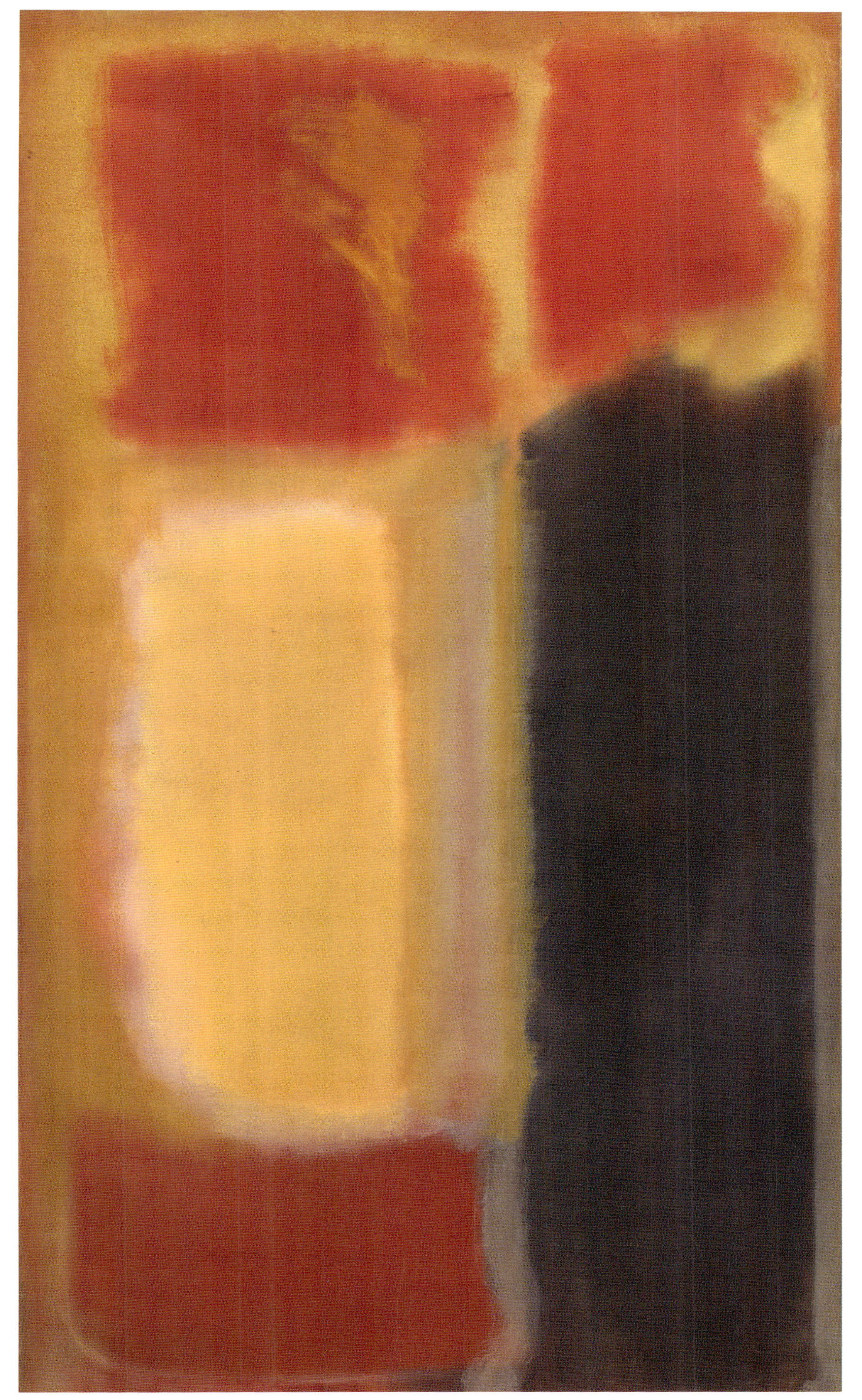

stillness & awe

The new elements that Rothko was seeking in his work were gradually to come to the fore over the following months, stimulated by his San Francisco teaching and particularly with the relationship and influence of Clyfford Still. Back in New York, he was inspired to experiment in his art work, pushing boundaries, searching for his personal, unique language of expression. As well as seeking to develop new ways forward in his art work, Rothko was inspired to put his ideas and thoughts on paper after receiving invitations to contribute to art journals.

Writings

In 1947, Rothko was given the opportunity to share more of his ideas and philosophy in two new art publications, *Tiger's Eye* and *Possibilities*. One of his most important texts, in which he discusses his own art, was published in the 1947–48 Winter edition of *Possibilities*, in an essay given the title of its first four words, 'The Romantics were Prompted.'

The contents of the essay make clear that in his works, Rothko is seeking to find a way to communicate the transcendental, that is a way to relate to a spiritual realm, something beyond the everyday human experience. Transcendentalism emphasizes the intuitive and the spiritual over and above the material world, which can be seen and touched. It also has the connotation not simply of seeking to experience what is beyond, but also seeking to explore what lies within us as human beings; in this sense, it involves the emotional and the expressive depths and possibilities of the innermost human self.

The title of the essay refers to the artists and perhaps also the musicians and writers of the Romantic movement of the late-eighteenth and nineteenth centuries who, as Rothko puts it, **'were prompted to seek exotic subjects and travel to far off places'** in a search for transcendental experience. Rothko considers: **'They failed to realize that, though the transcendental must involve the strange and unfamiliar, not everything strange or unfamiliar is transcendental.'** He argues that when the artist is freed from a false sense of security by not relying on his bank book, and the approval and support of others, then he is free to create a work that can lead to a transcendental experience. From his comments, it is clear that this experience of the transcendental is what Rothko is aiming to achieve in his work, although he is still seeking a form of expression that will allow him to fully realize this aim. He is still grappling with issues of form and shape, seeking a way to facilitate the creation of a transcendental experience.

Form and the Human Condition

In the same essay, Rothko goes on to give something of a rationale for how he has expressed his ideas formally so far in his career. He refers to the strange creatures and beings of ancient myth, underlining what he considers to be the fact that **'since the archaic artist was living in a more practical society than ours, the urgency for transcendent experience was understood and given official status'**. The human figure was thus legitimately able to combine with the monsters, hybrids and gods and demigods of ancient myth to communicate eternal truths of the human condition. Referring to our modern society, he stresses that in order to communicate these truths, 'the familiar identity of things has to be pulverized' so that the shrouds that cover these issues are destroyed and people are then able to see more clearly

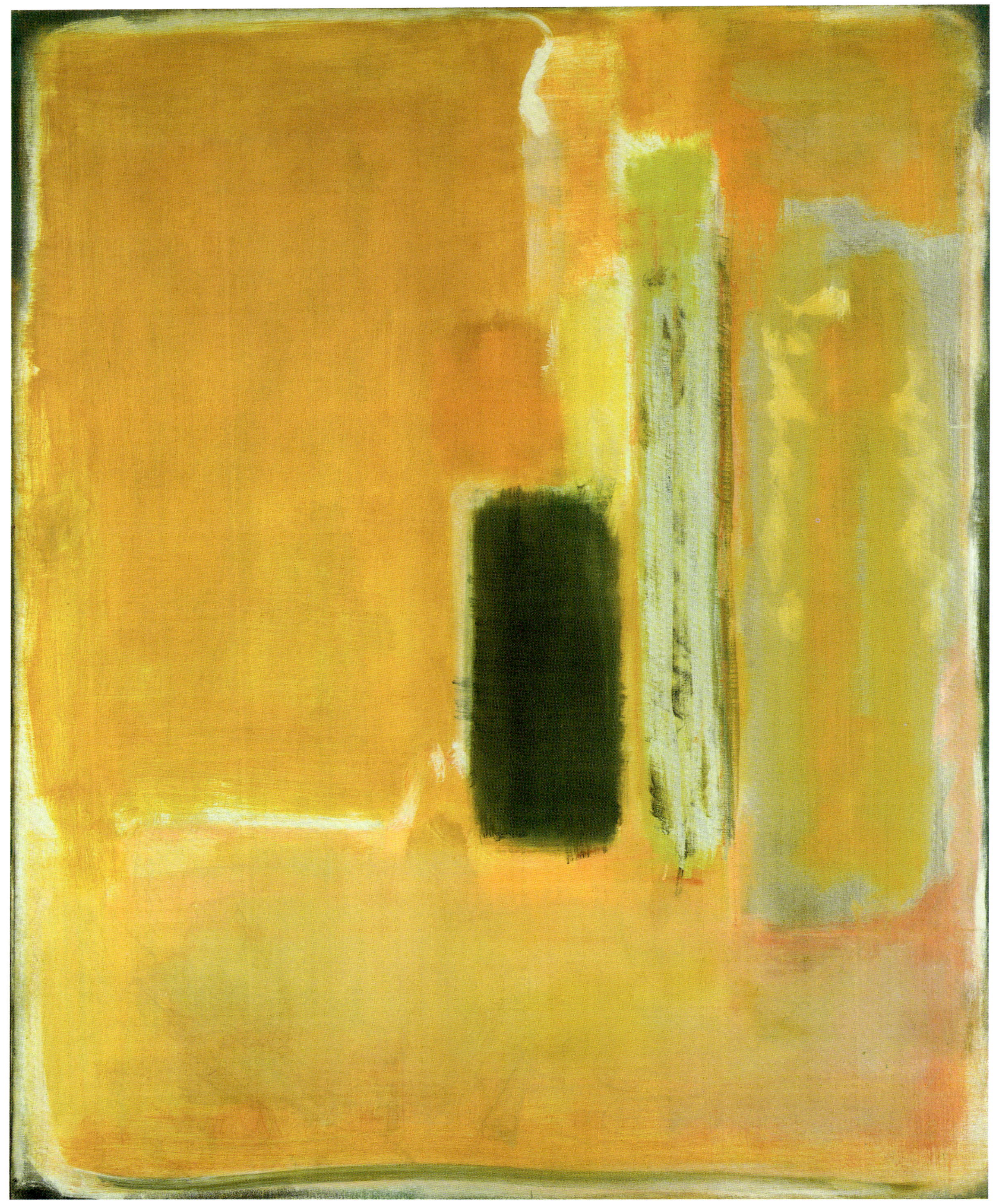

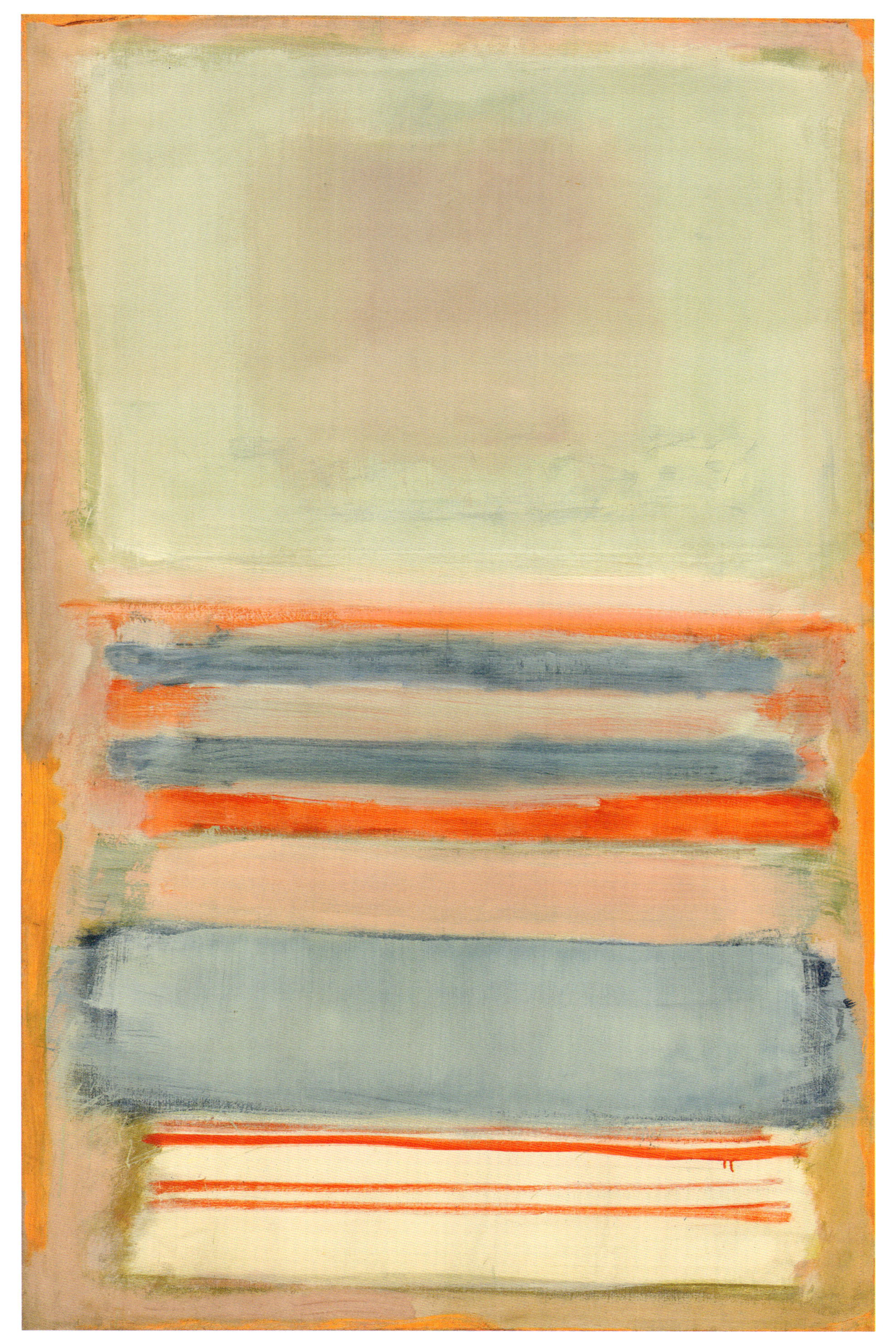

the important issues of human existence. He goes on to say that he considers the greatest achievement in the past was when the artist took the probable and familiar and represented the 'single human figure – alone in a moment of utter immobility.' For Rothko this exposes the essence of the human condition.

The Life of Shapes

Rothko continues by expressing his ideas on shapes, stating that: 'They are organisms with volition and a passion for self-assertion. They move with internal freedom and without need to conform with or to violate what is probable in the familiar world. They have no direct association with any particular visible experience, but in them one recognizes the principle and passion of organisms.' Throughout this discussion, Rothko has woven the theme of variety into the ways he has expressed his thoughts formally in his art. These include the representation of the human figure; the depiction of strange mythological creatures interacting with humans; the 'pulverization' of images of familiar things so that they create more impact and thus stimulate thought, reaction and action; and the life of shapes which appear to be living organisms, which have their own will and move freely. All these formal aspects have been used by Rothko in his art so far; his realist works, his mythological works, his surrealist works and his biomorphs.

Towards the end of the essay, he introduces the idea of the concept of the abstract, writing: **'I do not believe that there was ever a question of being abstract or representational'**. The end of the essay has perhaps inadvertently posed the question with which he was wrestling, that of seeking the best vehicle for his stated aim of enabling the transcendental, and it has perhaps also inadvertently given the answer in the word 'abstract'.

Search for Clarity

Part of Rothko's search for a new way to express his ideas was the search for clarity. In an article that was published in ***Tiger's Eye*** in October 1949, Rothko wrote that he considered the progression of his work was 'toward the elimination of all obstacles between the painter and the idea, and between the idea and the observer'. He goes on to give some examples of what he considers to be obstacles: **'I give (among others) memory, history or geometry, which are swamps of generalization from which one might pull out parodies of ideas (which are ghosts) but never an idea in itself.'**

It is interesting to note his examples of obstacles, all of which have been used in his own work; it is a clear indication that he is moving on from the kind of work he has done in the past and underlines that he is looking to a new way of working in the future. Although he only rarely spoke about the meanings of his paintings, he does express in this article a desire to be understood. This, he thought, would come about when he had eliminated all obstacles, stating that: **'To achieve this clarity is, inevitably to be understood.'**

After 1946, for the most part, Rothko stopped giving names to his works, and they were largely designated by numbers. Some have suggested that this is a possible link with music, which gives *opus* numbers to works to identify them. However, many were given numbers by exhibition curators as a means of identifying them. By refusing to name his works, Rothko was refusing to specify any possible meanings or to suggest possibilities of interpretation; he was beginning to leave the observers to suggest and experience meanings for themselves; a title became an obstacle that blocked the path for ideas and experiences to be revealed.

Search for the Abstract

During the transitional period, approximately 1946–49, when Rothko was moving away from surrealism through the biomorphs to full abstraction, he admitted that he struggled to leave behind his means of expression. In a 'Personal Statement' from the exhibition catalogue ***Painting Prophecy*** (1950), he writes: **'I quarrel with surrealist and abstract art only as one quarrels with his father and mother.'** He is drawn towards surrealism as it **'has established a**

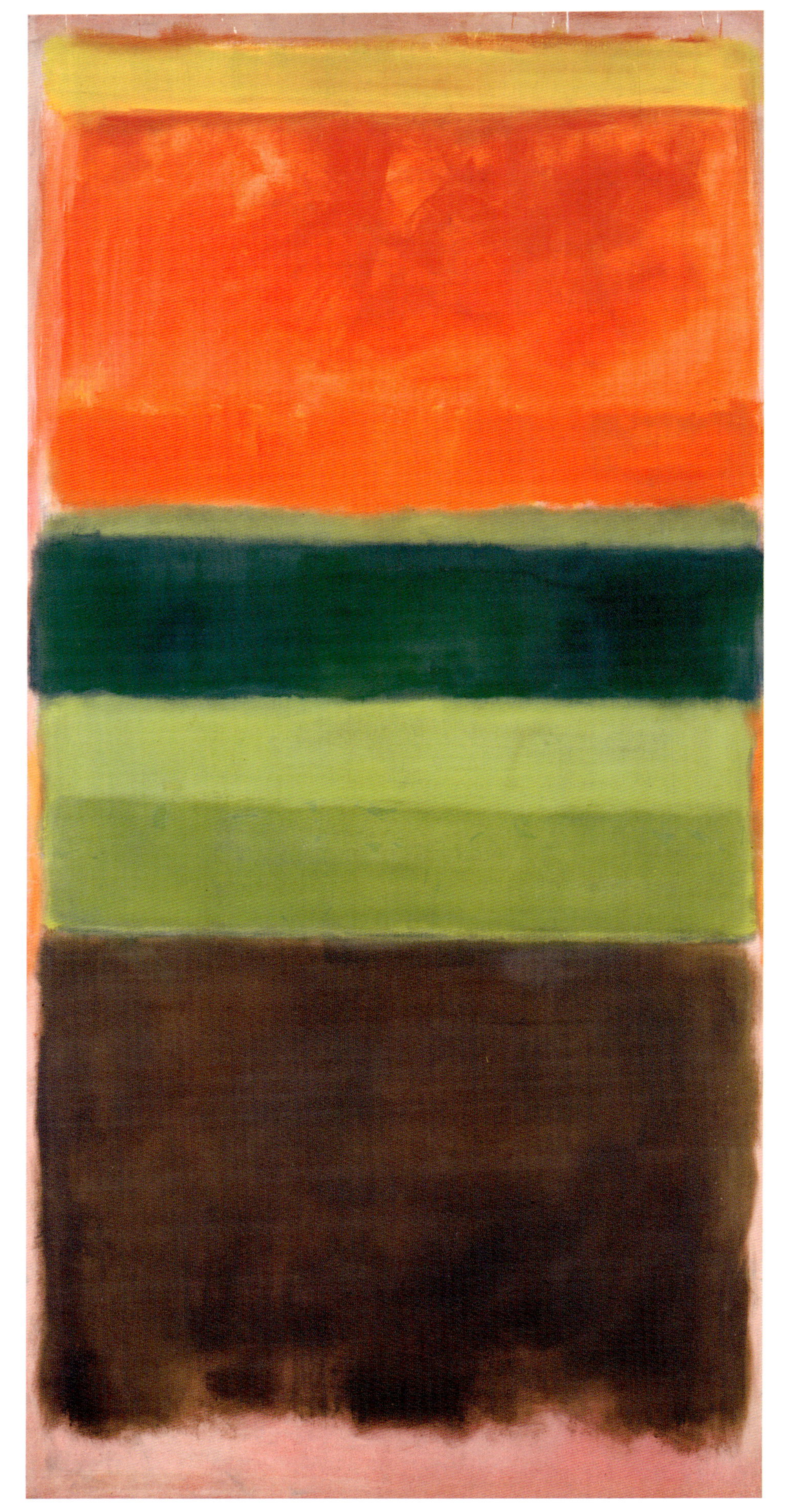

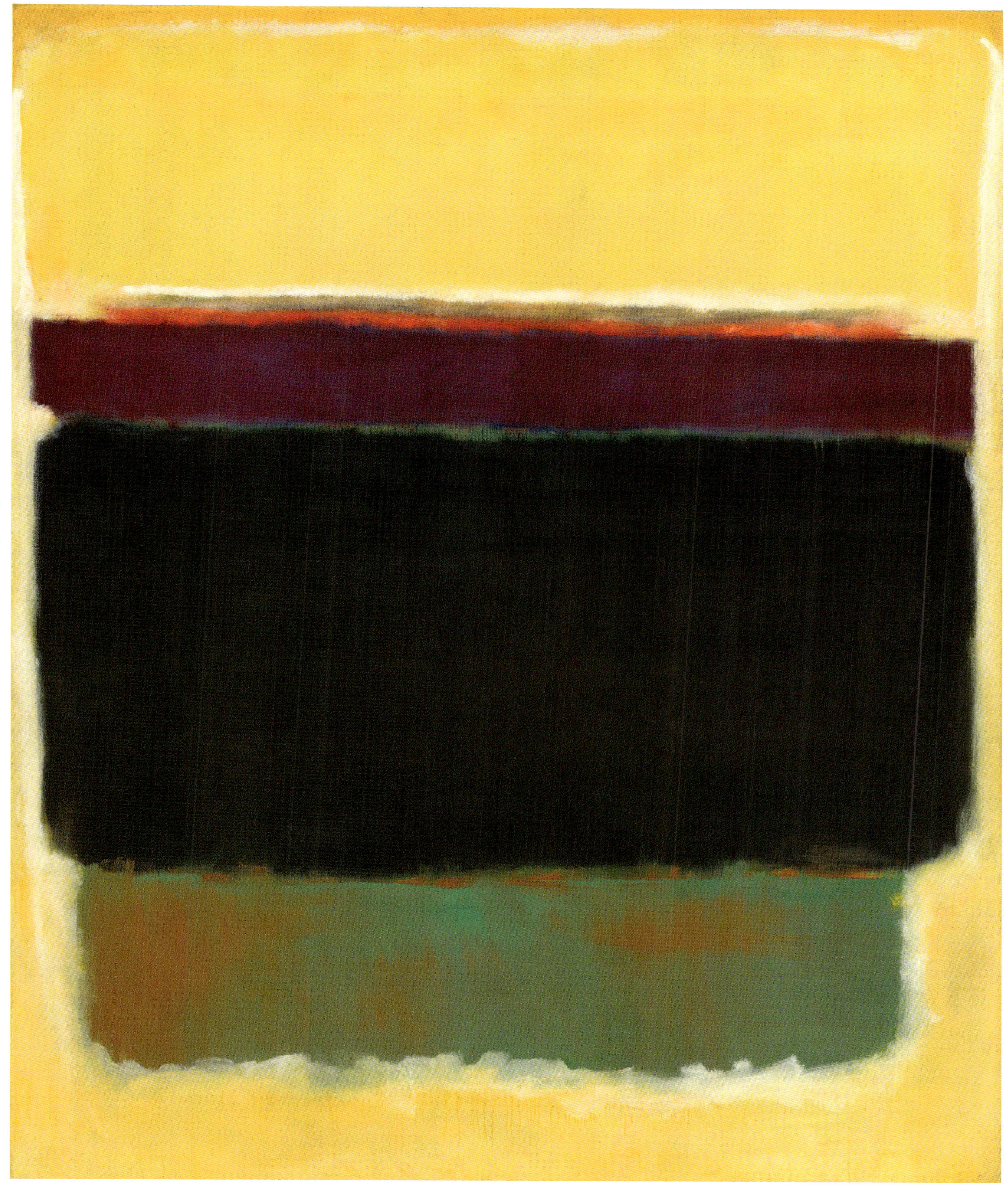

congruity between the phantasmagoria of the unconscious and the objects of everyday life'; he goes on to say that, for him, this 'constitutes the exhilarated tragic experience which for me is the only source book for art.' On the other hand, he respects the abstract artists for giving 'material existence to many unseen worlds and *tempi*.'

Eventually, Rothko realized that to be completely free and create a genuine art of the transcendent, he would have to adopt abstract art. This would release him from the tyranny of having to portray objects or people in whatever disguise he had done before, in whatever style he had worked in before. This would enable him, as he writes in 'The Romantics were Prompted', 'to produce miracles'. He considers that: 'Pictures must be miraculous; the instant one is complete, the intimacy between the creation and the creator is ended. He is an outsider. The picture must be for him, as for anyone experiencing it later, a revelation, an unexpected and unprecedented resolution of an eternally familiar need.' The progress to complete abstraction was to facilitate this freedom to create the miraculous.

The Multiforms

'Multiforms' is a term used posthumously to describe the works that Rothko produced in this phase of transitional abstract works, which can be considered as a pathway to his classic colourist works. From 1946 to 1949, he produced a large number of this type of work, which showed a wide range of variations within a consistency of approach (*see* figs. 21–36/pages 49–82).

In the catalogue for Still's exhibition in 1946, Rothko had written that in Still's work, 'Every shape becomes an organic entity, inviting the multiplicity of associations inherent in all living things. To me they form a theogony of the most elementary consciousness, hardly aware of itself beyond the will to live – a profound and moving experience.'

He found that the shapes in Still's work seemed to take on a life of their own, that they seemed to express a primeval force. This experience on viewing Still's work was to become a goal for Rothko to aspire to. In his multiforms, the canvases are covered with areas and patches of colour, which manifest as amorphous shapes of varying sizes and shades, not confined by lines but given scope for growth, blurred at the edges as if one colour was almost bleeding into the next.

The Drama of Colour Pools

In his mythological paintings, Rothko's forms had the appearance of being carved using shallow relief, which could be measured back to a shallow wall. In the multiforms, geometrical boundaries and biomorphic images have disappeared, and in their place are shades and pools which appear to float on the canvas, some overlapping, others seemingly drifting apart, creating a sense of movement and organic life forms. Edges blend so that one shape moves into the next or is silhouetted against a void of space behind it, which gives the impression of depth.

Clearwater considers that: 'The indeterminate space surrounding Rothko's areas of colour became an essential element of his paintings.' In 'The Romantics were Prompted', Rothko writes he considers that **'the shapes in the pictures are performers'** and that his pictures are 'dramas'. This idea that each shape is an individual entity, has a character and a role to play, confers life to them as if they are 'organisms', with a will and capacity for action. Rothko's goal is to have the canvas covered with pools of colour, as pulsating life forms, breathing and existing in a world of amoebic images and colour.

Luminosity

One way that Rothko created this effect of living organisms on his canvases was with his painting technique. On to the unprimed canvas, Rothko would brush a thin layer of binding solution with some pigments in it, then paint over this foundation with oils, which fixed it in place, allowing them to spread over the edges of the paintings. He no longer used frames, as this

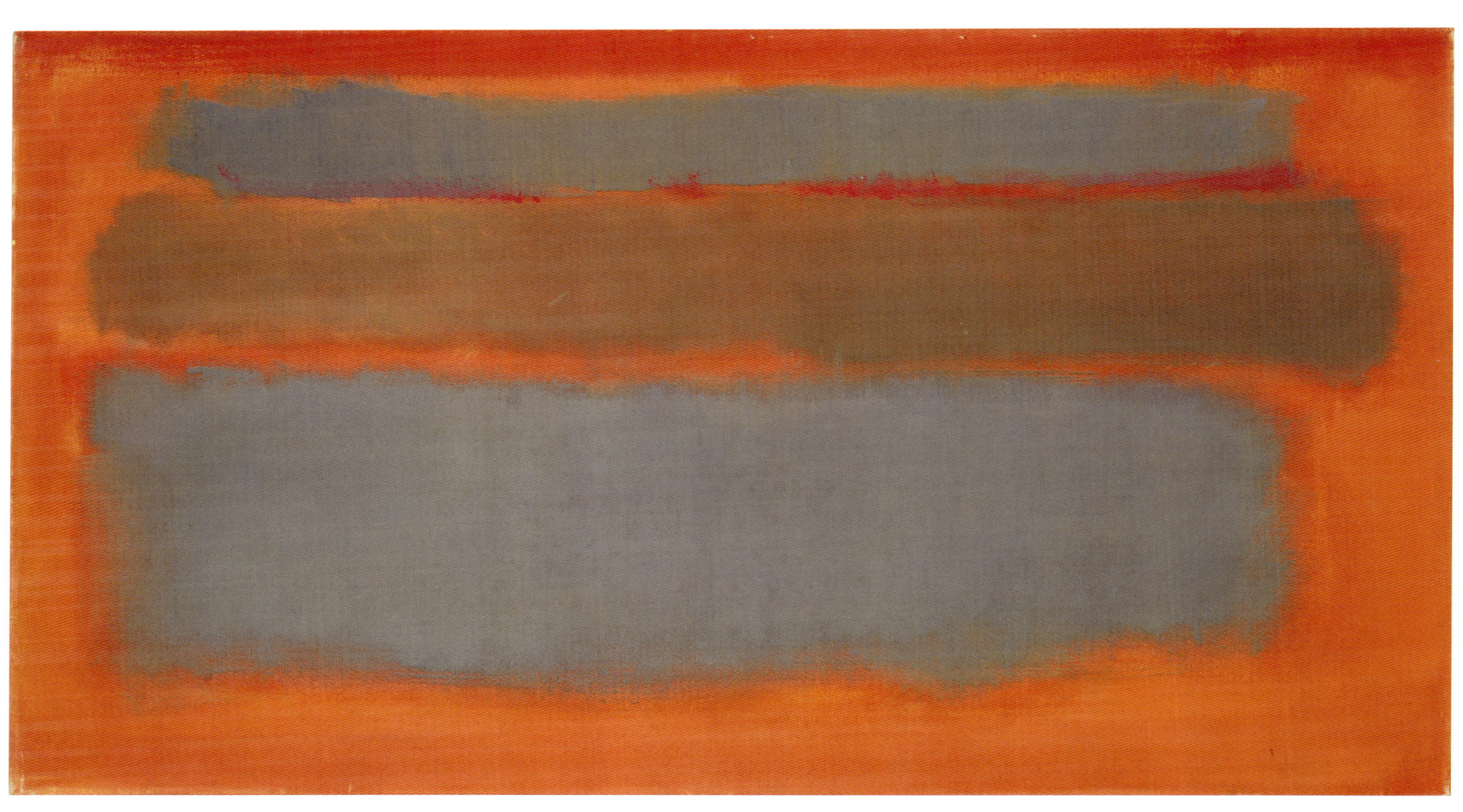

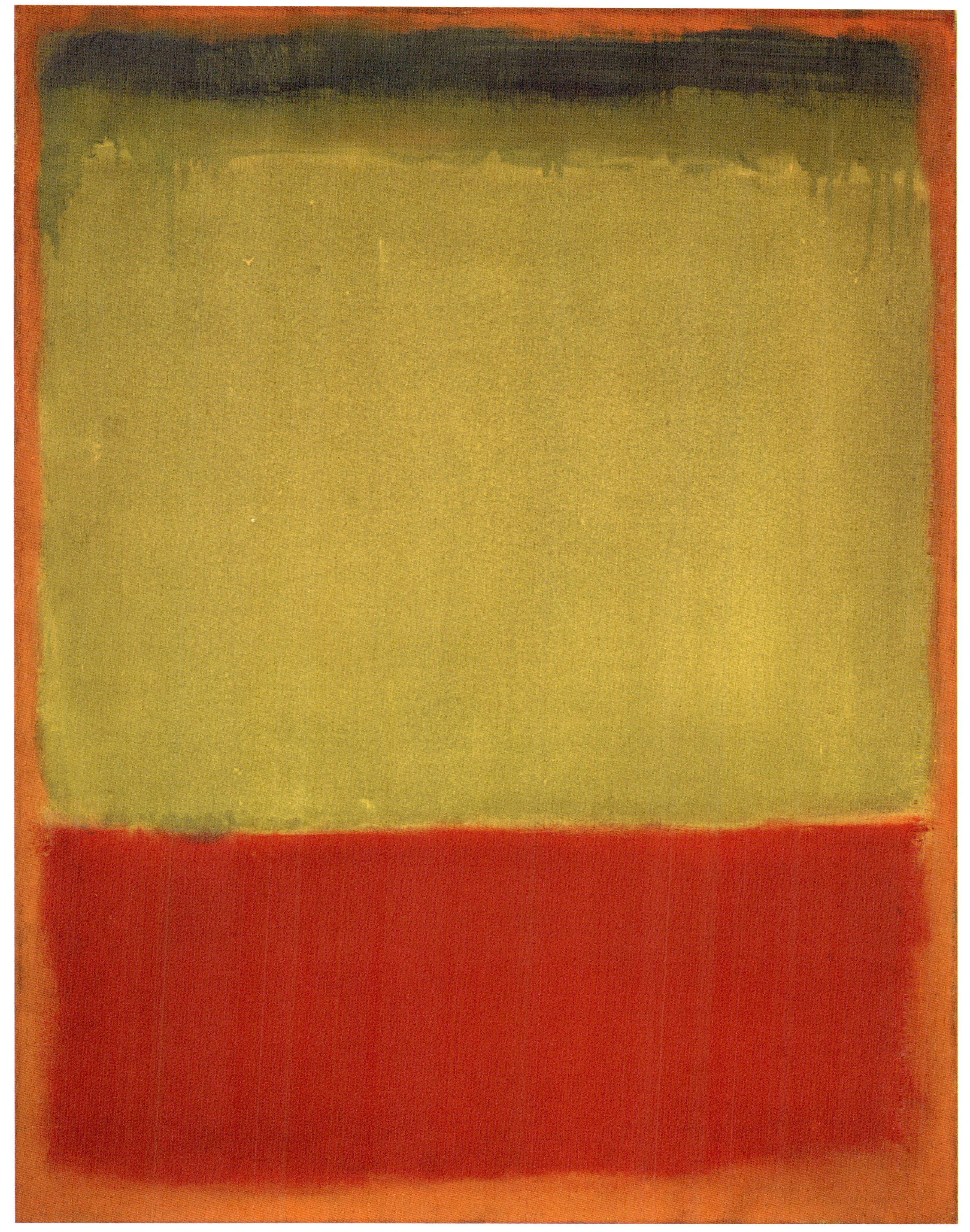

would give the sensation of a definite finished edge to the work, something he was keen to avoid, as he wanted to give the impression that the work could continue to grow and expand beyond the canvas. On top of this primer coat, Rothko would paint layers of colour on top of each other, which were so thin that the pigments in the mix would barely cling to the surface. Lower layers were able to shine through the upper layers, thereby creating a luminosity and transparency that enhanced the effect of movement in the paintings, giving a greater feeling of depth. Christopher Rothko writes that his sense of these layers is that 'they are a type of visual representation and expression of emotional complexity'. They are 'many-layered constructions of the inner world'.

Two Types of Space

Rothko's use of space is also critical in creating the sensation of movement on the canvas. In ***The Artist's Reality***, he writes about two types of spatial understanding. The first one he calls tactile space, that is **'one kind of space which gives us the sensation of things that can be felt by touch'**. He considers that tactile space in a painting 'gives the sensation of a solid'. He goes on to suggest the metaphor of a **'plate of jelly or perhaps soft putty, into which a series of objects are impressed at various depths'**.

He considers tactile space to be the predominant space in the art of Ancient Greece, China, primitive cultures and children, who show 'a complete unconcern with the representation of space in which the desired objects simply float anywhere on the paper'. What he calls visual space was made possible by the discovery of linear perspective, which aims to represent three dimensions on a two-dimensional surface so creating the illusion of objects as they appear to the eye. This includes such techniques as space receding to a vanishing point, forms at the front of the picture being painted larger than those at a distance and colours being more vibrant at the front of the picture and growing dimmer as they recede towards the vanishing point.

Spatial Theories

Clearwater details how Rothko based his theories on the work of William Mills Ivins Jr., first curator of prints at the Metropolitan Museum of Art, who shared his ideas in two books: *On the Rationalization of Sight* (1938) and *Art and Geometry* (1946). Rothko and Ivins agreed that both ways of spatial understanding were at work in a painting, and the mind has to choose which one to prioritize in order to perceive the relationship of forms and objects within the art work.

Ivins goes on to say that the way a culture chooses to view spatial relationships can even determine a philosophical viewpoint, pointing out that the Greeks' mistrust of visual space led certain philosophers, such as Plato and Socrates, to denounce the visual arts as falsehood. In his essay, Rothko points out that modern painters have rejected the illusory perspective of the Renaissance and chosen tactile expression as the most natural and honest expression; they have chosen 'the world of sensation' over 'the world of objectivity'.

Rothko's aim was to unite these two forms of space intuition so as to create a sense of movement. Linear perspective places objects in a fixed point in space, so by eliminating the fixed point and any other indications of measurement, Rothko is able to paint forms that appear to be shifting position, sometimes coming towards the viewer, at other times receding. This sensation is also aided by careful consideration of the size of the forms and the fact that the forms are for the most part overlapping. As Clearwater reminds us, this use of spatial intuition for Rothko is not an end in itself. All these considerations are subservient to Rothko's overall aim of his shapes assuming roles and performing in the unfolding dramas on his canvases.

Colour and Space

Rothko did not want to be known as a colourist. His work, as he saw it, was to be visionary, to open a way for viewers to experience aspects of the human condition and, like in Greek tragedy, to undergo a cleansing of the emotions, and as a result feel uplifted, confirmed in their human existence – in essence, a positive experience.

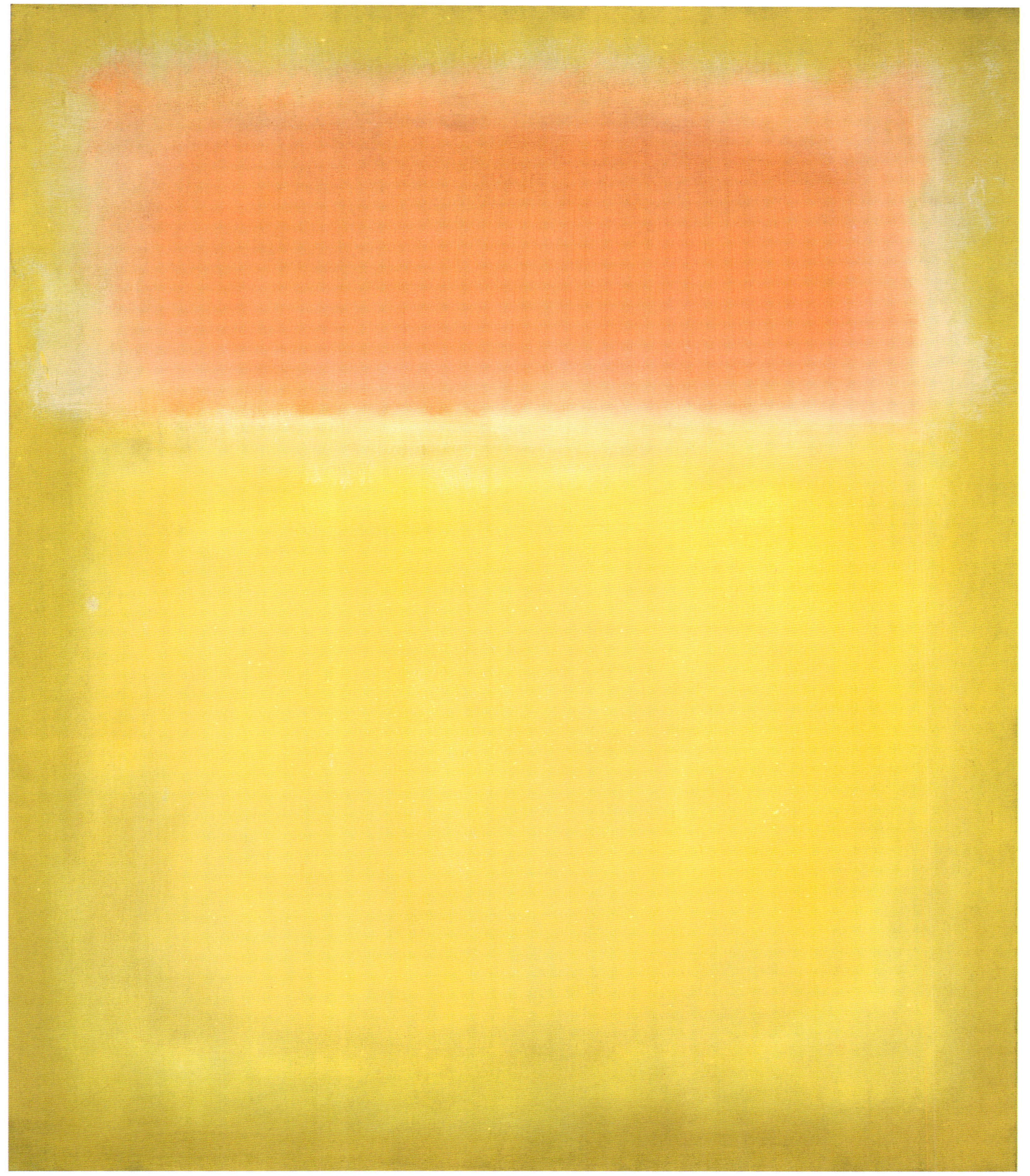

Colour, however, was clearly important, as this was one of the major tools by which Rothko was to achieve his goals. Even as early as 1940–41, when he was writing ***The Artist's Reality***, he linked the importance of colour to use of space. Holding up Giotto as an example of a tactile, visionary artist, he states: **'It is Giotto's colour … that produced the great effect of his tactility.'** He goes on to say: **'All the tactile painters have used colour with a knowledge of its tactile qualities.'** He compares the tactile painters' use of colour with that of the illusory painters **'whose illusion of recession is achieved by the graying of colour as it recedes into the distance'**.

Colour, therefore, gives the sensation of recession and advancement. 'The bluntest statement of this property is that cold colours recede while warm colours advance. It is this property that both Giotto and the Egyptians exploited. Colours which made no attempt to resemble atmosphere at a distance actually gave the sensation of coming forward and coming back.' Rothko considers that this use of colour made it possible to give to space 'that tangibly mucous character'. He goes on to say that this strengthens the tactile sensation, **'for every motion in any direction is always resisted by a sensed mass or solid space'**. This he considers to be much more powerful than movement in a vacuum, as it creates resistance that makes the figures exert force and so creates a sense of movement.

The Red Studio

In 1949, the Museum of Modern Art acquired ***The Red Studio*** (1911) by Matisse. This was at a time when Rothko was spending many hours studying paintings in the New York galleries and museums. He recalls standing in front of this work most days over a period of months. Many other artists have been influenced by this work and it has been considered to be a significant point in the history of art, where representational, figurative art of the past, which essentially looked outwards, shifted towards art that began to look inwards to the life of the artist as the reference point, which in turn increasingly became the reference point for the art of the future twentieth century.

Its flattened perspective alters reality, as well as altering the viewer's perception of space. Matisse painted the world as he perceived it, in a personal way, creating a personal reality unique to him. He has recreated his studio, which we are allowed to visit. We enter his world and see it from his viewpoint; some of the paintings he is working on are displayed for us to see, his work tools, including his easel and his brushes, show us the tools of his trade.

Colour Immersion

One of the most striking features in *The Red Studio* is Matisse's use of colour. The colour red provides the backdrop for the objects depicted, but it is more than that. The canvas seems to be saturated with a glowing, intense red on which the objects in the room have been placed; to cover the canvas with just one colour before depicting objects on top of that colour field was unprecedented at the time.

Rothko said of this work that 'you became that colour, you became totally saturated with it as if it were music'. Rothko, as mentioned earlier, would sit for many hours listening to music, internalizing it, allowing it to wash over him and becoming one with it. He links *The Red Studio* with the experience of being totally consumed. In many ways, it can be considered a major creative source of Rothko's multiforms and later classic works. In that same year, 1949, Rothko created a multiform (*No. 21*) which is a glowing red colour field covering the canvas, interspersed with some darker colour elements but portraying no recognizable objects. The colour red almost hypnotically and powerfully draws the viewer into its depth of red space.

Science, Psychology and Colour

In *The Artist's Reality*, Rothko makes a number of references to scientific experiments in psychology and psychiatry, and had a clear interest in developments in these areas. After the war, psychological discoveries and insights from the early twentieth century were widely disseminated, discussed and studied; given Rothko's already stated interest, it is quite possible that he kept up with these debates.

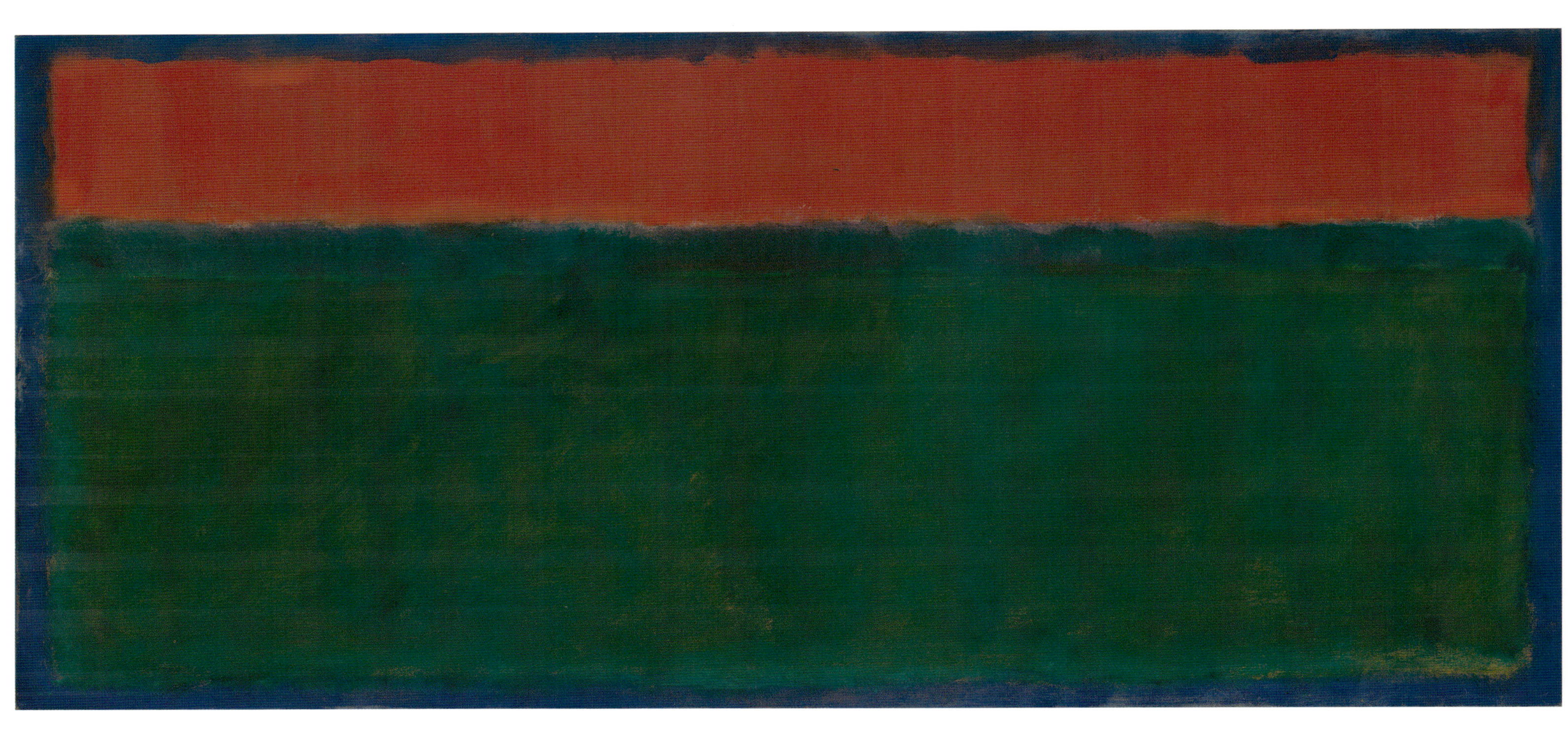

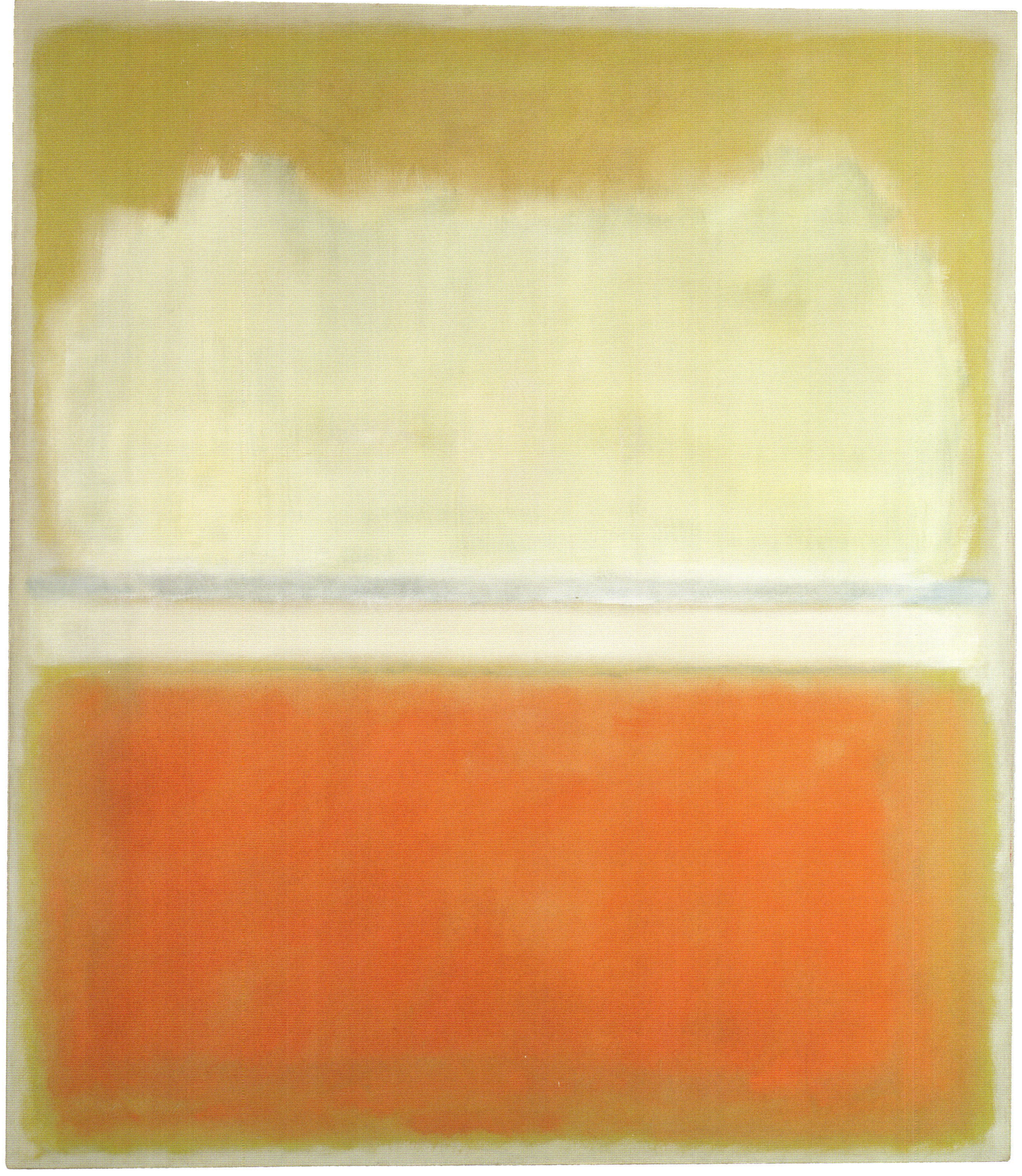

Clearwater draws attention to the doctoral dissertation 'Abstract Expressionist Painting in America' by William Seitz, written in the early 1950s, in which Seitz suggests certain developments in the study of perception could have significantly impacted Rothko's work. A study entitled ***The World of Color*** (published in English in 1935), by David Katz, discussed the similar results of experiments carried out by both scientists and artists. It is not known if Rothko read this work, but some of its results and discoveries do seem pertinent to Rothko's developments in the use of colour. One such discovery, which Seitz considers to be significant in Rothko's case, is Katz's summary of the discovery of three different ways of using colour: 'A given tone can resemble a solid surface, a transparent film, or a volume.'

Surface and Film Colour

Seitz considers that the differentiation between surface colour and film colour has a special significance for Rothko. He summarizes: 'Surface colors are those which are encountered most often on objects of paper, cloth, wood, or metals; they embody the tangibility of everyday artifacts.' Surface colour 'presents a barrier beyond which the eye cannot pass'. On the other hand, film colours 'have a spongy texture just short of transparency, like the blue of the sky, they are seen ... as colored light.' With these 'one feels that one can penetrate more or less deeply into the spectral color.' Seitz also noted that Katz highlighted that other things can affect the viewer's perception of colour. Katz noted that a 'lack of sharpness' can affect surface colour so that it appears to recede. Rothko's increasing use of blurred edges at the boundaries of colour areas creates such a lack of sharpness. Katz also noted that surface colour can be transformed into film colour when a framing device is placed around it. Rothko, in his early experiments with colour-field abstract painting, would place a narrow border at the edge of his work, thereby creating such an effect.

The Importance of Size

Although Rothko did many drawings, watercolours and sketches on smaller pieces of paper, he is best known, as are many other abstract expressionists, for his large, if not enormous paintings on panel and canvas. In an interview which was held at 'A Symposium on How to Combine Architecture, Painting and Sculpture' at the Museum of Modern Art, New York, 19 March 1951, Rothko acknowledged his use of the large picture format and noted that this could be construed as something 'very grandiose and pompous'.

He explains that the reason he uses such large formats is, in fact, the opposite: he wants to be 'very intimate and human'. Painting a small picture, he considers is, **'to place yourself outside your experience to look upon an experience as a stereopticon view or reducing glass. However you paint the larger picture, you are in it.'** His aim is to surround the viewers and almost overwhelm them with size, so that they are not just looking at the work but are actually in it, experiencing it from the inside. He continues: **'Since I am involved with the human element, I want to create a state of intimacy – an immediate transaction. Large pictures take you into them.'** The paradox is that the small, intimate picture leaves the viewer on the outside, while the large format draws the viewer in, enabling the creation of an intimate experience. He further expands his views by saying: **'I think that small pictures since the Renaissance are like novels; large pictures are like dramas in which one participates in a direct way.'** As Rothko has expressed his view that his pictures are in fact dramas about the human condition, it follows that he would prefer to use large formats for his work, as he considers large formats to facilitate both drama and the participation of the viewer in the drama.

Travels

In 1950, Rothko and Mel were able to fund a five-month trip around Europe, using money from an inheritance when Mel's mother died. This was Rothko's first trip abroad since leaving Russia as a child; they travelled to England, France and Italy, visiting the most important galleries and museums.

Although Rothko expounded the need for a new American art, he still held the art of Europe in very high regard. After the physical work of painting, it seems he was looking to refresh his enthusiasm and gain new ideas and possible approaches through these

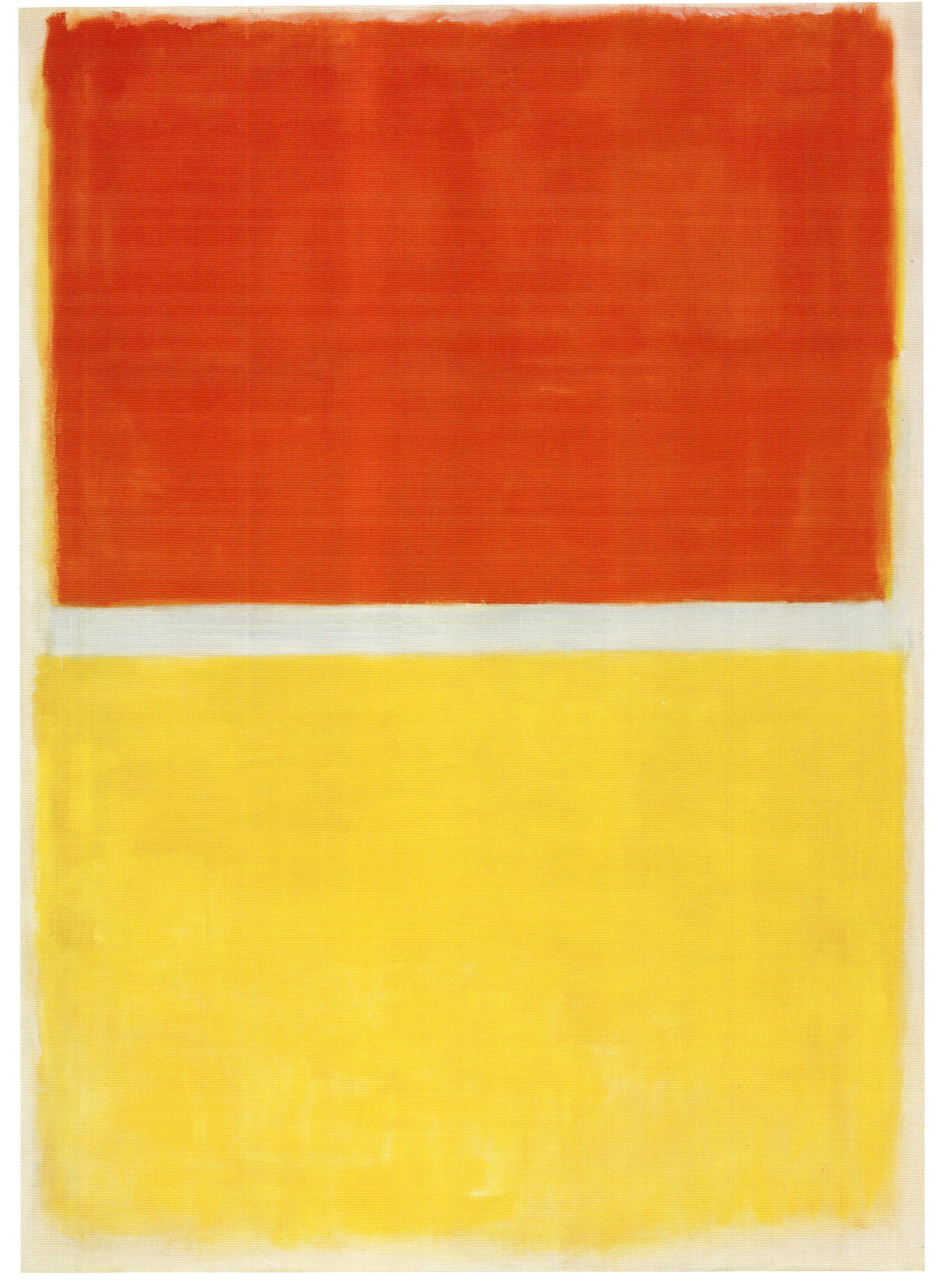

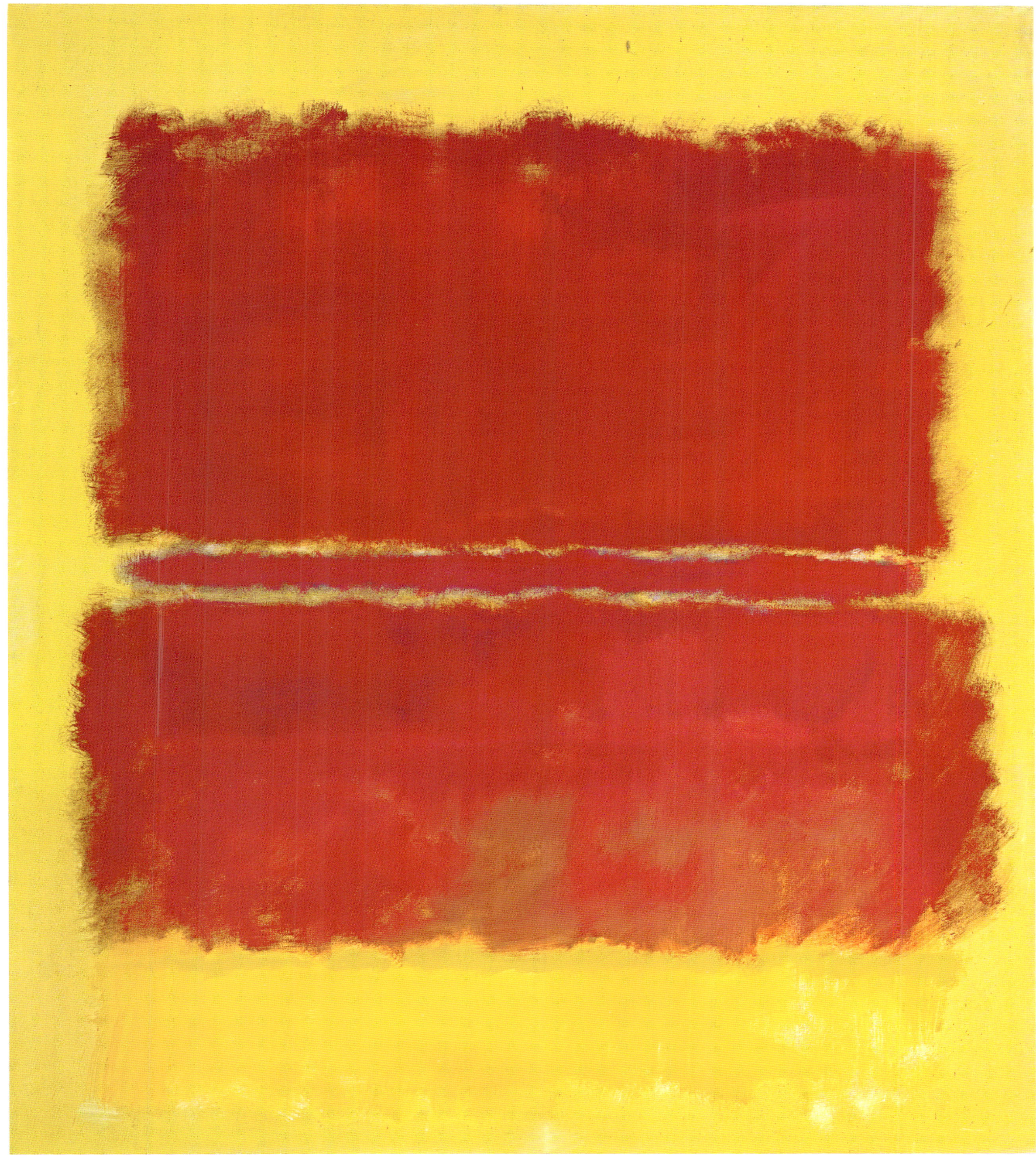

travels. He was gradually gaining recognition as an artist and his work was beginning to sell; one painting had sold for $1,000 and his works were represented in a number of shows in the States, as well as in Tokyo, Berlin, Amsterdam and São Paulo, but he was still struggling to support himself and Mel financially.

It appears that Rothko was disappointed with Paris, the city where so many new artistic developments had originated over the past century. In a letter to Newman, he writes that the differences between the Paris and New York art scenes were even greater than he had imagined. **'Never did I ever conceive that the civilization here would seem as alien and as unapproachable as the actuality as it appears to me … our reluctance to send pictures over here seem to have been correct.'**

Meditative Frescos

In Italy, they visited Venice, Florence, Siena and Rome. In Florence, Rothko was very impressed by the early Renaissance frescos, particularly those by Fra Angelico in the cells at the monastery of San Marco, responding to their meditative style intended for the monks to reflect upon as they sat alone in their cells.

On this trip, he also had the opportunity to view some of Giotto's works, which he had studied, admired and referenced in **_The Artist's Reality_**. As the time came to return to New York, Rothko seems to have been increasingly anxious; in particular, he seems to have been concerned about divisions between the New York artists. In London, he wrote to Newman: **'we must find a way of living and working without the involvements that seem to have been destroying us one after another. I doubt whether any of us can bear much more of that kind of strain.'** It was during this trip to Europe that Mel became pregnant and their daughter, named Kathy Lynn (Kate) after Rothko's mother, was born on 30 December 1950 after their return to New York.

The Irascibles

During the trip, Rothko had kept up with developments in the New York art world through contact with his colleagues back in the States. The Metropolitan Museum of Art was preparing to stage a show entitled ***American Painting Today***, the first of a series of open national art competitions. Eighteen painters and 10 sculptors, including Rothko, had sent a letter to the president of the museum protesting that the contents of the show would be chosen by a jury, which would inevitably, in their opinion, go against those artists working in a more avant-garde style.

A photograph of the group was taken and published in ***Life*** magazine in the edition of 15 January 1951, which was published at the time of the announcement of the winners of the competition. This photograph was given the title of 'The Irascibles' and has become an iconic image of this group of indignant artists. Rothko had continued his participation in artists' groups after the break-up of The Ten, clearly finding the company, and the discussions and debates, stimulating. Artists would throw themselves into the robust discussion about the activity of painting, and the conversations would often be passionate and provocative, as well as, at times, confusing. Avant-garde artists had been meeting informally in the Cedar Street Tavern in Greenwich Village and in a group officially known as Studio 35, but referred to as the Club, which continued the Friday evening lectures started by the Subjects of the Artist school in 1948. Most of the artists who became part of what would be called the Abstract Expressionist movement were members. Rothko had given a lecture there in 1949, entitled 'My Point of View', although he does not seem to have been committed to the group, referring later, in 1955, to an artist who attends such groups as a 'kind of egotist'.

Exhibitions

As early as 1946, Rothko had been included in exhibitions at his old adversary the Whitney Museum of Art, in its annual shows of contemporary art. However, from the early 1950s onwards, it was clear that Rothko's star was in the ascendant, with an increase in exhibitions and invitations. In 1952, he was included in the exhibition ***Fifteen Americans*** at the Museum of Modern Art in

105

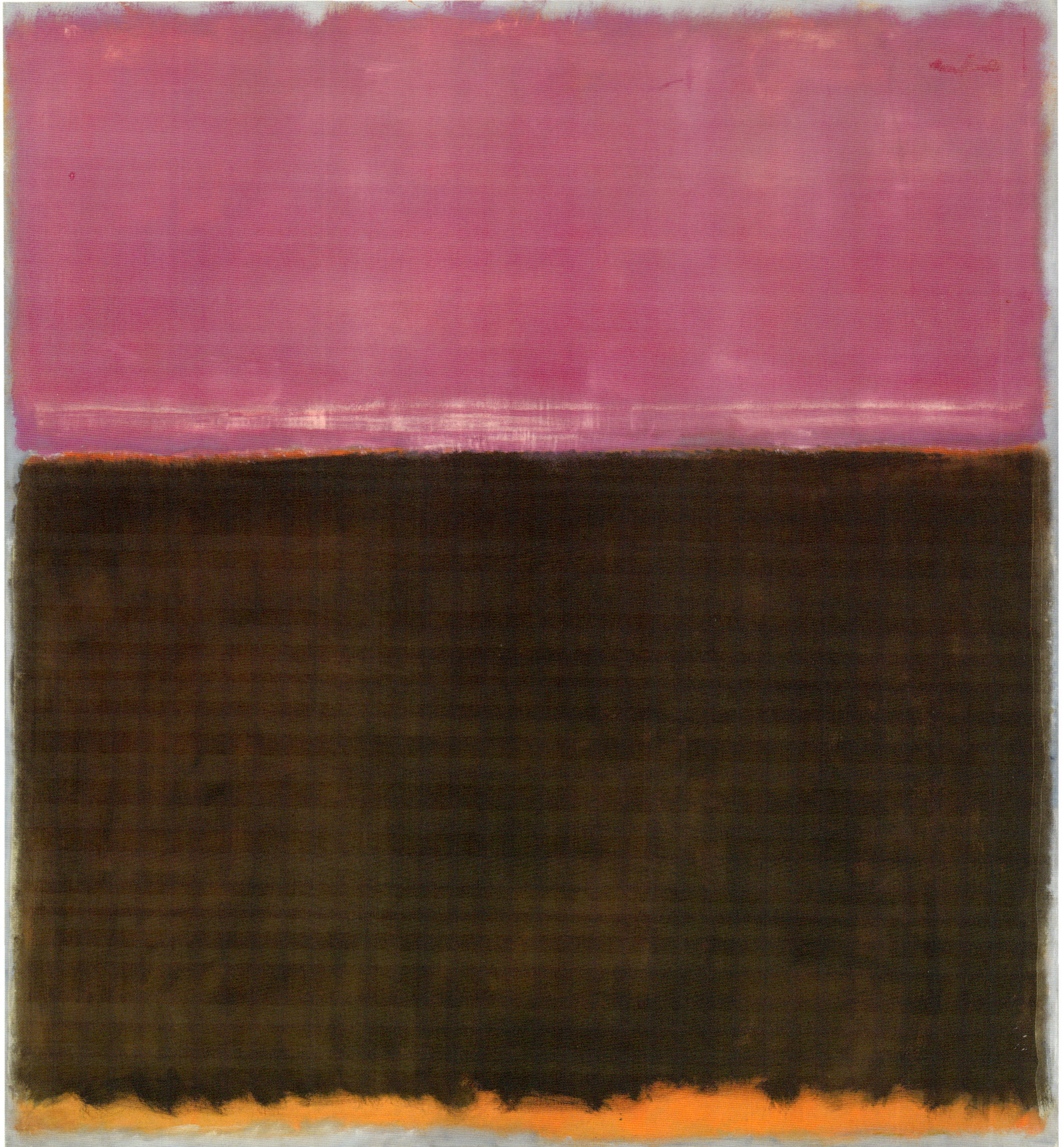

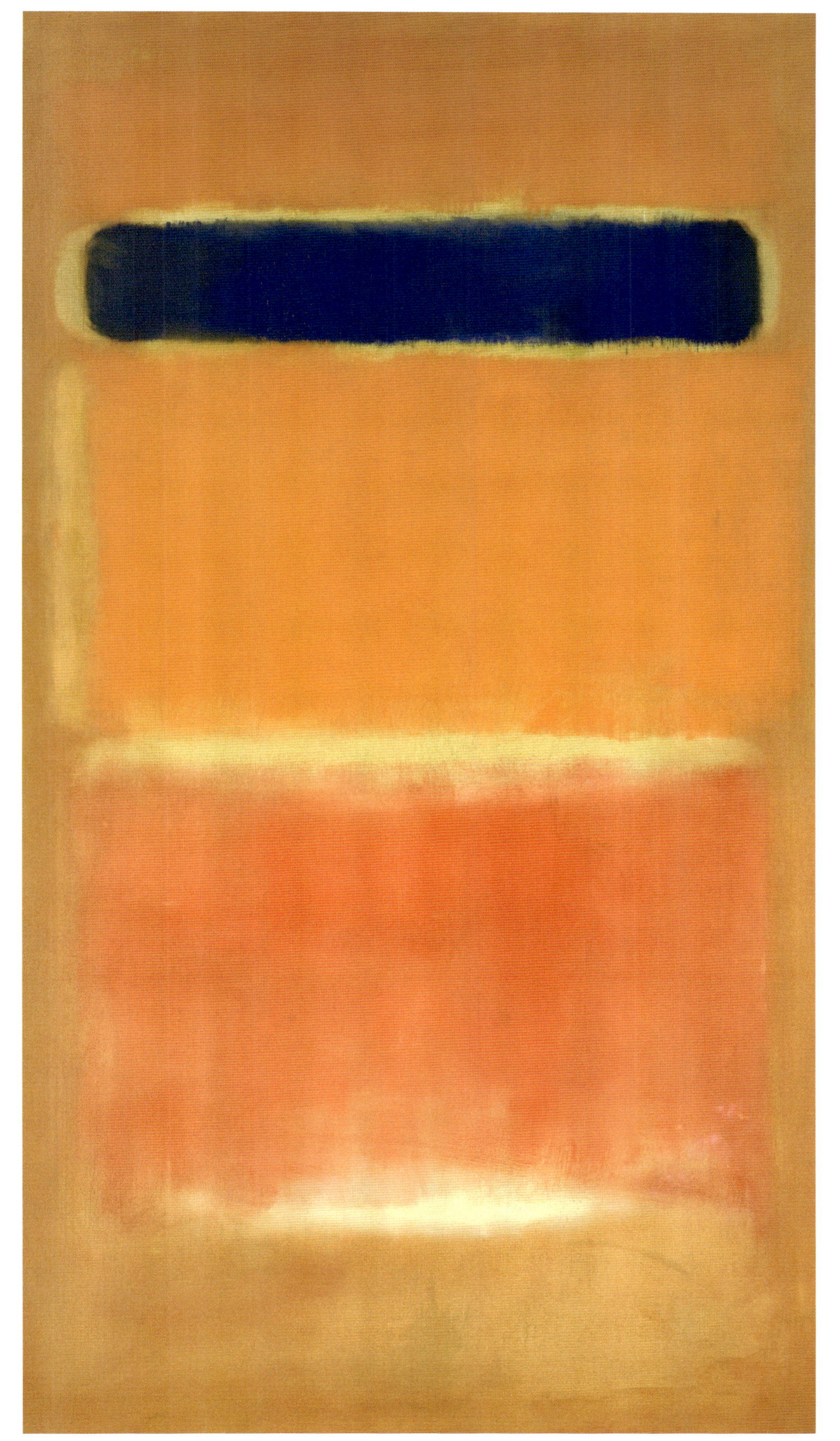

New York, where he was given his own room. Dorothy Miller, the curator, chose the works, but Rothko altered her selection and wanted to have the walls completely covered with paintings touching each other, presumably to give the viewer the effect of being totally absorbed in the world of his creations.

He also wanted control over how the works were illuminated, insisting they were lit by brilliant lighting, something which he was particular about in the early years of displaying his classical colourist works. This bright illumination can startle the viewer to begin with and slow them down, and can initially blur the details and variations in the colours, which then gradually reveal themselves as the viewer adapts to the lighting. Rothko was to change this approach as time went on. Miller was unhappy at his suggestions, fearing that they would disturb the overall unity of the show and, ultimately, it took the intervention of the museum's director to persuade Rothko to accept Miller's plan. Rothko, however, refused to let his works travel to Europe when the exhibition was to tour there, as he would have no control over how they would be presented.

More Exhibitions and Lectureships

Over this same period, Rothko was promoted by exhibitions at the Betty Parsons Gallery and then, after leaving Betty Parsons' stable of artists, he joined that of the very successful New York art dealer Sidney Janis. For his first exhibition at the Janis Gallery, he was included in the show entitled *9 American Painters Today* in 1954; this was followed by his first solo exhibition with Janis in 1955, which was a huge success, thus confirming his international importance in the post-war art world.

Rothko himself arranged the hang; it appears to have been what he had wanted to do at the Museum of Modern Art exhibition, before being overruled. The paintings were crammed together on the walls of the gallery, from floor to ceiling, and the lighting was bright. Unusually, compared to his later thoughts on the display of his works, Rothko had chosen to place pieces next to each other, which would create a colour clash, thereby igniting a dissonance between the works.

Reviewers noted the glowing light produced by the paintings and the overall effects, created by the works as an ensemble, leading to the impressive impact of the show. Apart from his success in exhibitions, Rothko received more invitations to speak and teach. He had earlier spent two summers, 1947 and 1949, teaching at the California School of Fine Arts in San Francisco, and in 1951, he was appointed Assistant Professor of Design at Brooklyn College. In 1955, he taught for eight weeks as a guest lecturer at the University of Colorado, Boulder; was visiting artist at Newcomb Art School, Tulane University, New Orleans in 1957; and in 1958 was invited to deliver a lecture at the Pratt Institute, New York.

Chicago

A significant step forward for him was when the Art Institute of Chicago proposed a solo exhibition, entitled **Recent Paintings by Mark Rothko**, to be held in 1954. The curator of the Chicago exhibition was Katherine Kuh, with whom Rothko was to develop a mutually respectful, professional relationship. She initially wanted to publish a book, which would detail their correspondence, and thus shed light on Rothko's ideas and way of working.

Eventually, he decided against this, as he was reluctant to discuss his works on the grounds that it would constitute a barrier between the viewer and the work; it would **'tell the public how the pictures should be looked at and what to look for'**. He stated that it would lead to **'the paralysis of the mind and the imagination (and for the artist a premature entombment)'**. In the end, Kuh was to use just two excerpts from Rothko's letters in her brief essay on the exhibition. However, her archived papers contain correspondence she carried out with Rothko, so his ideas have subsequently been made available to us. Rothko again wanted to control the installation, but working at a distance handicapped him in this respect, and he compromised by just giving her guidelines from his experience of hanging his works.

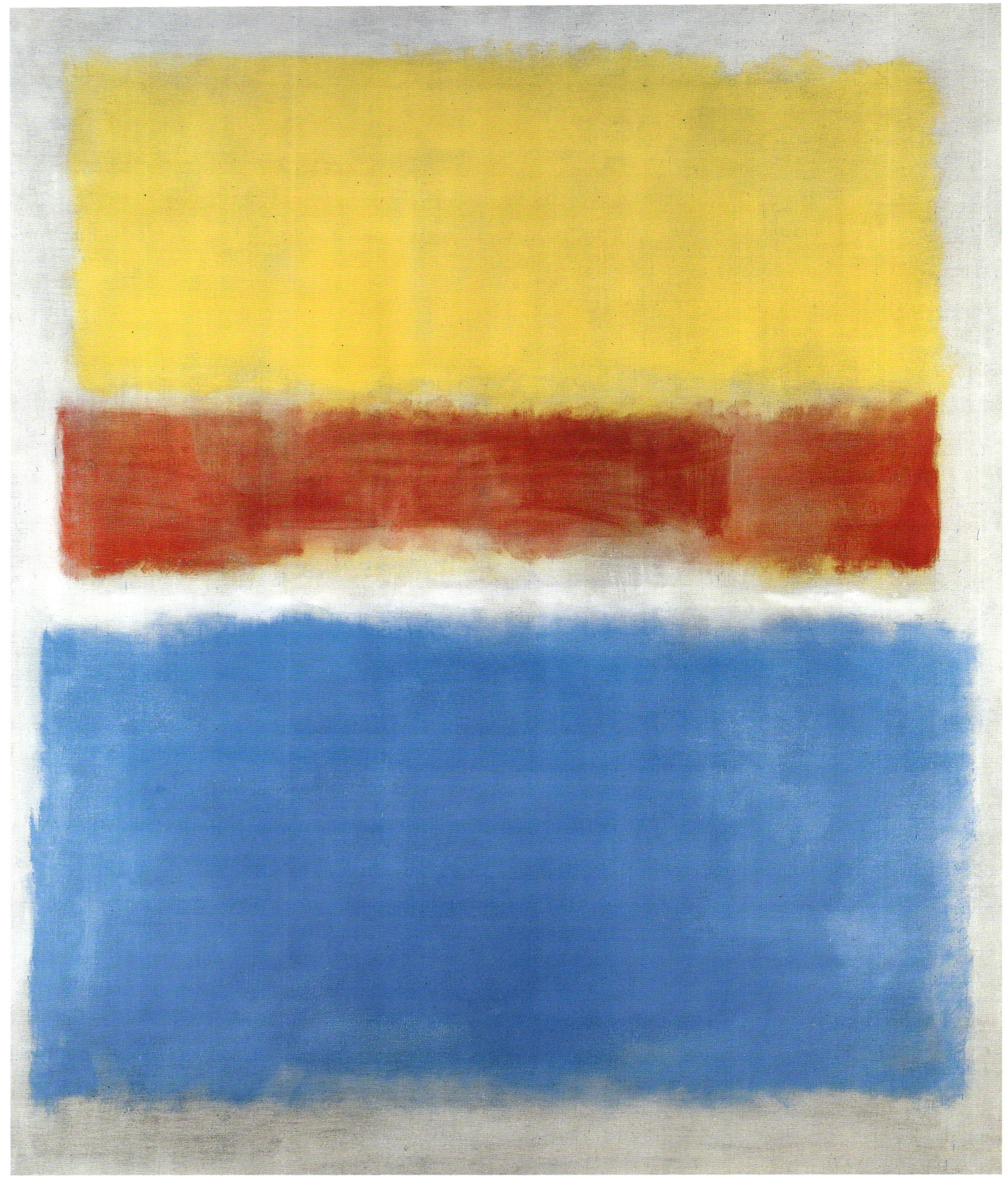

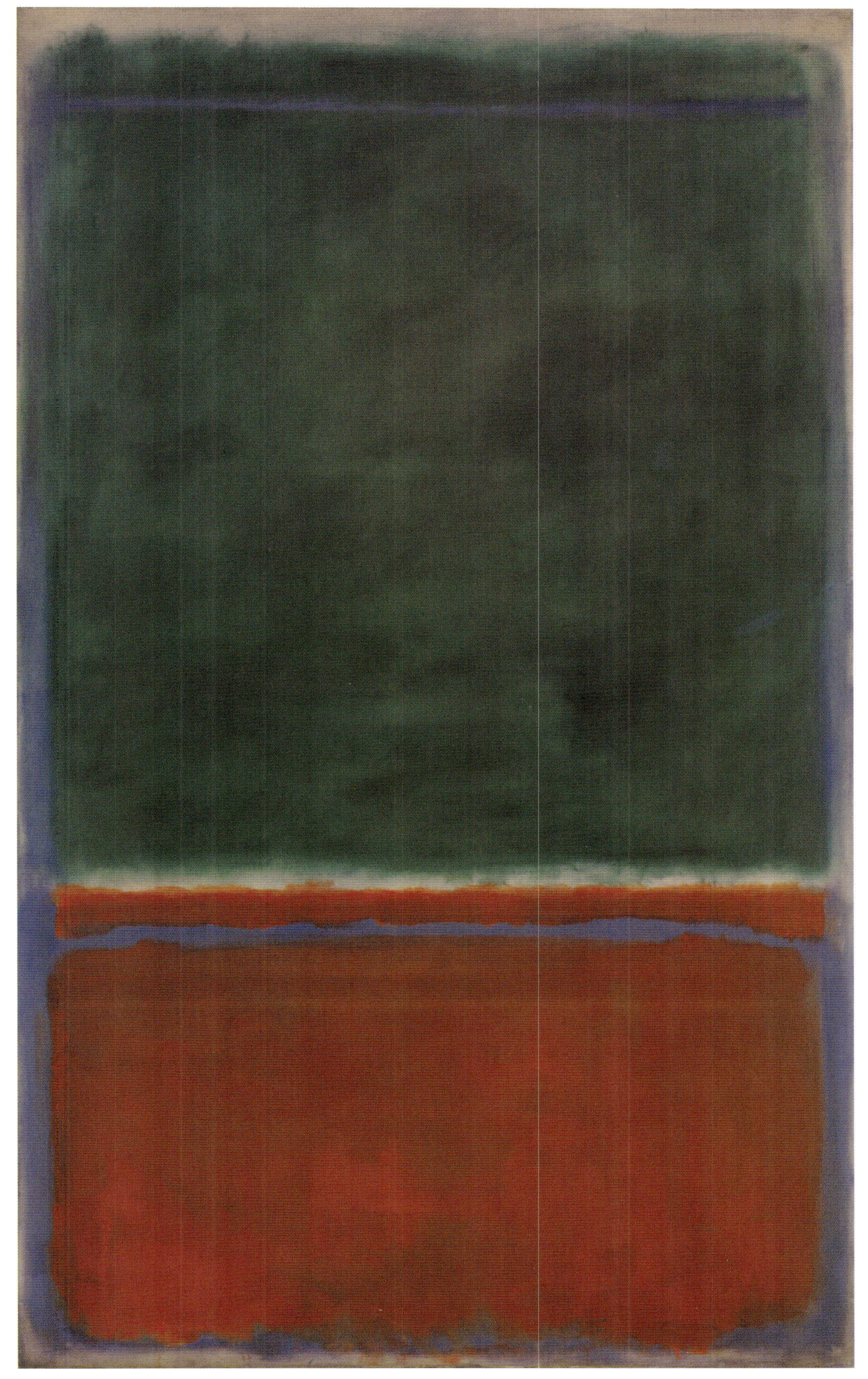

Impact

In his correspondence with Kuh, Rothko explains that his greatest fear was that his works would simply be decorative, writing: **'Since my pictures are large, colorful and unframed, and since museum walls are usually immense and formidable, there is the danger that the pictures relate themselves as decorative areas to the walls. This would be a distortion of their meaning, since the pictures are intimate and intense, and are the opposite of what is decorative.'** He explains that he had found out by experience that if he used more works or larger works, it would **'crowd the show rather than making it spare. By saturating the room with the feeling of the work, the walls are defeated and the poignancy of each single work ... become[s] more visible.'**

He was clearly concerned about his work making an immediate impact on the viewer. He wrote to Kuh that he would place **'the largest works so that they must be first encountered at close quarters, so that the first experience is to be within the picture'**. Two other features he cites as helpful are the positioning of the large works, in particular, 'as close to the floor as possible', and to make the display space as confined as possible. This initial powerful impact of positioning, he considered, **'may well give the key to the observer of the ideal relationship between the viewer and the rest of the pictures.'**

Disturbed Relationships

The increasing success of certain members of the New York artists' group put severe pressure on relationships within the group. Originally bound together to assert themselves against the art establishment of the times, and to promote a new way forward, difficulties arose when their art was becoming increasingly acceptable and recognized. The result was that the group began to fall apart; it had lost the purpose which had bound it.

Rothko's close friend Newman had not received good reviews for his shows, possibly partly due to the fact that he rarely showed his works. When he did, the viewers had not been able to keep up with how his style had been developing and so were perplexed and confused, despite the explanatory notes he had provided. He eventually withdrew from Parsons' gallery after a second disappointing show in 1951, which received poor reviews and sold little. This was at a time when Rothko was continuing to receive favourable reviews and beginning to sell more works. Relationships within the wider group of artists became increasingly tense as discussions began to focus on integrity and the problems that were arising from the acceptance of the avant-garde by a wider social group. People wearing designer label clothes began to arrive at exhibitions in fancy cars wanting to buy a painting by the 'new' abstract artists for their flashy Manhattan apartments.

Disputes

Newman and Still accused Rothko of selling out to the idea of a bourgeois existence and eventually labelled him a traitor to the cause. Each of them wrote a letter to Janis before the opening of the 1955 first solo exhibition, explaining why they refused to come to the opening, Newman writing: 'I am frankly bored with the uninspired or to put it more accurately, I am bored with the too easily inspired.' Baal-Teshuva notes that Still wrote to Rothko, demanding he return the pictures Still had given him over the years. This Rothko did, but it marked the ending of the friendship, which Rothko found hard to take. Despite efforts on his part at *rapprochement*, the relationship did not improve. Rothko increasingly refused to be identified with the New York School of artists, strongly denying he was an abstract painter in an interview with Selden Rodman in 1956. In 1957, he objected to being called an action painter in an article by Elaine de Kooning for ***Art News***, one of the most influential art journals in the US. He rejected the term 'Action Painting', coined by the critic Harold Rosenberg to describe the new American school of abstract painting. He wrote:

'to classify is to embalm. Real identity is incompatible with schools and categories … To allude to my work as Action Painting borders on the fantastic … Action Painting is antithetical to the very look and spirit of my work. The work must be the final arbiter.'

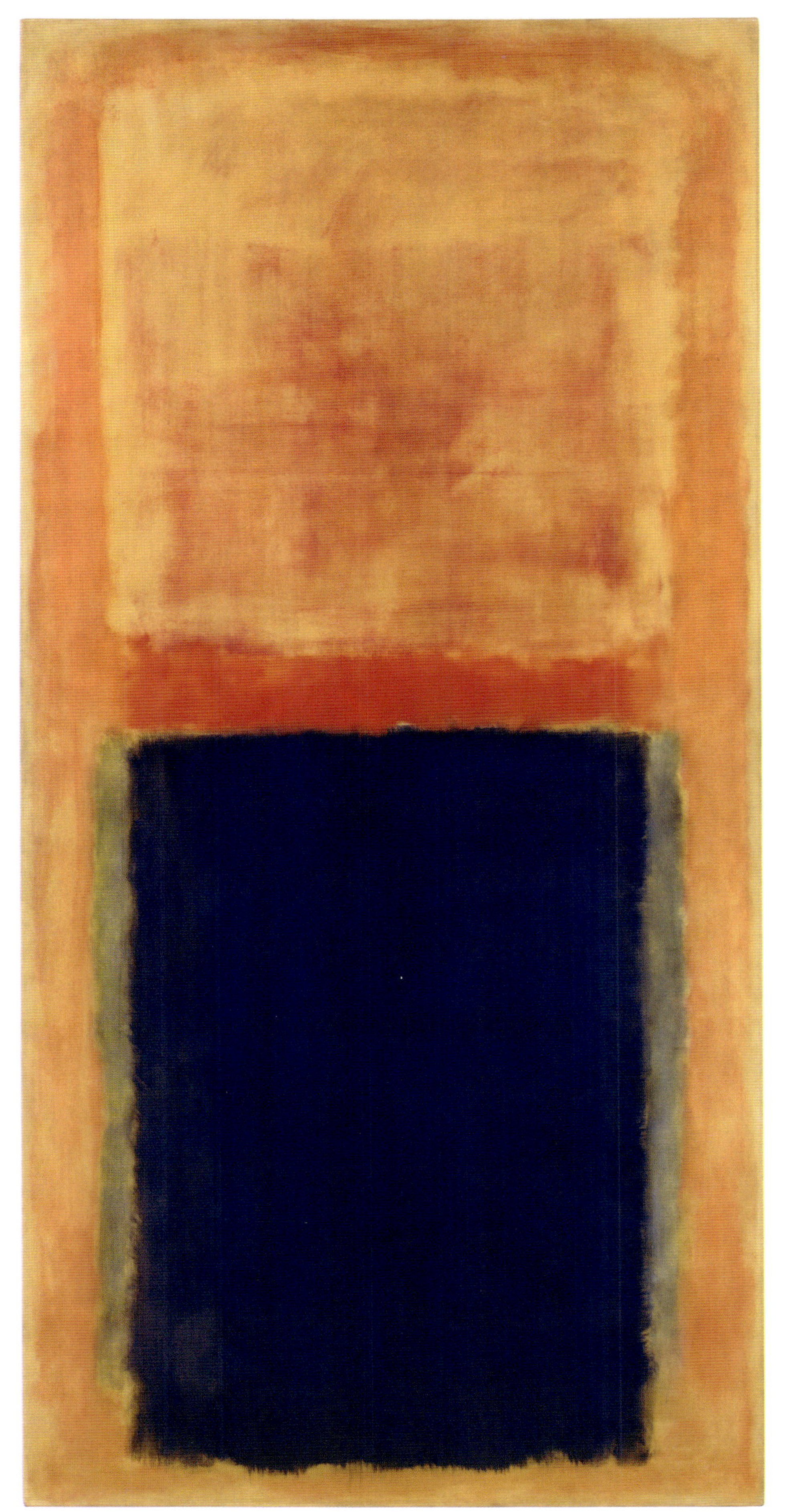

The Seagram Murals

In 1958, Rothko was commissioned to paint a series of murals (*see* figs. 74 and 75, pages 160–61) for a room in the Seagram Building, Park Avenue, New York. This newly finished building, an iconic bronze and glass tower, 39 storeys high, belonged to the Seagram Company Ltd., which was the largest distiller of alcoholic beverages in the world. The company became defunct in 2000 and was broken up, and its assets sold to such companies as The Coca-Cola Company, Diageo and Pernod Ricard. The building today is owned by RFR holdings, a company belonging to Aby Rosen, a real estate investor and developer.

The structure was designed by the German architect Mies van der Rohe (1886–1969) and the lobby and internal arrangements, including The Four Seasons restaurant and the Brasserie restaurant, by Philip Johnson (1906–2005). It has been hailed as one of the finest examples of functionalist architecture, that is the functional aspects of the building's structure are visible, and as a masterpiece of corporate modernism. No expense was spared and, at the time, the costs of construction made it the world's most expensive skyscraper. This was clearly a prestigious and demanding commission for Rothko; the enormous fee of $35,000 was agreed with $7,000 as an advance.

Problems

From the start, the commission was problematic in a number of ways. The room was to be used as a restaurant, known as The Four Seasons, which would have an elite clientele, a group of people who Rothko at times struggled to find a way to relate to. The room was long and narrow, a difficult shape to work with, plus the fact that his paintings would have to hang above the level of the seated diners' heads, not in his favoured position of just above the floor.

In addition, it may have occurred to him that his works would essentially function as decoration for the room. He may well have been attracted to the commission by the fact that it involved the design and execution of a whole set of related works for one room, working together to achieve an overall effect and on permanent display to a large number of people; an aesthetic and design challenge, which resonated with his artistic goals.

Shortly after his death, Mel reportedly said that as far as she could remember, Rothko did not know what the room's purpose was to be when he took on the commission and certainly not that it was to become a restaurant. It is possible that Rothko thought it was to be a staff dining room where at least one wall could be seen from the main cafeteria where the workers ate, which was on a slightly lower level, thus creating something akin to a stage set.

The Panels

Whatever the misgivings he may or may not have harboured, Rothko did accept the commission, immediately renting a large studio where he erected scaffolding to replicate the exact dimensions of the room. He threw himself into the work and, in fact, in the following eight months created not one but three series of the enormous wall panels that would be needed. Unusually for him, he made painted sketches as preparatory studies beforehand.

He chose a warm set of red and brown tones for his colour palette, creating the paintings to function as a horizontal frieze with the elements within the canvas in a vertical position. His student assistant at the time, Dan Rice, said that this arrangement was reached simply by turning the classic pictures on their sides. It is also possible that Rothko chose this arrangement because it echoed the architecture of the room, which had three large square-shape openings into the main dining room. The arrangement of the areas of colour within the canvases suggested architectural elements such as columns, windows, doors and walls, thus giving the viewers the feeling of being in a confined space but able to reach out to a wider world beyond.

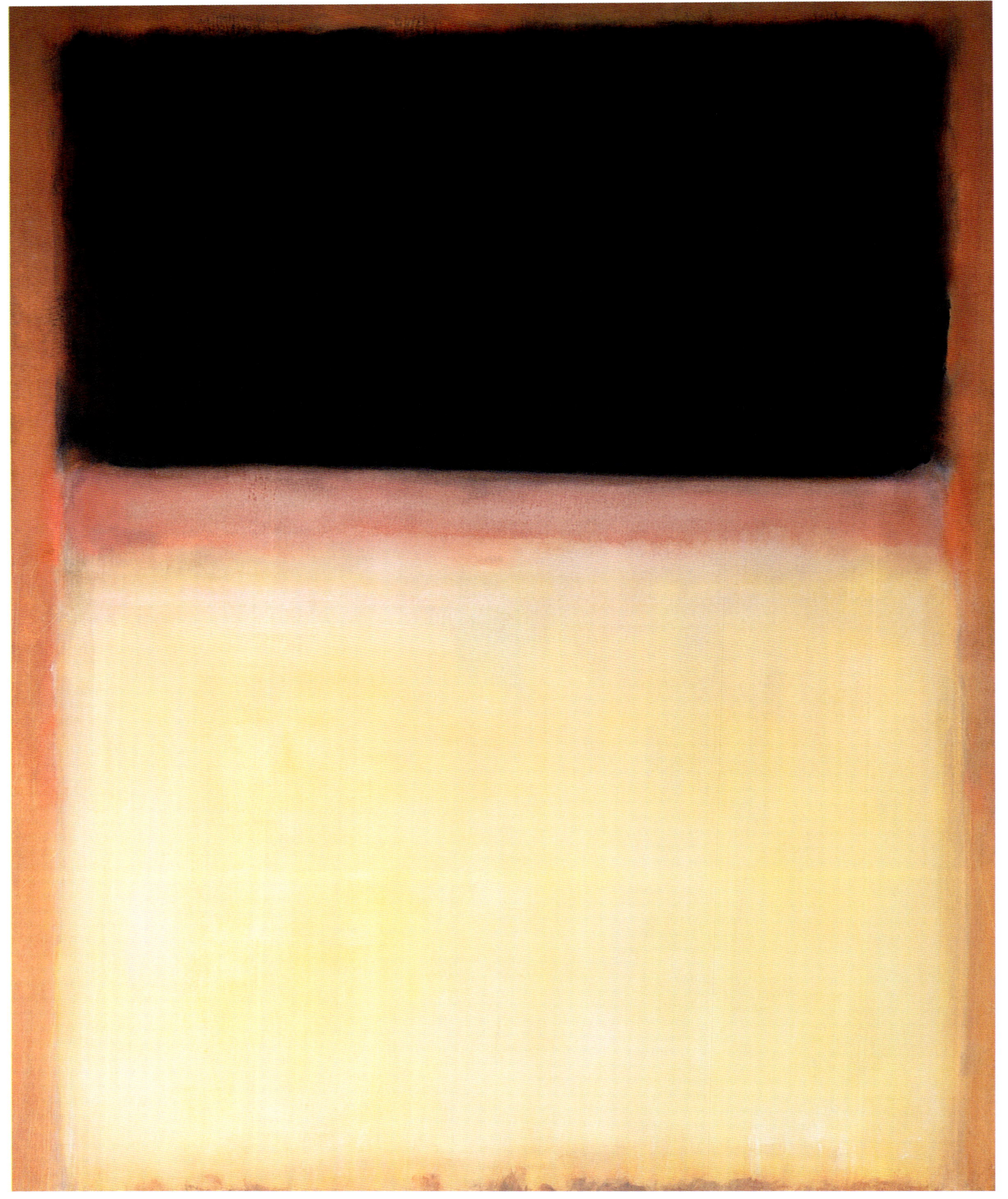

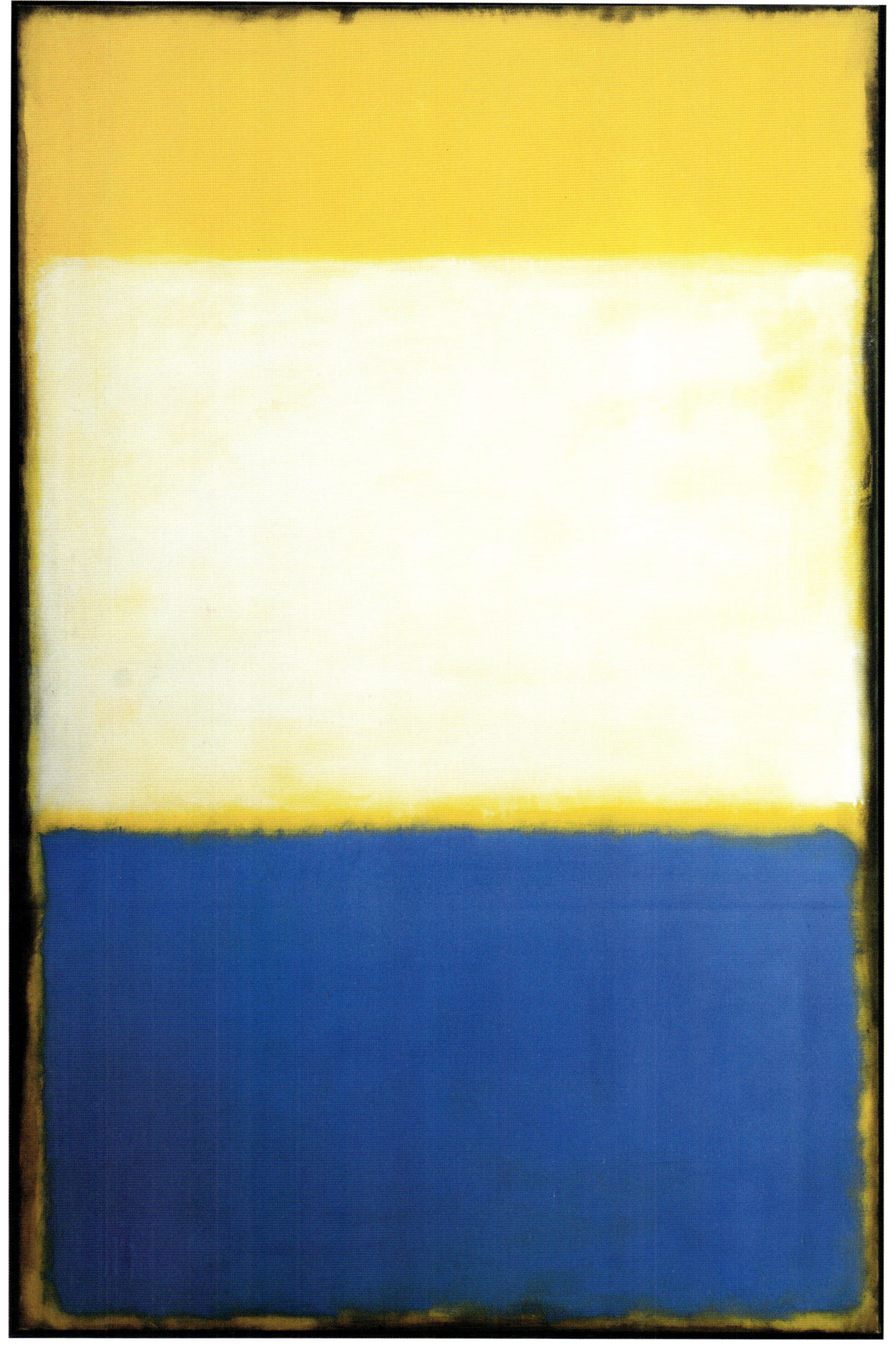

Europe

After a year working on the Seagram project, Rothko broke off to go on a European tour with his family, crossing the Atlantic on the SS Independence, leaving in June 1959. Onboard the ship, he became friends with the writer John Fischer. Fischer reports that in their conversations, Rothko said that he only took the Seagram commission so that he could paint something 'that will ruin the appetite of every son of a bitch who ever eats in that room'.

The Rothkos and the Fischers went ashore at Naples and visited Pompeii, where Fischer reports that Rothko said he saw 'a deep relationship' between the murals for the Seagram project and those of the Villa di Misteri. The Rothkos then travelled to Rome, Florence and Venice. In Florence, Rothko once again visited the Medici library as he had done on his earlier trip and was deeply impressed by Michelangelo's staircase, where the blind-window effect gives the stairwell a claustrophobic atmosphere.

According to Fischer, Rothko said: **'After I had been at work some time I realized I was much influenced subconsciously by Michelangelo's walls in the staircase room of the Medicean Library in Florence. He achieved just the kind of feeling I'm after – he makes the viewers feel that they are trapped in a room where all the doors and windows are bricked up, so that all they can do is butt their heads forever against the wall.'**

Windows

The window theme had already been used in some of Rothko's early works of the 1920s and 1930s, but in the Seagram murals he returns to it in a much more sophisticated way. The darker shapes, which seem to imply windows, draw the viewer in, but due to the way light and dark colours have been modulated, the viewer advances only to feel trapped in another `space. As Clearwater writes: 'The endless journey through this frieze of paintings traps viewers in a claustrophobic labyrinth.'

Rothko's sketches for the murals show that the effects of the bright orange window shape intensifies the effect of the area of dark red colour that it contains and makes it 'appear simultaneously as surface and as deep recesses in space.' The dark reddish area is the same colour as the surrounding 'frame', with the result that the frame and the dark red area within the orange 'window' work together and appear to engage in a co-ordinated shifting movement, vying with the orange window to gain dominance. Clearwater notes that the orange area is brushed and rubbed to create further shifting effects of light and that Rothko scatters highlights over the picture surface to create a shimmer effect, perhaps echoing the effects of candlelit churches on Renaissance frescos.

The Four Seasons Restaurant

In the Seagram paintings, a sensation of pulsating movement occurs between the light and dark areas according to the different sizes of the window spaces that are visible, so causing the forms in the viewer's eyes to either increase or diminish. Once more, this is playing with the philosophical and perceptual understanding of space as discussed above. With the Seagram murals, these perceptions were placed with consideration of the height at which they would be displayed, as well as the creation of a complete environment. With a classic Rothko painting, the viewer stands in front of the work at the centre; with the Seagram frieze, one views the paintings from one end of the whole set to the other end. The Four Seasons restaurant was officially opened with much publicity in July 1959, and Dan Rice recalled that Rothko told him that he was going to take Mel to dinner there 'and look the place over.' Rice continues: 'I had arrived early in the studio the morning after and he came through the door like a bull, as only Rothko could, in an absolute rage. He said explosively,... **"Anybody who will eat that kind of food for those kind of prices will never look at a picture of mine".'**

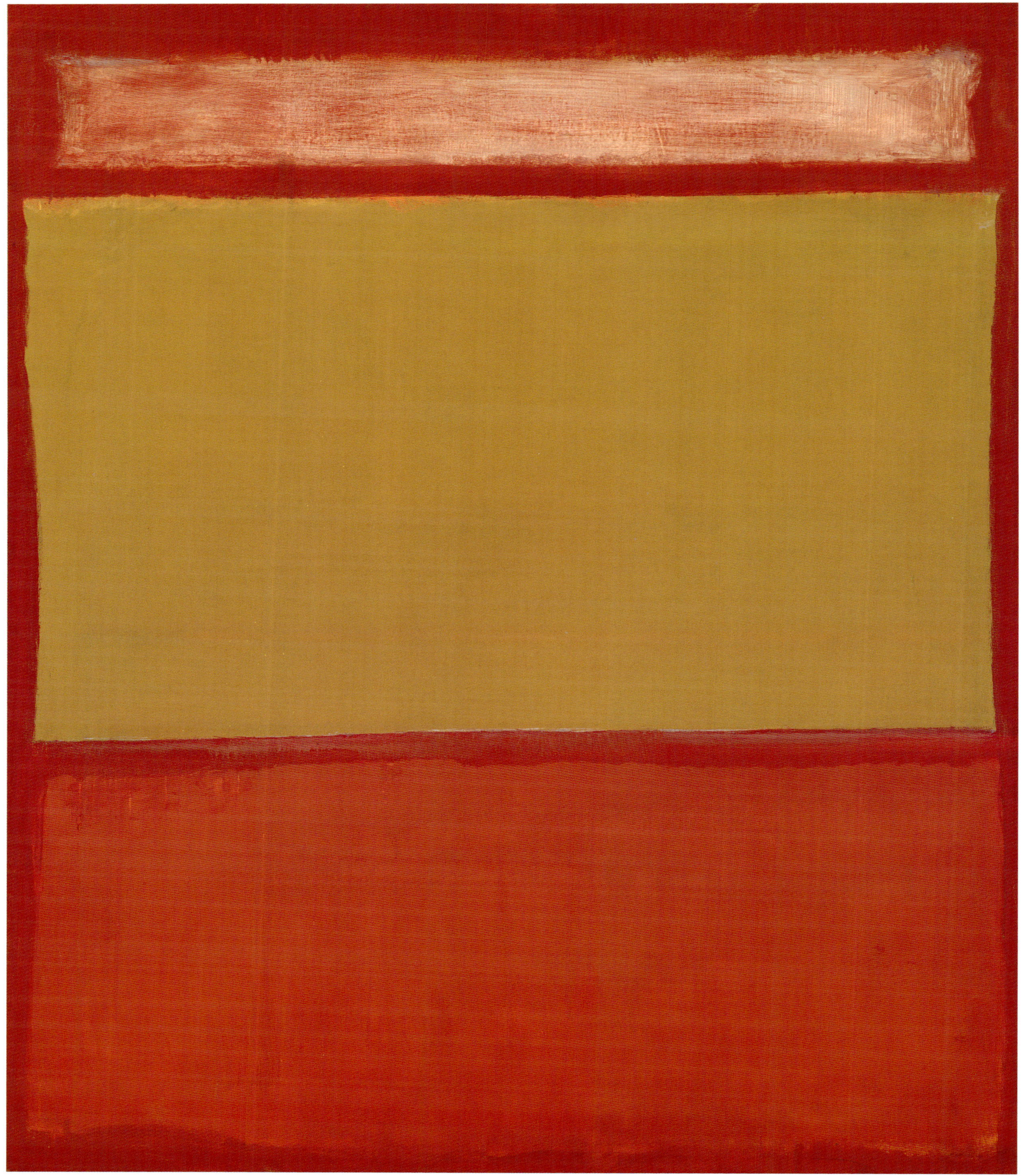

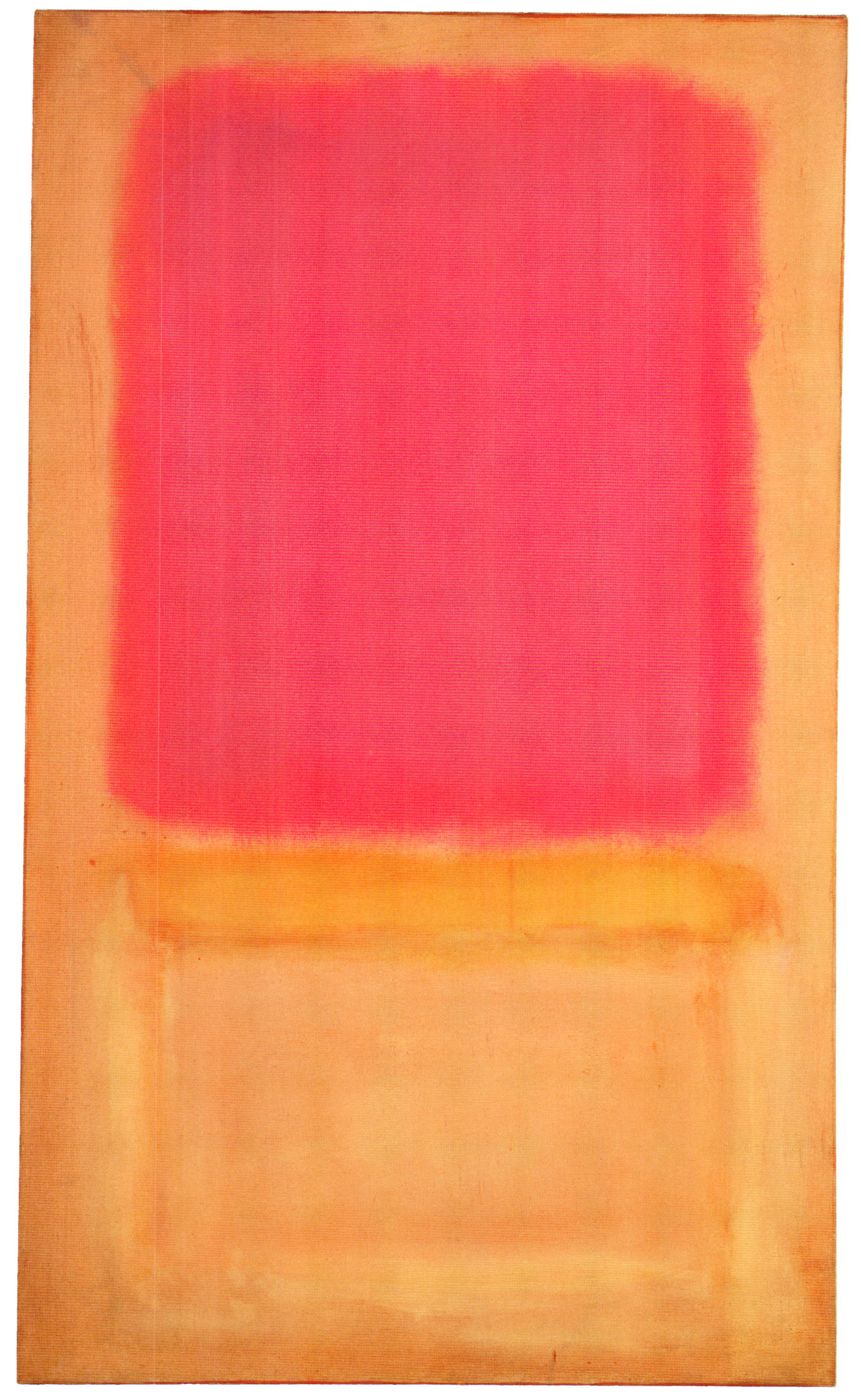

Rothko withdrew from the project and returned the money he had received; at this point in his career, he was not financially dependent on the commission.

His personal moral compass and philosophical leanings had triumphed over his aesthetic desires and aspirations. The affair received a lot of press coverage and created a lot of interest. It is no longer possible to recreate the original presentation concept, as Rothko never made a final choice as to which of the canvases should eventually be part of the final group. One group hangs in the Rothko room at the Tate Modern in London, another group hangs in the Kawamura Memorial Museum in Japan, while others are in the collection of the National Gallery of Art in Washington and in the collection of Rothko's children.

The Phillips and Harvard

Rothko was now well known and financially independent, his works were in demand and his studio was frequently visited by private collectors; among these were Duncan and Marjorie Phillips from Washington. The Phillipses used their Washington home as a gallery space and in 1960 had organized an exhibition for Rothko. Duncan Phillips wanted to create a Rothko room in his gallery space and in the same year bought four paintings from Rothko with this end in mind. This space was the first one where Rothko was able to achieve his ambition of being in control of both the room and the viewer's experience in order to create an environment where the viewer could engage with the paintings both physically and emotionally as Rothko intended.

Also at around this time, Rothko was given another opportunity to design a public room exclusively with his own works. In 1961, Harvard University, Cambridge, Massachusetts offered him a commission to furnish the penthouse room of the Holyoke Center, a 10-storey office building, which was to be used as a dining room for the Society of Fellows of Harvard College. The canvases are each eight and a half feet high, and they hung on the east and west walls of the penthouse room, while the other two walls had picture windows displaying spectacular views. From the start, Rothko realized that light from the windows would likely damage the murals and he agreed only on condition that fibreglass curtains be installed to protect them from sun damage.

The Harvard Murals

There are five works in the frieze, a triptych and two single but related panels (*see* fig. 79, page 169 for ***Panel One*** of the triptych). By using vertical oblongs, Rothko has created what appears to be a colonnade with dropped keystones, giving the appearance of a Classical architectural feature. The lines are sharp, unlike the blurred edges of the Seagram murals, and the parade of sharply defined verticals is reminiscent of the early subway paintings. The colours vary from crimson to black, but the strong orange of the Seagram murals is missing. Rothko has varied the width of the 'columns', thus affecting the perception of their density. The verticals appear to project from the panels through Rothko's use of contrasting colours.

Clearwater links this technique to Gestalt psychology, which has demonstrated that the mind can only perceive an ambiguous image one way at a time. If the viewer perceives the larger painted areas as solid, then the verticals look like voids. Conversely, if the viewer concentrates on the verticals, and allows the darker painted areas to recede, the verticals appear as solid. In this way, in the original frieze, Rothko has created 'the uncanny effects ' of a fluctuating pattern of light and dark.

Turning off the Rothkos

In an article in the ***New Yorker***, 1 April 2015, 'Watching Them Turn Off the Rothkos', Louis Menand writes that people visiting the penthouse room liked the views and so the curtains were rarely closed, and diners inadvertently splashed particles of food and drink on to the canvases or caught them with their chairs as they got up to leave the table. By the end of the 1970s, the room was being rented out as a function room for parties and the murals began to receive dents and tears. No one department at the university seemed to be taking responsibility for them. By 1979, they had lost most of their colour and were taken down and put in storage.

Because of Rothko's methods of using different coloured layers of underpainting, it is not possible to restore the paintings using conventional methods. A technique known as 'compensating illumination', pioneered by the conservator Raymond La

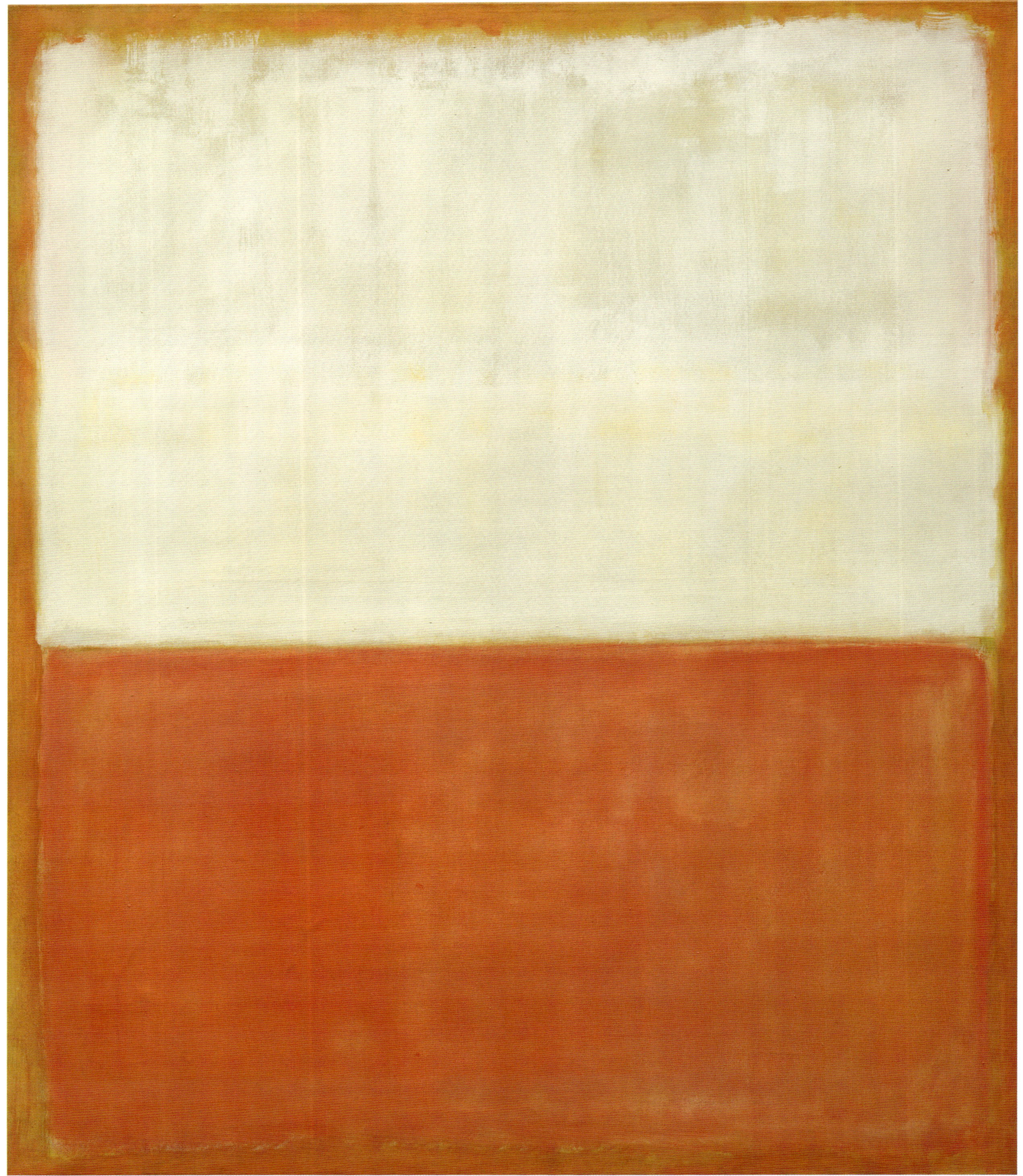

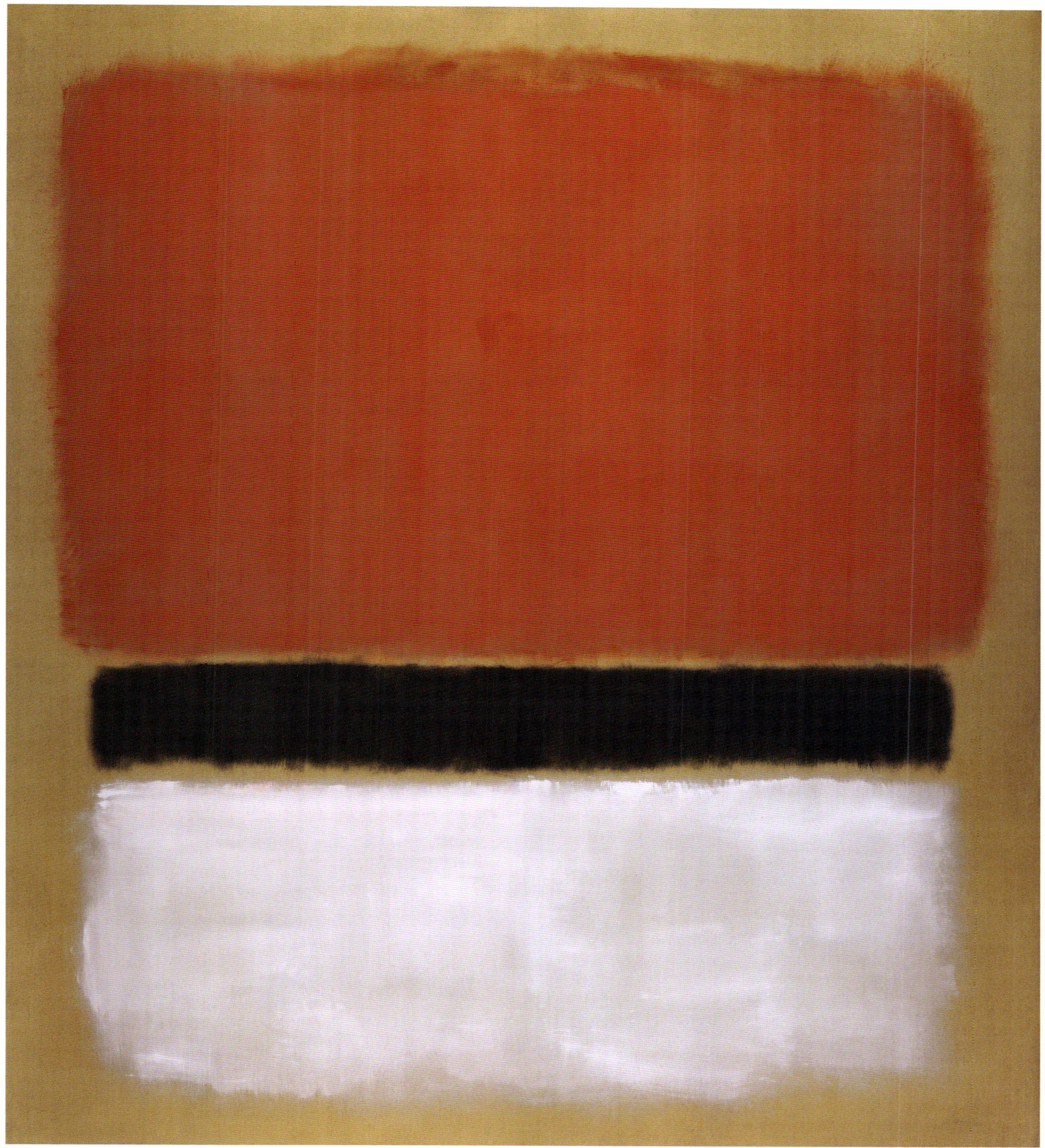

Fontaine, has been used by the Harvard Art Museums, where five digital projectors light up the canvases so that the original colours appear. At the end of the day, people gather to see the projectors turned off one by one, and the colours revert back to their present-day muddy blacks and greys; the architectural bones of the works are there, but the glowing colour is gone. This 'back from the dead' approach has fascinated people as it raises a number of philosophical issues. In a way, it creates a new work of conceptual art, although it has been pointed out that projecting light on to a canvas is different to light emanating from the canvas. The one missing element, considers Menand, is that the murals were site-specific; with Rothko's works on two walls and fantastic views on the two other walls, it must have provided a spectacular setting. One wonders what Rothko himself would have made of all this.

Threats

Around the beginning of the 1960s, it was becoming clear that the star of the American Abstractionists was beginning to wane. A new generation of young artists, led by such people as Andy Warhol (1928–87), Roy Lichtenstein (1923–97) and others, was rising up and for the most part, they appeared to represent many of the things that Rothko and his contemporaries held in disdain.

Pop Art had originally come from Britain, but had been enthusiastically embraced by the new American artists and spread rapidly. It arose from the brash, aggressive world of advertising, the expanding mass media and the developing consumer culture. The artists would take everyday things, including the banal and profane, and use them in provocative and at times ironic, even sarcastic ways.

Suddenly, the New York school of Rothko's world looked to be old establishment, of the past, high-minded, even pompous and elitist. Rothko was of the opinion that these new artists were 'charlatans and young opportunists'. Sidney Janis gave the new artists a show at his gallery in 1962; after seeing the show, Rothko, together with Kline, Motherwell and de Kooning, were furious at what they had seen and broke ties with the gallery. Rothko, summing up what they felt, posed the question: **'Are these young artists plotting to kill us all?'**

Honours

The late 1950s and early 1960s, however, were also for Rothko personally a time of wider recognition and honour. In 1958, he was chosen to represent the United States at the XXIX Venice Biennale. In 1961, as a cultural leader, he was invited to attend the inauguration of John F. Kennedy as the President of the United States and was deeply moved by this recognition of his work and his career. At the ball, which took place after the ceremony, he was placed next to Joseph Kennedy, the President's father, a singular honour.

Also in 1961, the Museum of Modern Art mounted a highly successful retrospective exhibition of his career, selecting 48 paintings. Rothko visited the exhibition on many occasions, intently studying his own work. When the exhibition was over, he was happy to hand over a number of the paintings to form part of a touring exhibition, which as well as visiting certain American cities, went on to the Whitechapel Art Gallery in London, Amsterdam, Brussels, Basel, Rome and Paris; he had truly arrived.

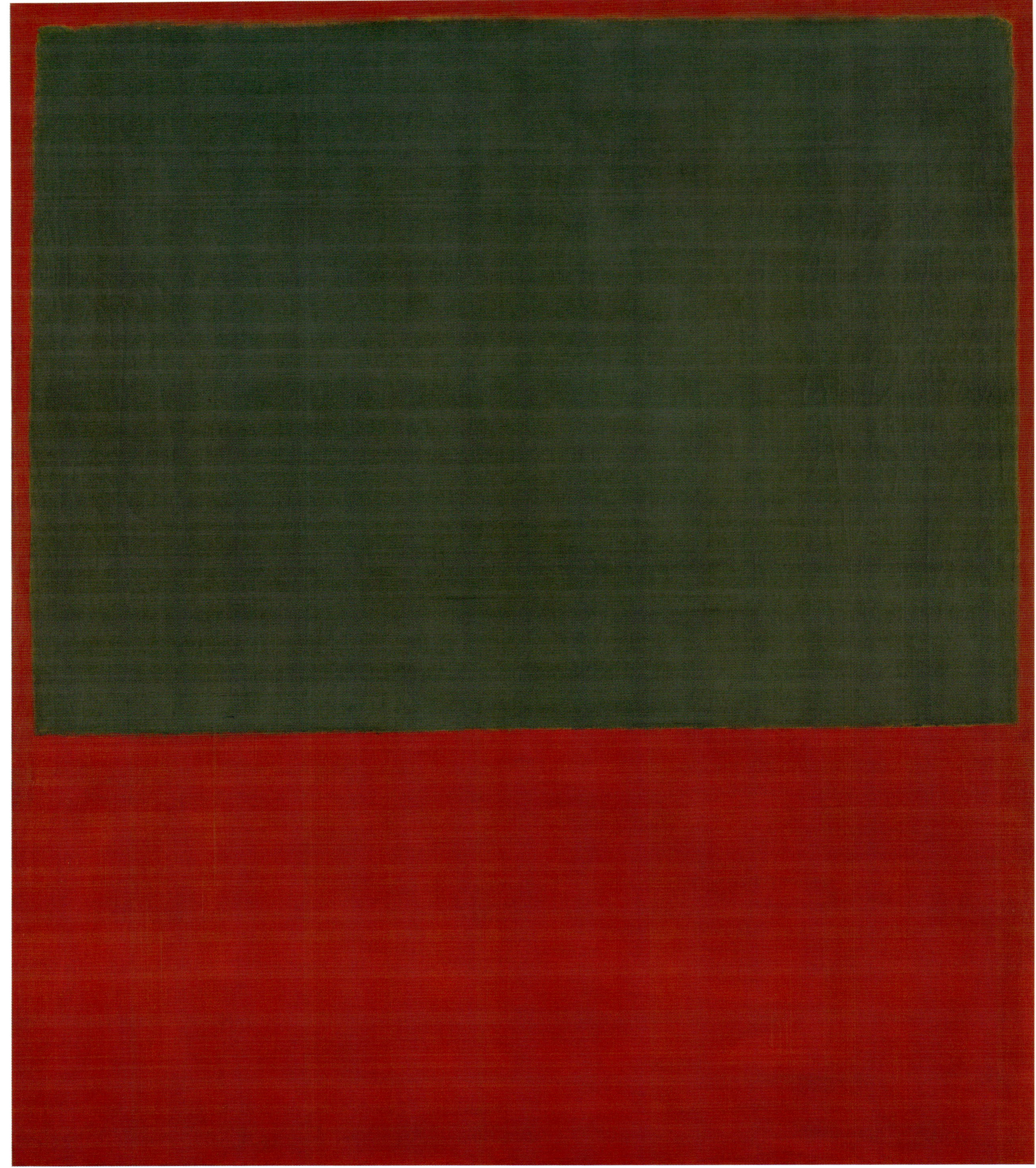

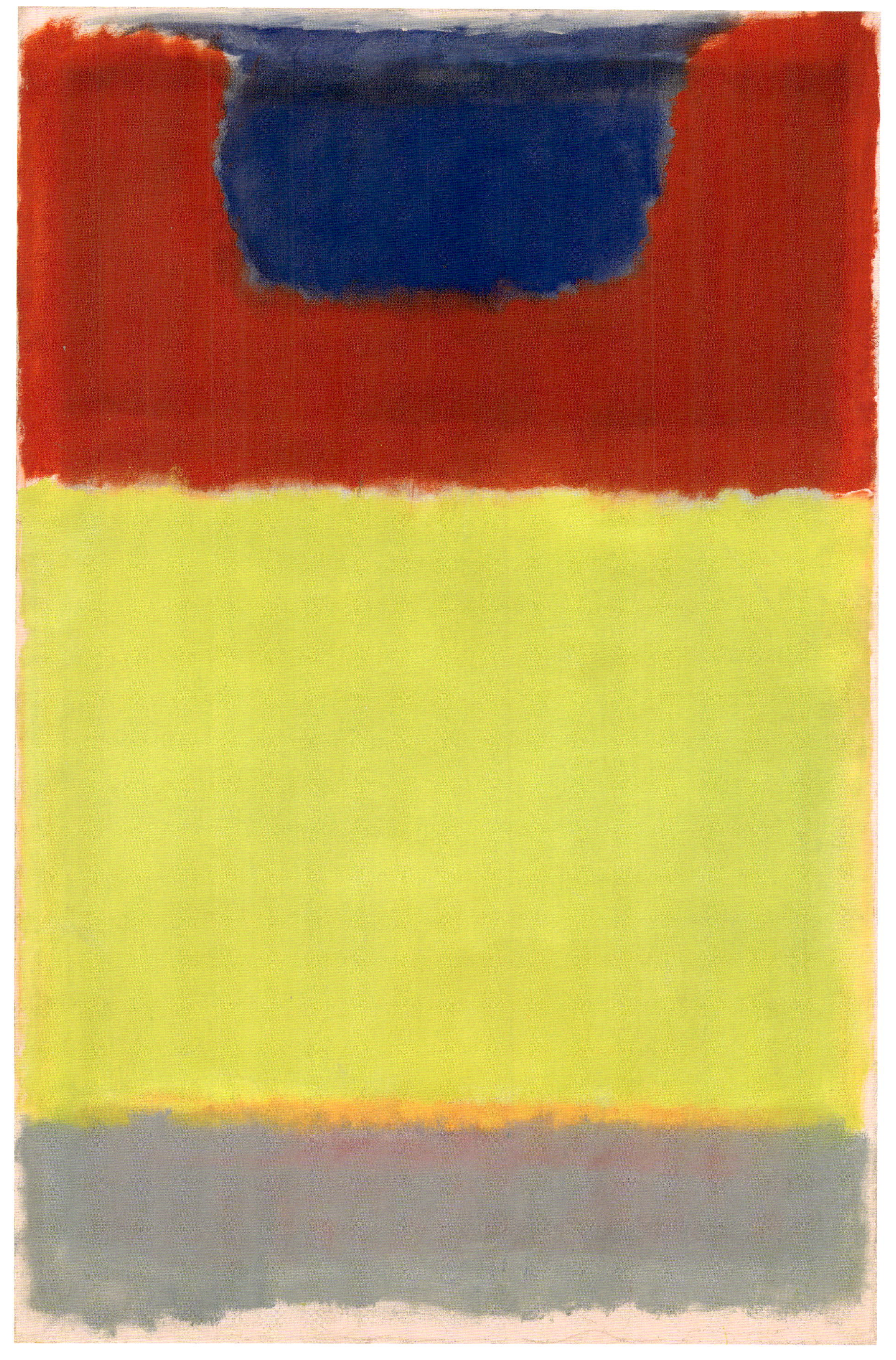

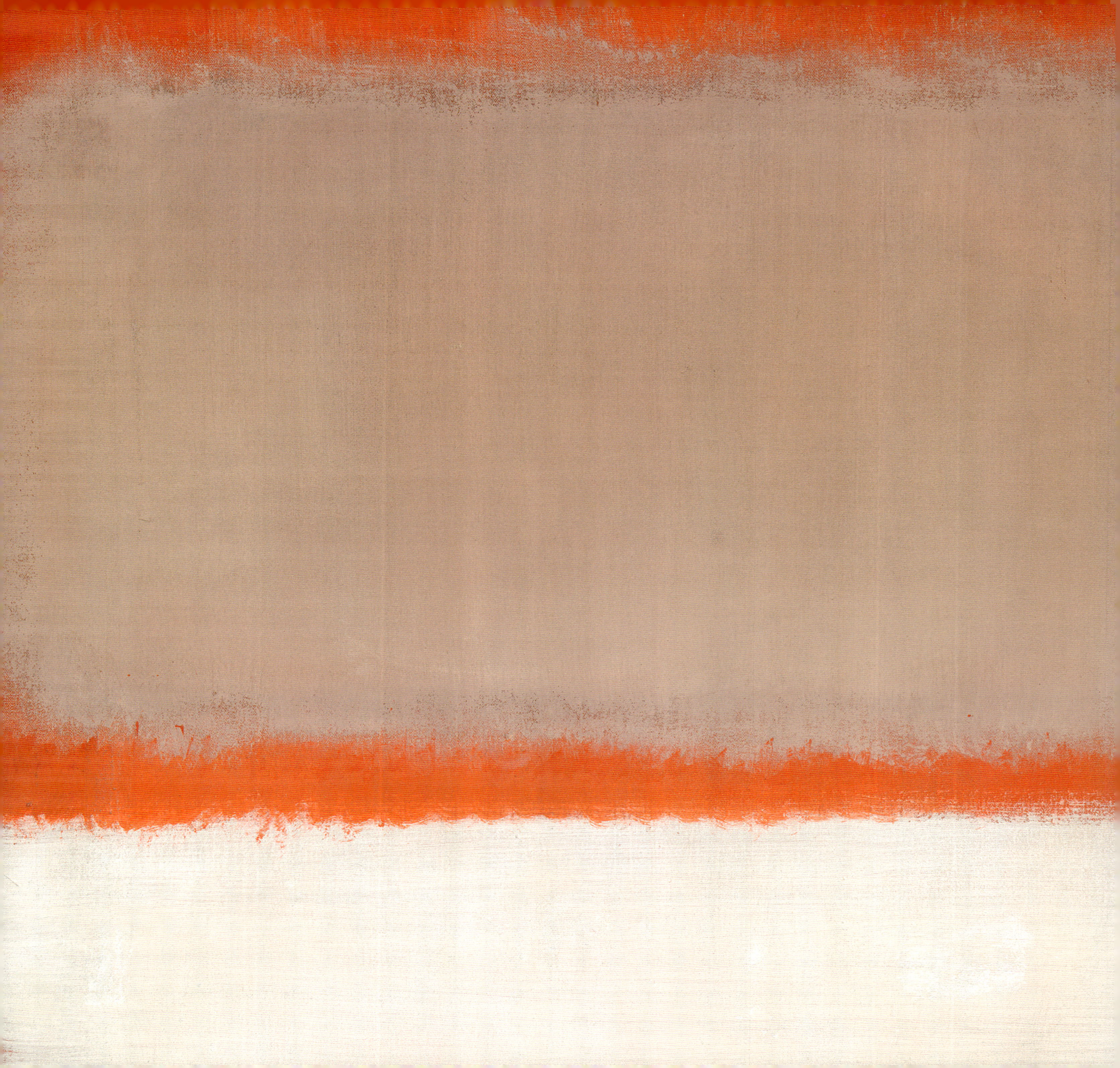

an inner light

What brought Rothko the most fame and recognition and cemented his reputation as one of the most significant artists of the twentieth century were the works that have become known as his classic works.

In the summer of 1948, he had invited some friends and artists to view his new 'multiforms', which were very well received. The art historian Harold Rosenberg recalls finding these works 'fantastic' and described his visit as 'the most impressive visit to an artist' in his life. Over the following months, Rothko worked at developing this way of artistic expression, experimenting with shapes and simplifying his use of colour; he reduced the colour pools of the multiforms to two or three rectangular-shaped areas of colour, which appear to hover in the foreground of the painting, thus creating the basic template for the layout of a 'classic' Rothko. He continued to deny that he was an expressionist painter, an abstract painter, colour field painter or any other sort of painter. Just as he had given up for the most part naming his works, he refused any categorization as an artist, thereby giving the impression that his work was basically unclassifiable and by definition had something of the enigmatic and mysterious about it.

Classic Works

By 1950, Rothko had found his ultimate style of expression in which he continued to work for the rest of his life. His classic works of the 1950s are full of bright colour contrasts and vivid juxtapositions, appealing and sensuous. These are what people tend to think of when they refer to a Rothko work. Although at first his style may appear abstract, for Rothko, form and colour were significant only as they represented a higher truth. He wanted to follow in the great tradition of intellectual European art, art which has something to say, to communicate higher values and meanings about the human condition.

The striking characteristic of his early classic works is two or three floating rectangles on top of each other (*see* figs. 37–39, pages 83–87, for example); the contrasting horizontal and vertical bands of the multiforms have disappeared. Spatial illusion is limited, although his floating forms appear to hover just above the colour field on which they are painted. This colour ground at times shows through the shapes painted on top of it; the almost feathery application of paint on the rectangles gives them an almost transparent surface. Because they are so delicate and seem almost weightless, they can seem to move towards the viewer. This process of reduction and clarity in Rothko's works, tending to the essence of simplicity, together with their large scale, endows them with something of grandeur and nobility.

Repetition and Variety

From 1950 to around 1956, the works he produced were remarkably restricted in style, but they were at the same time remarkably varied; for all the seeming repetition, there were variations in Rothko's work. Colour palette changes led him to use different hues and colour combinations at different times, borders and edgings appeared and disappeared, at times soft-edged rectangles were replaced by sharp-edged colours, canvas size differed, works were on paper as well as on canvas. Although the general format of his works was very limited in the variety and number of shapes and their placement on the canvas, the variation in canvas size and the display of a vast range of colours and colour combinations, with shapes slightly altered in size from picture to picture, created changes. Within these parameters, Rothko was able to suggest a wide range of moods, atmospheres and emotions. The simplicity and unity of the classic works give a sense of continuity, suggesting that they have been there for ever. The picture shapes float in a space that gives the impression at times of being fluid, at other times of being thin and immaterial. Round-edged, soft and unthreatening, they rise and sink, almost hypnotically at times. Using his method of staining the canvas and painting many layers of very thin washes of paint, he achieved the implication of a hidden light source, almost an inner light emanating from the central

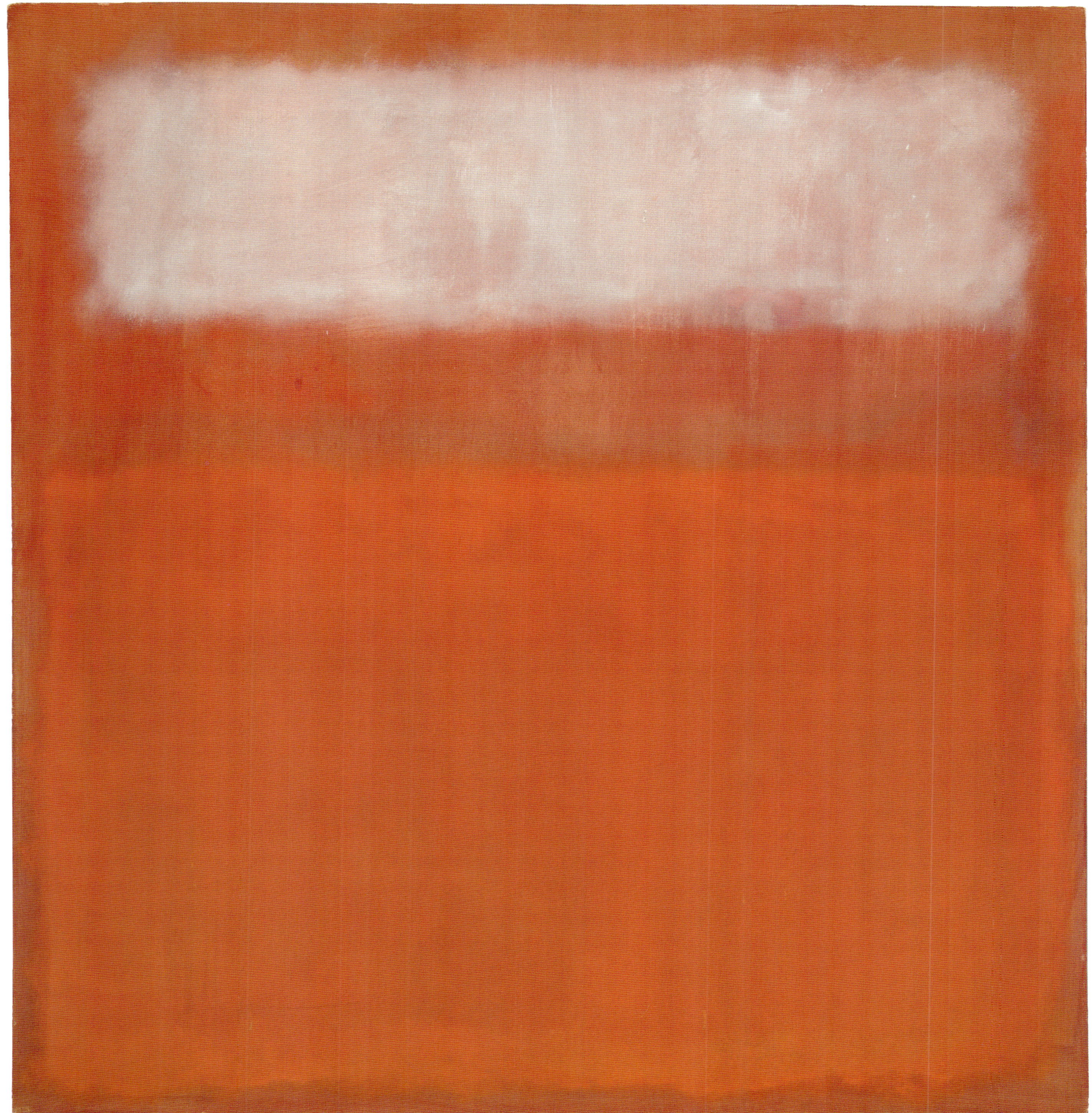

core of the work, something akin to the effects created by Rembrandt (1606–69), one of the artists he so admired. His mastery of nuances of form and colour were revealed as the 1950s progressed.

Rust on Blue

The author Diane Waldman has contrasted two of these early works to demonstrate the different effects Rothko could create while using the same techniques within his choice of restricted form. In ***Brown, Blue, Brown on Blue***, also known as ***Rust on Blue*** (1953), painted on a square-shaped canvas, a dark rusty blue rectangle at the top and a smaller light brown shape at the bottom are separated in the middle of the canvas by a vibrant blue area that melts into a slightly darker blue, which provides a frame around the edge of the whole painting. The darker areas of brown keep the blue colour from bursting out and taking over and so provide a sense of stability, while the blue surround holds everything together, creating unity. The shifting relationships between foreground and background, shallowness and depth, create a feeling of movement.

Waldman considers that the clever use of shades of blue and reddish brown, the balance between forms and the tension between depth and shallowness, create a masterly effect, making it, despite its large size, accessible at both an intimate and expressive level. The components of 'measure, balance, shape, textuality, tonality – cannot adequately express its breathtaking beauty'. The viewer is stimulated to experience a sense of awe, a feeling of mystery. She considers that in this type of work, 'Rothko creates the contemporary spiritual equivalent of the great Renaissance painters he revered', whose paintings 'were meant to inspire the beholder not merely with their formal perfection but also as reminders of an order beyond man and matter'.

Homage to Matisse

Homage to Matisse (1954; *see* fig. 53, page 115), using similar means, creates a totally different effect. Here, Rothko uses a tall, narrow canvas. Again using blue, but of a darker shade, he creates a large rectangle at the bottom of the canvas. Around this rectangle floats a sea of shades of yellow mist. In some areas, an underpainted field of red shows through, which has a blue tinge to it. There is a section of clear red that may have been painted on top of the canvas. Because of the colour tones and hues, the result is implausible, as red and yellow always produce orange. Rothko is experimenting with colour, creatively changing the rules, reinventing new effects, inspired by Matisse.

Waldman also suggests that there may be a symbolic and spiritual dimension intended. The deep blue rectangle is physically bold and strong, while the golden yellow surround is 'evanescent, incorporeal' like a shimmering halo. 'Thus, the painting speaks of form and space, of the real and immaterial, the physical and sensual yet disembodied presence of paint.'

The Aura of Mystery

The variations that Rothko created over the period of the 1950s are multiple. Waldman notes 'the size of the field and the interior configuration' differ in their relationships to each other, the width of the spaces between the colours varies, colours range from bright to dark, but the mood is rarely sombre, with only a small amount of black used. Paint is used loosely, with edges of colour blocks blurred and feathered so as to give a soft edge. Sometimes Rothko allows the paint at the edge of colour blocks to 'bleed' into the next colour area, which thus encloses it. The canvas is also painted at its edges and as the works are unframed, the whole painted area is visible.

Most pictures are left untitled by Rothko, given identifying numbers or colour names by curators. Even the colour names inform the viewer what to look for and thus suggest things to the viewer's mind. Rothko keeps this aura of mystery, of not knowing, with the aim that the viewer is swept into these larger-than-life canvases, 'drawn into the space that exists somewhere between himself and the picture plane and is engulfed in an overwhelming emotional experience'. Although these works did involve much effort, particularly with working on such large canvases, it is clear why Rothko does not fit the description of 'action painter.'

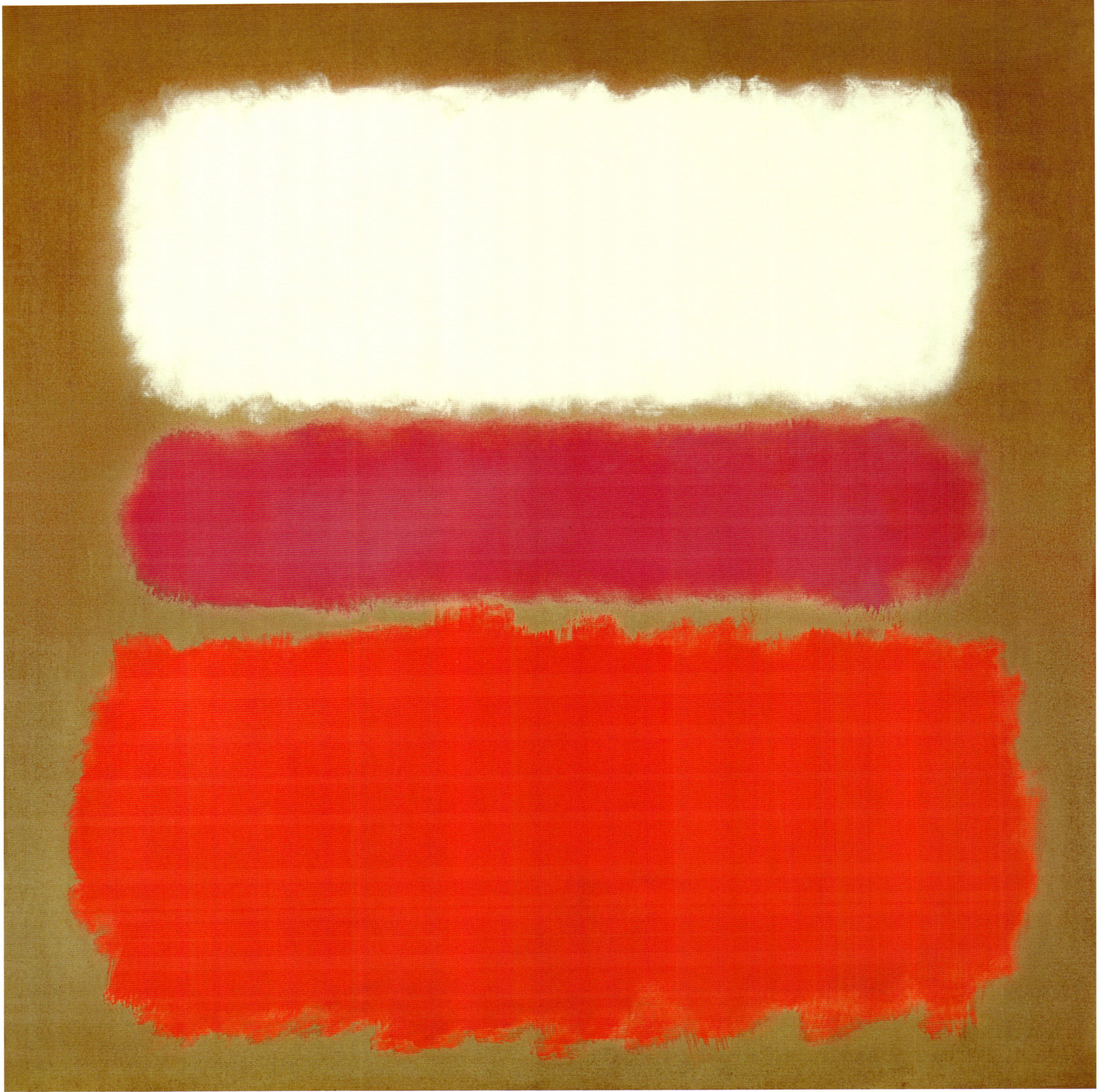

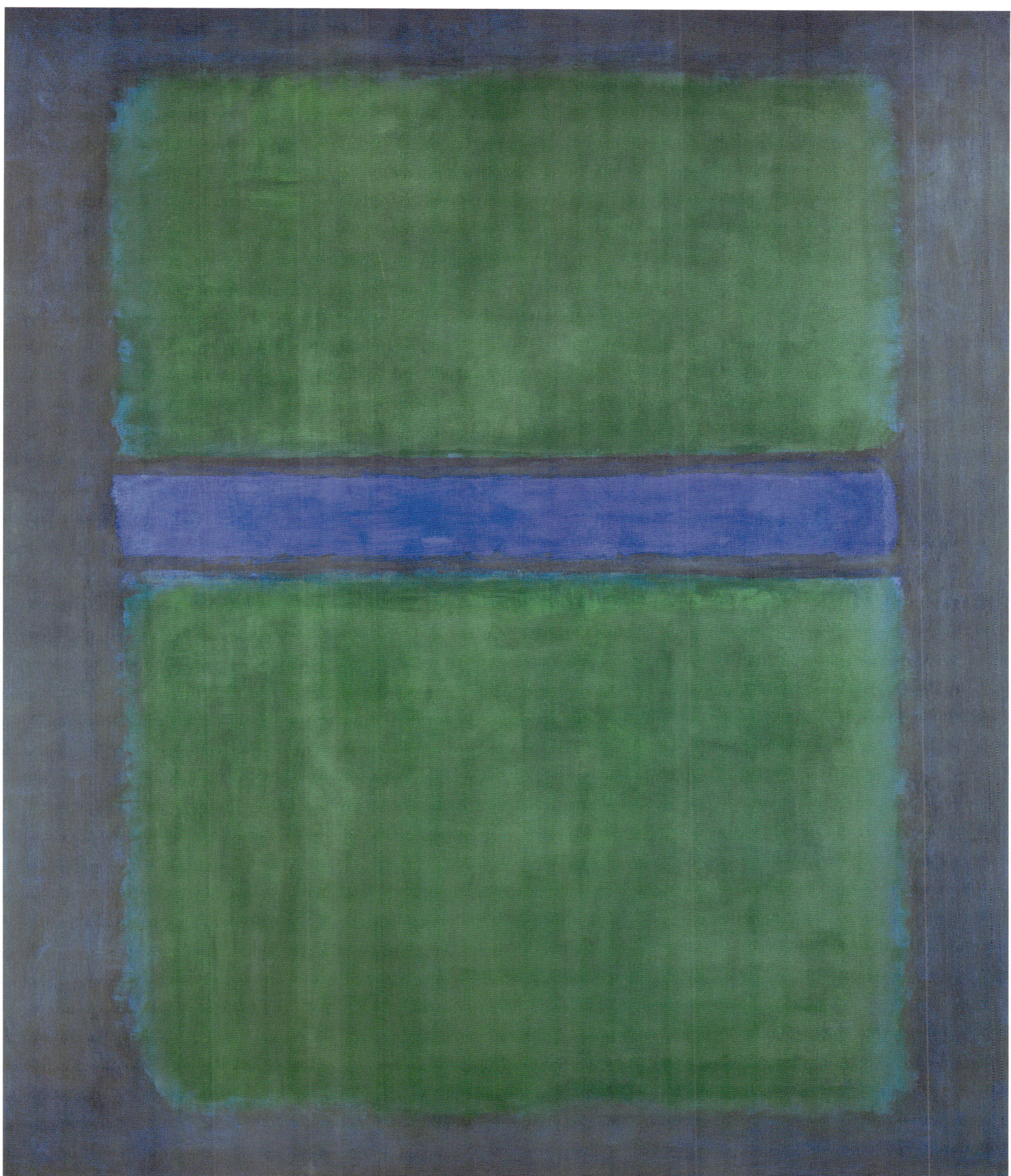

Waldman links his desire to create this exalted, transcendental experience with the works of Still and Newman, as compared to the works of 'action painters' such as Pollock, de Kooning and Kline. For them, the actual physical act of painting was the most important thing: 'the canvas must reflect the very act of painting'. Pollock was seen as the quintessential action painter, walking around his works, pouring and dripping paint on to the canvas, continuously in movement.

Rothko had a very different style, expending much energy on painting and then contemplating his works for long periods before starting to paint again. Over the timespan of the 1950s leading up to the commission of the Seagram murals in 1958, Rothko's canvases grew larger, he hardened the edges of his forms and he began to experiment with darker colours.

Works of the 1960s

By the 1960s, Rothko had become a more subtle exponent of his adopted means of expression. His works were more subdued, less sensuous and opulent, more economical in their language. The viewer is not so overwhelmed or seduced by the painting, but has to work harder to connect.

Rothko himself suggested that 18 inches was the ideal distance to stand away from his paintings to get the maximum benefit of their effect, so that their hidden depths of colour and meaning could begin to be revealed. His ideas about lighting also changed as his career progressed, as he began to insist that the lighting be dim so that initially the viewer is disorientated but gradually adjusts to the semi-obscurity, then begins to make out the works in the dimness and so the works in turn gradually begin to reveal their effects.

Emphasis is put on a more geometric approach to the depiction of the rectangles and on a feeling of weight. Less emphasis is given to the effect of colour. Symmetry is more closely observed than in the works of the 1950s and a clearly defined edge marks boundaries. A simplification, a clarification leads him to a more pared-down communication of the essential. Christopher Rothko suggests that because the works of the 1950s had been so well received, Rothko may have considered that he had made them too accessible, too sweet and his work of the 1960s was a way of correcting this.

His use of colours was widely praised; he was being called a colourist painter. So his new use of colour would show that it was not this that interested him overall, but that, for him, the idea behind the painting was paramount. His works are intended to make the viewer reflect on what it is to be human, and they do this by inspiring the viewer to contemplation. Discovery of the painting's heartbeat, its underlying rhythms slows down the heartbeat of the viewer; as viewer and painting find common ground, the viewer begins to listen, and the painting can begin to communicate.

More on Music

Museum director Thomas M. Messer suggests that Rothko finds empathy with the world of music in its immateriality, in its use of rhythmic structures (in the work of art, these are articulated through use of space and, as we have seen with Rothko, with a sense of movement) and the use of modulated tone colours. He suggests that like many of the great composers – Haydn (1782–1809) with his 104 symphonies springs to mind – Rothko uses a structure within which he creates a multitude of richly varied effects. Messer goes on to compare him to the great Romantic composers, from Schubert to Brahms. We might say that this modulation of colour leading to a musical effect could describe the works of the 1950s.

Christopher Rothko also uses a musical metaphor when discussing the works of the 1960s, but this time, the comparison is with Bach's works of the 1740s, the comparison of late Rothko with late Bach. Using the effects of proportion and structure, Bach's pieces of this period are 'darker, sparer, less overtly emotive ... Intellectual rigor is paramount, and Bach adds nothing that will interfere with the purity of his line, the beauty deriving from the contrapuntal argument itself'. Just as late Bach is not generally for the novice, so Christopher Rothko suggests that beginning with 1960s Rothko is a challenge, but as the viewer begins to understand where the works came from, how they developed, their secrets begin to reveal themselves.

Art Critics

The basis of art criticism at this time was formalism, that is the art critics would discuss the works in the context of what they looked like, their shape, form, line, colour. One of the most influential modernist critics of the time, Clement Greenberg (1909–94), in common with other critics, would largely confine his comments to how the painting appeared and how the painter achieved his effects.

In his essay 'American Type Painting', he gave Rothko credit for being the first to eliminate the problem that occurs spatially when pigment is applied to the canvas. Recognizing that Rothko achieved his effects by layering colours on top of each other, he wrote that Rothko 'seems to soak his paint into the canvas to get a dyer's effect and avoid the connotations of a discrete layer of paint on top of the surface'. Greenberg's stance, as was that of most other critics at the time, was that art should only be a visual experience and make no reference beyond itself; this idea was quite alien to Rothko. In his Pratt Institute lecture of 1958, Rothko stated of his paintings that it was not his intention 'either to create or to emphasize a formal colour-space arrangement'.

A Subjective Response

William Seitz, when interviewing Rothko for his doctoral dissertation, has some understanding that Rothko wants to go beyond simply innovating formally and that he is looking for a subjective response from the viewer. He notes that Rothko emphasizes 'that his variously shaped colour areas are simply "things" placed on a surface. From this viewpoint, spatial and atmospheric phenomena are subjective responses of the spectator'. He also recognizes Rothko's aim of creating movement within his works, writing: 'the shapes are more independent ... though intermittently one or more of the areas appear strikingly dense and impenetrable as a mass of concrete; but as the eye moves upward or downward – the only directions which the balanced format will permit – the spatial and physical effects shift, and what was mass becomes mist'. On hearing Seitz talk about his paintings, Rothko tried to move him on in his understanding, asking: 'But what do they mean to you? Just because an area [is] like undulating silk, is this important? Lots of people can make [sic] like undulating silk. Writing should look into the writer and find out what the painting really means.'

Emotional Need

In his interviews with Seitz, Rothko told him that what he was looking for was 'pure response in terms of human need. Does the painting satisfy some human need?' He believed that his viewers would respond much more to this emotional reaction, than to formal analysis. Rothko was aware that people were still looking for recognizable objects in paintings and he himself had spoken of the challenge and struggle he had experienced when he had decided to give up the depiction of the human figure, which for hundreds of years had been the expressive format for raising issues about what it means to be human and the human condition.

In his Pratt Institute lecture, he still referred to his paintings as portraits, because he was painting the eternal human action and drama, in which the human figure was central; even in his mulitforms, the colour spots have some affinities with individual figures. The transition of realistic figures in his early works into biomorphic configurations, and then eventually into planes of colour in his classic works, completes the metamorphosis. He had stated that 'memory' was one of the things he wanted to eliminate in his works, so that there should be no point of reference within the work itself that would encourage viewers to refer back to other things they already knew and then bring that perspective to the work of art they were looking at.

There was also the difficulty of positioning colour areas. An upright band of colour could possibly suggest a vertical object such as a person or a tree, while a horizontal colour area could be construed as a landscape or a horizon; Rothko wanted to eliminate all such reference points. He wanted to create something that had never existed before, something that would deliberately not suggest any other person, thing or natural phenomenon. He also did not want to prescribe what the viewer should experience emotionally through his paintings. He said: **'If people want sacred experiences they will find them here. If they want profane experiences they'll find them too. I take no sides.'**

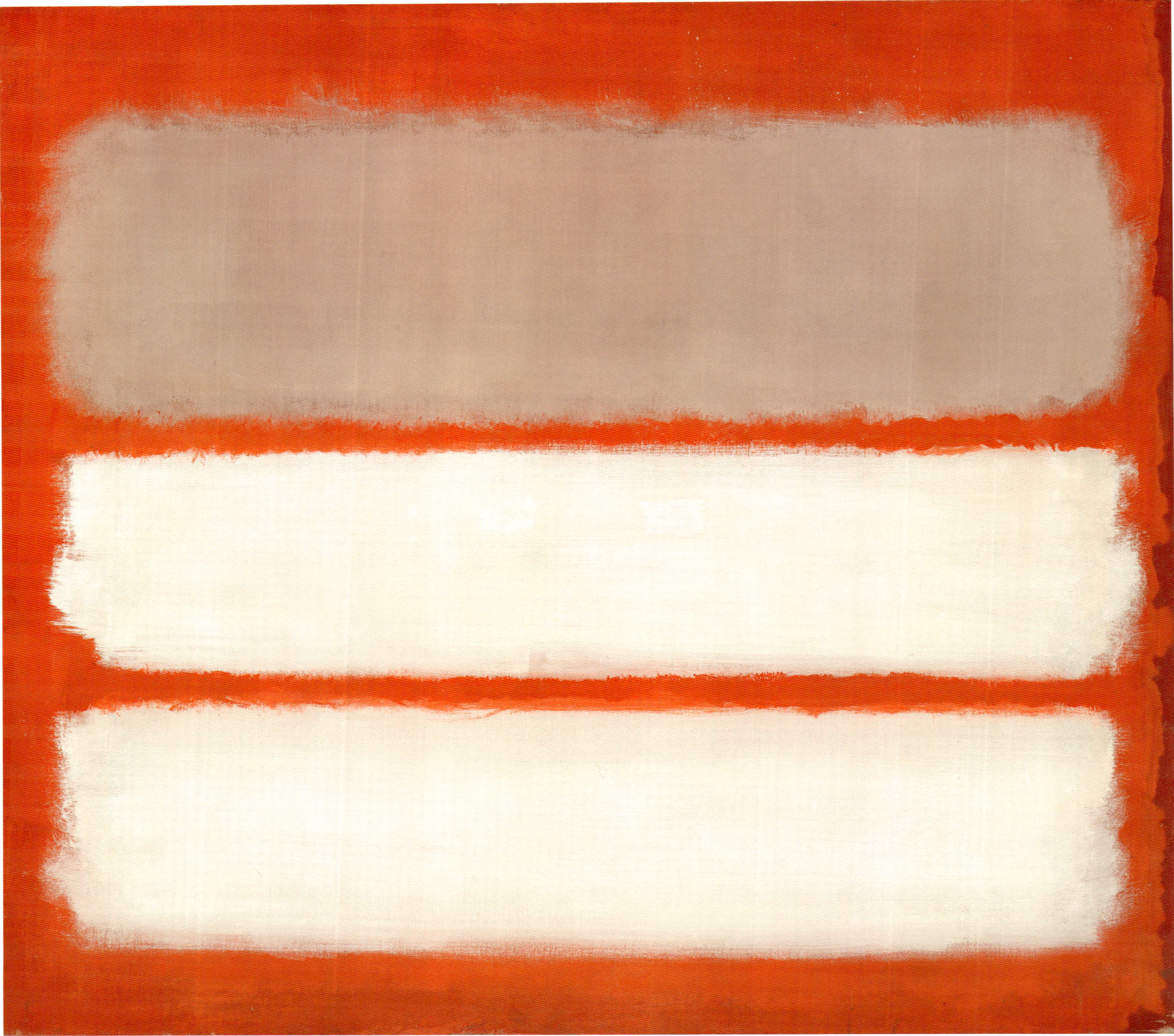

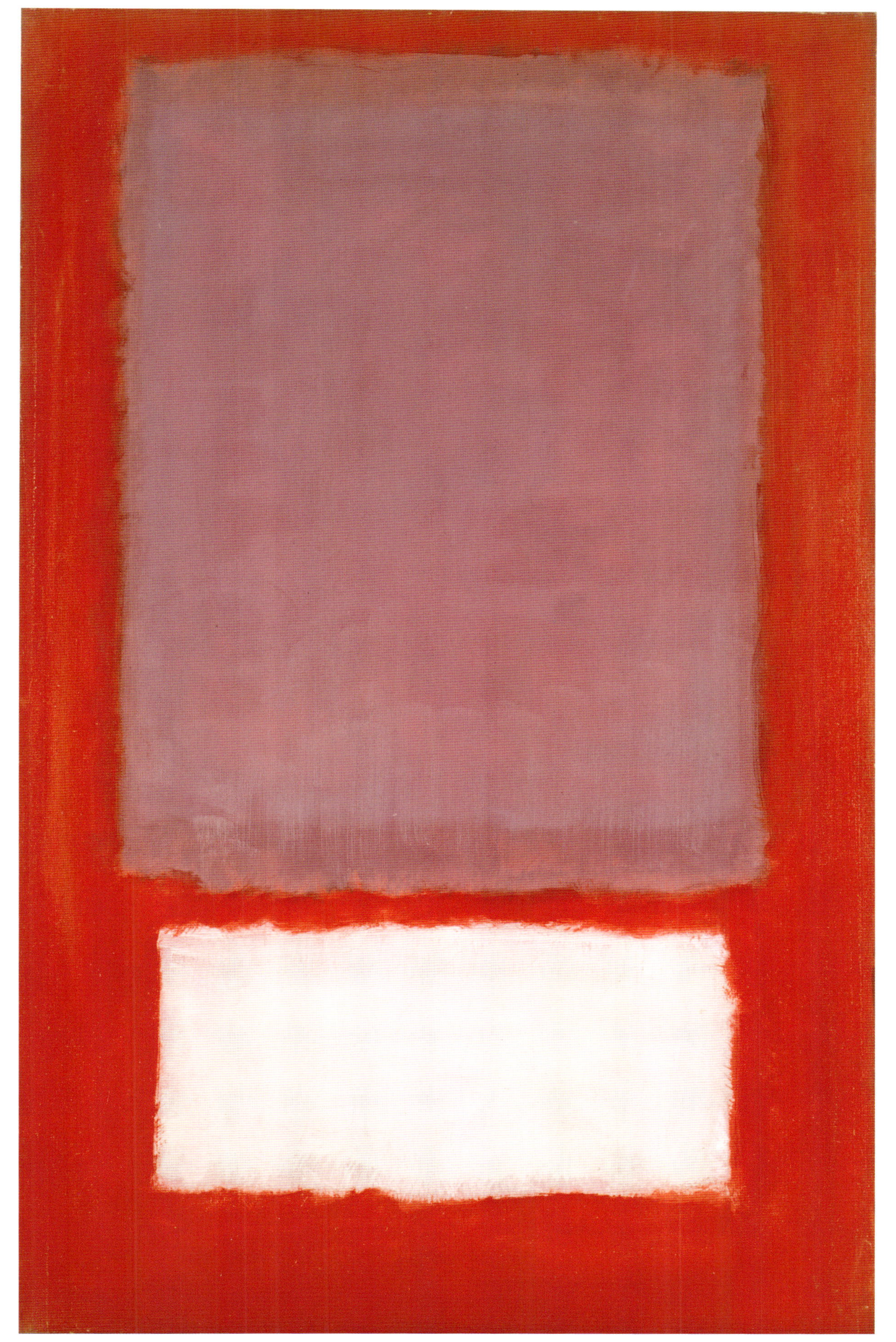

Colour-Atmosphere

Many people enjoy the paintings of Rothko's classic period for their glorious colours, and although this may not be totally pleasing to Rothko, as he had deeper issues in mind, it is certainly a valid approach. The individual viewer can feel uplifted and affirmed by the experience of taking pleasure in the wide variety of shades and tones, which Rothko uses in his own unique, creative way.

The Venetians were famed for their effects of colour and atmospheric light, sometimes referred to as the Venetian Secret. Through his readings and study, combined with his own reflections and thoughts, Rothko writes in ***The Artist's Reality*** of how the Old Masters, in particular the Venetians, used colour. He gives us some insight into his use of a background colour covered with layers of other colours, by writing: **'in order to create the one color tonality ... the Venetians worked on colored backgrounds wherein the basic color was allowed to function everywhere through the other colors superimposed upon it'.**

He also praises the Venetians for their use of 'an exploitation of human feelings through the representation of expression and the heightened effect of these through the discovery of atmospheric light'. Duncan Phillips, who created the Rothko room in his extended home gallery in Washington, when writing of Rothko, referred to the great master of colour and light in Venetian painting Giovanni Bellini, saying: 'Color-atmosphere in painting is as old as Giovanni Bellini and his mountain backgrounds.' He goes on to say that Rothko achieves similar effects: 'But in Rothko there is no pictorial reference at all to remembered experience. What we recall are not memories but old emotions disturbed or resolved.'

Colour Palette

Rothko's palette ranged from hot bright tones to misty lilacs, vibrant orange, shades of whites, pink, delicate greens and blues, and later on in his career, shades of grey, brown, dark purple and black. Red was a particular favourite and he used every hue available. Red can be used for many significant events and dramatic points in the human story: birth, lust, the violent glare cf the sun, sacrifice, revelation, death.

We have already noted the influence of Matisse's **Red Studio** on Rothko; Kandinsky (1866–1944) said of red that 'it rings inwardly with a determined and powerful intensity. It glows in itself, maturely'. Colour is a universal language, although it often has different meanings in different cultures. The impact of adjoining colours can create a vibrant clash or initiate a gentle meeting; different colours bring out subtle hues in other colours. Colours can replace the human figure, they make connections or push apart, they are powerful and energetic or peaceful and gentle. Even on a superficial level, they mirror the human story in a thousand disguises.

Colour and Emotion

William Scharf (b. 1927), a painter and friend of Rothko, said: 'You have to remember that Mark did not want to be a great colorist, he wanted to be a visionary.' If there are no recognizable visual objects to refer to, no actions or symbols to read, no cultural references, then colour is the one thing left to comment on for critics and viewers alike. John Gage (1938–2012), writing in 1988, attempted an analysis of Rothko's colours to try to extrapolate meanings from Rothko's work. Knowing of Rothko's earlier explorations of the Apollonian/Dionysian contrast, based on Nietzsche's philosophy, he suggested that Rothko's contrasts of vivid red and green may express this conflict. He offered support for this view by referring to Rothko's deep interest in the depiction of the Dionysian legend in the murals of the Villa of Mysteries at Pompeii, which include music, dance and sacrifice.

Rothko's juxtaposition of colours certainly creates tension and also, conversely, a relaxation of tension. Rothko denied that he was interested in colour and form, saying: **'if you say ... you are moved only by color relationships, then you miss the point'**. His statement underlining that he was interested 'only in expressing basic human emotions – tragedy, ecstasy, doom' points towards his use of colour to facilitate the exploration of emotions.

151

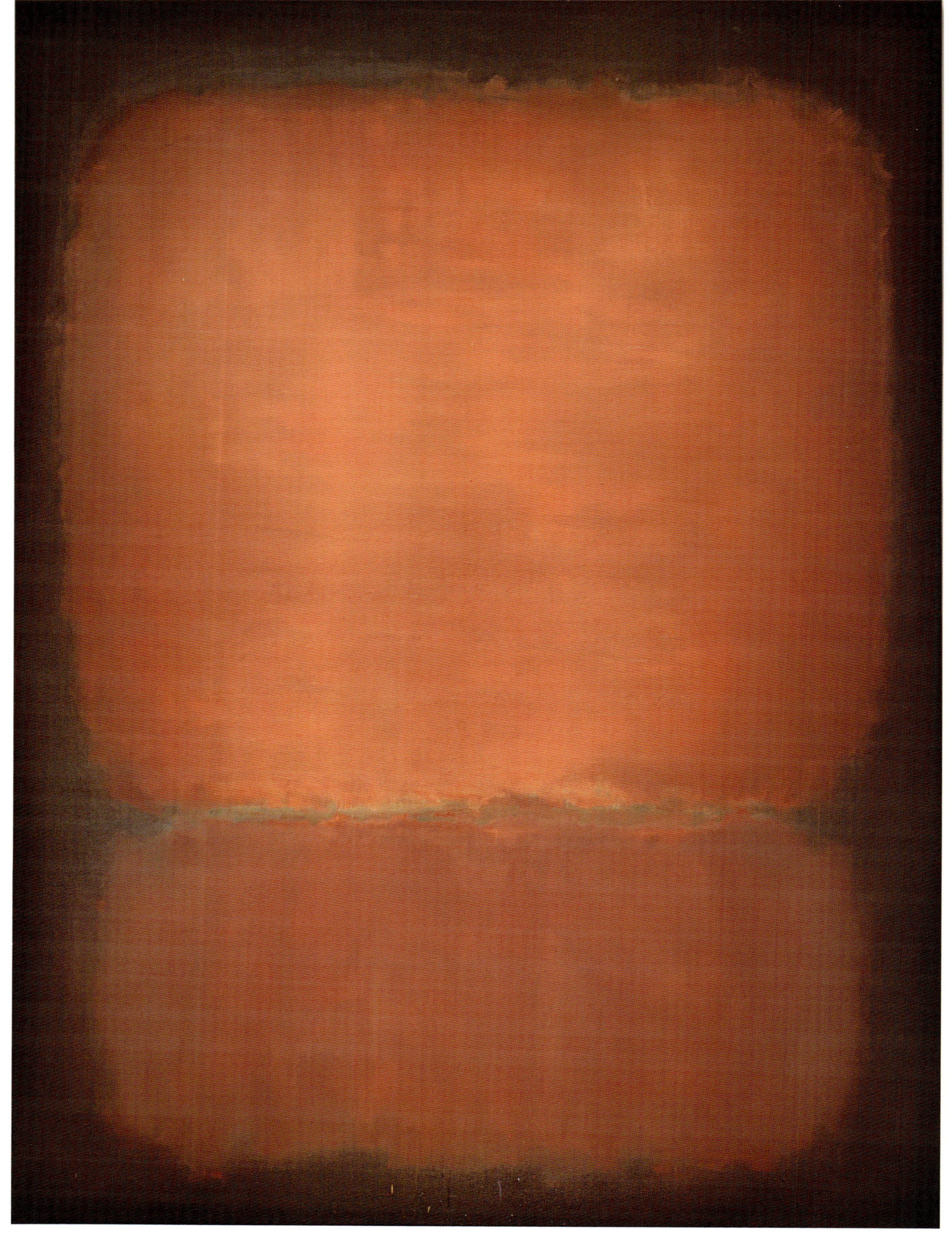

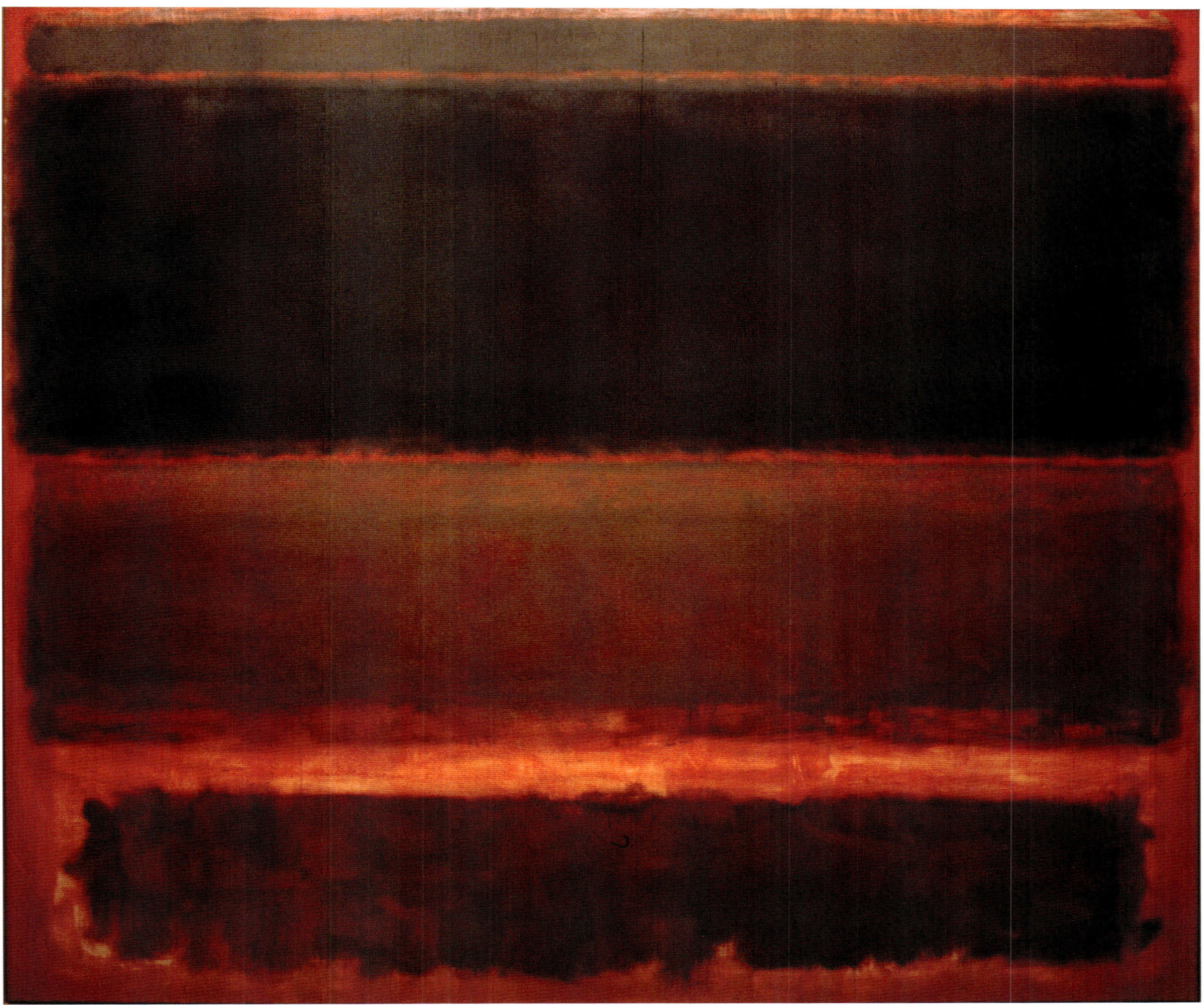

Colour Relationships

Clearwater succinctly points out: 'The colour relationships were instrumental in the way they produce the pulsating tension of forms pulling towards each other and pushing away. Thus the physical force produces the sensation that a conflict of life and death – the essence of human existence – is being acted out on the canvas.' As colour areas take on a quasi-biological existence, they appear to possess life, to become biological, conscious entities; interestingly enough, this is all illusion, perhaps just as much as linear perspective or realistic depiction of people and objects.

Ultimately, it is just as fake as all the other illusions art opens up to the viewer. However, Rothko was a pioneer in the use of these effects in art, but that is what they are – effects achieved by the manipulation of shape, form, colour and light. That this pulsation, reminiscent of a beating heart perhaps, affects the emotions, is one that viewers have to experience for themselves. Rothko acknowledges that he has opened up this opportunity for the viewer by saying: **'... the fact that a lot of people break down and cry when they are confronted with my pictures shows that I can communicate those basic human emotions.'**

The Transcendental

Rothko, though brought up initially to be strictly Jewish, was a non-believer. However, he had a religious temperament. He saw himself as a visionary and appears to have yearned after transcendence. His classic works can perhaps be considered to be one way he attempted to reconcile his religious early childhood upbringing with his atheism, and with the collective tragedies of the twentieth century. This unattainable synthesis drove him on to continue to work, always attempting to reach the essentially impossible. His non-representational works have been widely recognized by his admirers as making a strong spiritual impact, even being referred to as contemporary icons in the Byzantine tradition – in other words made for inspiring meditation and contemplation.

An early commentator on his work, one of the few at the time to look beyond the formal properties of his paintings, was the art historian Robert Rosenblum (1927–2006). Rosenblum wrote an article in 1961 entitled 'The Abstract Sublime' and went on further to develop this theme in an influential book, published in 1975, ***Modern Painting and the Northern Romantic Tradition: Friedrich to Rothko***. Rosenblum considered that Rothko shared certain affinities with Casper David Friedrich and J.M.W. Turner. He wrote that: 'Rothko, like Friedrich and Turner, places us on the threshold of those shapeless infinities discussed by the estheticians of the Sublime.'

Ungraspable Mysteries

Rosenblum proposes that Rothko continued the work of Turner (1775–1851) and Friedrich (1774–1840) 'to depict the awe-inspiring infinities of the natural world as a metaphor of the supernatural world beyond'. Both Turner and Friedrich, he considered, 'pursued ... the creation of a pictorial world without matter, usually conveyed through a vision of landscape, seascape or skyscape that would free us from the pull of terrestrial gravity and immerse us, without ruler or compass, in some primordial element of water, cloud, color, light or a fusion of all these ungraspable mysteries of nature.'

Although Rothko was not using realistic or even abstract landscapes, Rosenblum felt that they created a similar transcendental experience for the viewer. Indeed, Rothko indicated that the actual painting of works was at times a religious experience for him, saying: **'The people who weep before my paintings are having the same religious experience I had when I painted them.'** Rothko's paintings have undoubtedly become, in many people's opinion, works to be meditated on. Certainly the rise of interest in Eastern religions, with their strong element of transcendental meditation, during the period when Rothko was producing his classic works and showing no signs of abating today, may have been a factor in the development of this approach. The aim has become that you silence the words in your head, still the activities of the brain, relax the body, let go of tension, open yourself to a new experience, a fresh discovery, a new encounter and contemplate the painting, allowing it to work on, in and through you.

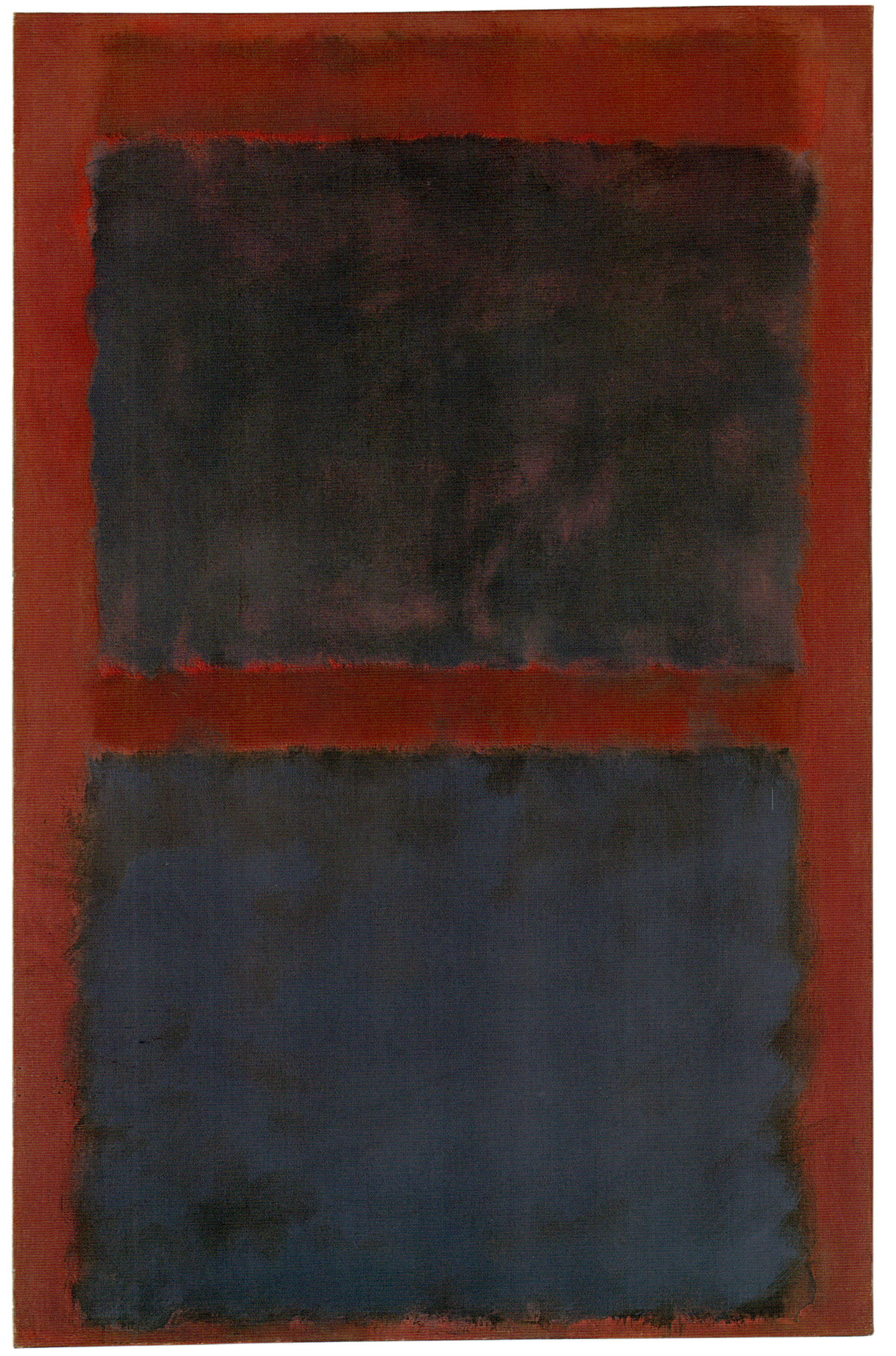

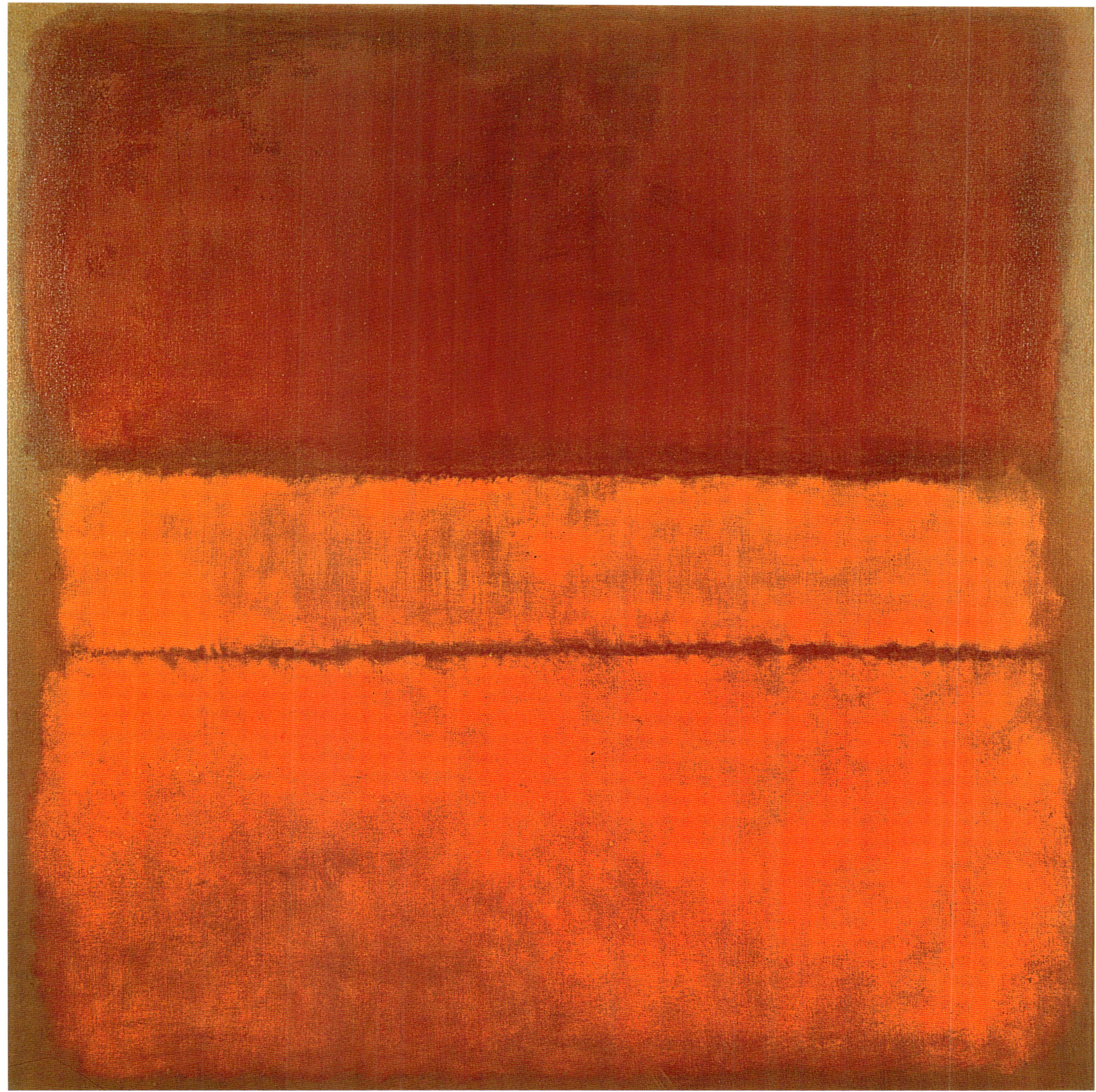

The Human Drama

Having discovered his particular way of communicating through art and all that he wanted to convey of the basic human condition and emotions, Rothko kept doing it again and again with variations throughout the rest of his career, that is for 20 years. For him, he had found his perfect way of expressing the human drama, almost an absolute meaning or truth for him; it was so vital to him that he had to keep on repeating it. Perhaps it could be considered almost like a ritual, formally creating the space/colour continuum and bringing into play some new gestures, some new movement; perhaps it was the experience of being taken out of himself as he worked, experiencing a personal revelation.

Some critics have made the point that Rothko could be considered to have painted himself into a dead end, that there was nowhere else to go. It seems, however, that for Rothko, having at last found his epitome of personal expression, his unique language, a way of expressing poignancy through paint, communicating directly to the viewers' emotions and so moving from the tangible world to the intangible, was enough for him. He seems to have shown no inclination to paint in any other way, but, for 20 years, found a continually renewing freshness based on the same basic method which kept him motivated and engaged.

That his works resonated with people and found a wide and appreciative viewing public, bringing him recognition and honours, was also a reward in itself and a stimulus to further creativity in the same area, along the same lines. Although he was never materialistic in outlook, it also enabled him at long last to provide for his family on a steady and consistent basis.

Wit, Play and Irony

The fact that Rothko considers there is wit, play and irony in his works may come as something of a surprise. He included these points in his lecture at the Pratt Institute, where he suggested a list of seven points or ingredients for painting; in this list were 'wit and play'. He says: 'In a way my paintings are very exact, but in that exactitude there is shimmer, a play in weighing the edges to introduce a less rigorous play element.' He considers that wit and play, together with hope, also on the list, make 'the tragic concept more endurable'.

In music, Rothko was always known to prefer Mozart to Beethoven, his reason being 'because of Mozart's wit and irony'. Comparing it to Beethoven, he said Beethoven's music was 'a farmyard wit'. He also considered irony was present in his work, giving this as another of his seven points. He explained this by saying irony allowed him to distance himself from his work and endow it with its own life, by giving it, therefore, its own independence. He expanded on the concept of irony in an interview with Peter Selz (b. 1919), the German art historian, in 1960, where he expressed the fact that as he had become older, Shakespeare had come to mean more to him. 'Shakespeare's tragic concept embodies for me the full range of life from which the artist draws all his tragic materials, including irony; irony becomes a weapon against fate.'

Clearwater considers that there are, in fact, many ironic elements in Rothko's work: 'The canvas is flat, yet spacious; the paint is thinly applied yet seems formidable; the physical size of the paintings is large, yet the experience is intimate; the pigment may be dark, but filled with light and although the image is static the tension pulls the forms asunder.' She goes on to say that this irony is based on the human condition. Rothko's works 'reveal the fallacy of our vision – the conflict between what is seen and what is felt.' Rothko's paintings, she considers, reveal to us these many contradictions, summing up by saying: 'The fallacy of our vision is our tragic flaw.'

The de Menils

Jermayne MacAgy (1914–64), for a time the wife of Douglas MacAgy (1913–73), the dynamic young director of the California School of Fine Arts, where Rothko had taught at the summer schools, moved to Houston as director of the Contemporary Arts Museum, and had organized a Rothko exhibition there in 1957. She had encouraged the Houston art collectors John (1904–73) and Dominique (1908–97) de Menil to engage with contemporary art works, in particular promoting Rothko. The de Menils had developed a

friendship with a Dominican priest, Father Marie-Alain Couturier, who had made it his mission to see religious art and architecture combined as they had been in the past. The way to do this, he considered, was to commission art from the greatest living artists, regardless of their private convictions, for use in radically designed new churches. Father Couturier had taken the de Menils on a tour of French churches in Vence, Assy, Audincourt and Ronchamp to promote the aesthetic and spiritual values of combining contemporary art and architecture.

The de Menils had been very impressed with the Seagram murals when they had paid an earlier visit to Rothko in 1960, and now felt that the tragic grandeur of Rothko's style would be ideal for a chapel they were having built at the University of St. Thomas, Houston. The chapel was originally conceived as a Catholic place of worship, although today it is used as an area for meditation and contemplation.

The Houston Chapel

The de Menils approached Rothko in 1964 with an invitation to create murals for the chapel, which he willingly accepted, seeing this as a fulfilment of a lifetime's ambition to create a monument in the great tradition of Western religious art. In the octagonal-shaped building, initially designed by Philip Johnson, Rothko planned to mount three triptychs and five single panels, using a dark palette of black, mulberry and plum. The triptychs had clear resonances with church altarpieces; indeed, Rothko said that he was inspired by the basilica of Santa Maria Assunta on the island of Torcello in the Venetian lagoon.

This twelfth-century church has a mosaic of the Madonna and Child in the apse over the main altar, which faces a huge depiction of the Last Judgment above the entrance on the facing wall at the other end of the church. The octagonal plan of the new chapel, suggestive of early Christian baptisteries, encloses the viewer in the centre of an almost circular space, equidistant from the walls on which the panels hang; natural light enters through a central skylight, partially filtered by a canopy.

Rothko had considerable control over the architecture of the chapel, which led to Philip Johnson leaving the project and being replaced by Howard Barnstone (1923–87) and Eugene Aubry. For Rothko, the octagonal plan was a way of creating a new viewing space, where the viewer is fully surrounded by equidistant works. No other works except those of the same series can impinge on the viewer's sightline.

The Chapel Murals

Rothko, aided by assistants, was to work for three years on the panels, which resulted in physical and psychological strain. He set up a full-sized model of part of the chapel in his studio so he could examine the interaction between the paintings and the chapel structure as he worked, using a parachute to replicate the lighting effects. Unsatisfied with some of the panels, he would destroy them and start again, painting, repainting and reflecting. Eventually, he was to deliver three triptychs and nine panels, from which he chose five for the chapel (*see* fig. 1, page 4); the other four are now in the Menil Collection in Houston.

Rothko's experiments with space, colour, perspective and illusion are highly complex, but have been studied in depth by Sheldon Nodelman in his book *The Rothko Chapel Paintings: Origin, Structure, Meaning* (1997). On entry to the chapel, the murals appear totally dark and monochrome as they stand out against the light chapel walls. The panel on the south entrance wall and the east-wall and west-wall triptychs have a single dark, hard-edged rectangle surrounded by another colour. The black central rectangle is so large that it seems to dominate the whole canvas, but the south-wall panel is edged with a dark red area and the west-wall triptych with a dark mulberry colour. The longer the viewer observes them, the more the slight contrasts and differences in colour become visible. The apse triptych and the remaining panels are single-form and totally monochrome, the pigment being stained into the canvas, which causes the tones to modulate against the background of the white wall, thus creating a subtle atmospheric effect. Clearwater suggests this may have been inspired by the light flickering on the mosaics in the Santa Maria Assunta basilica.

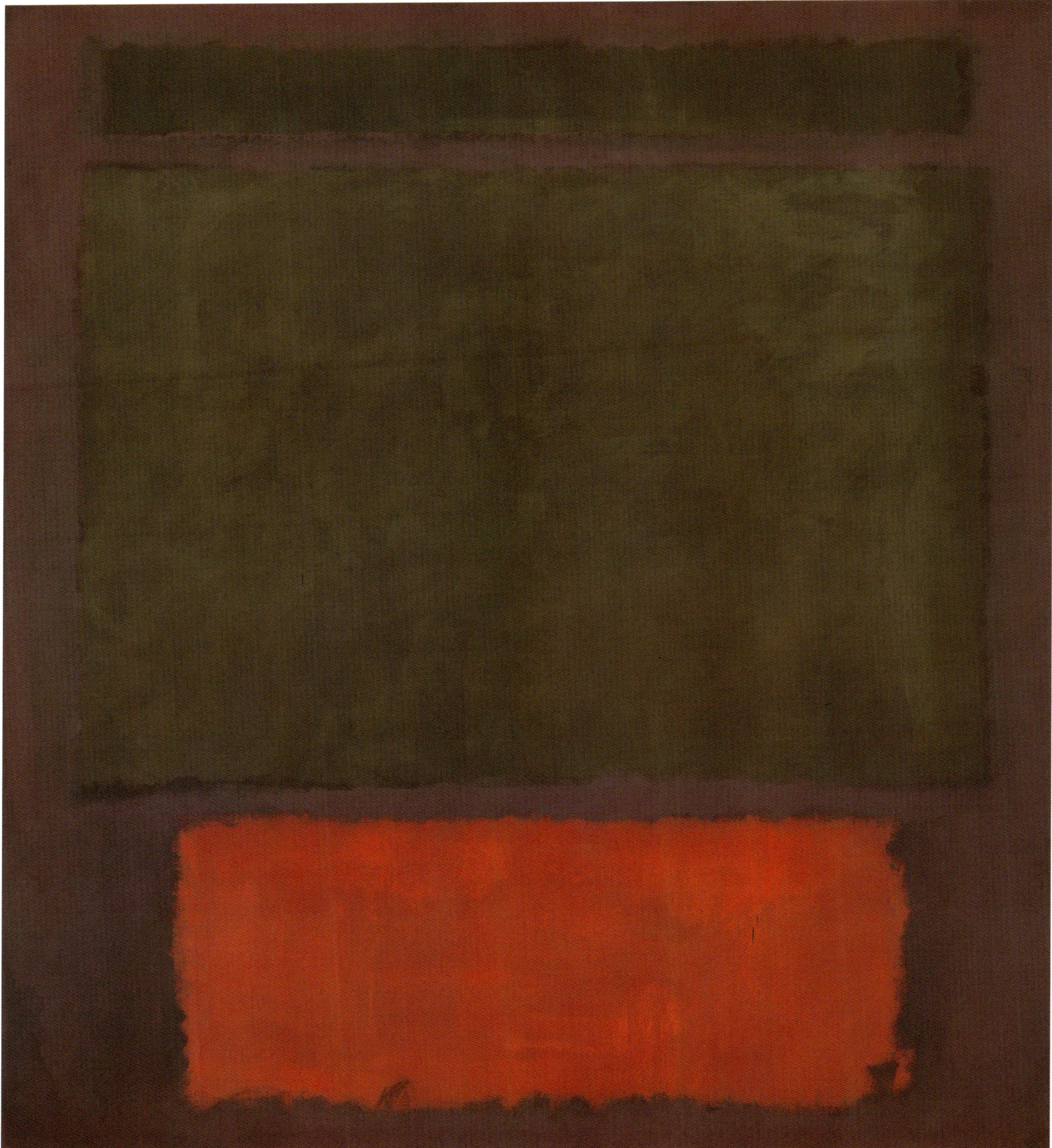

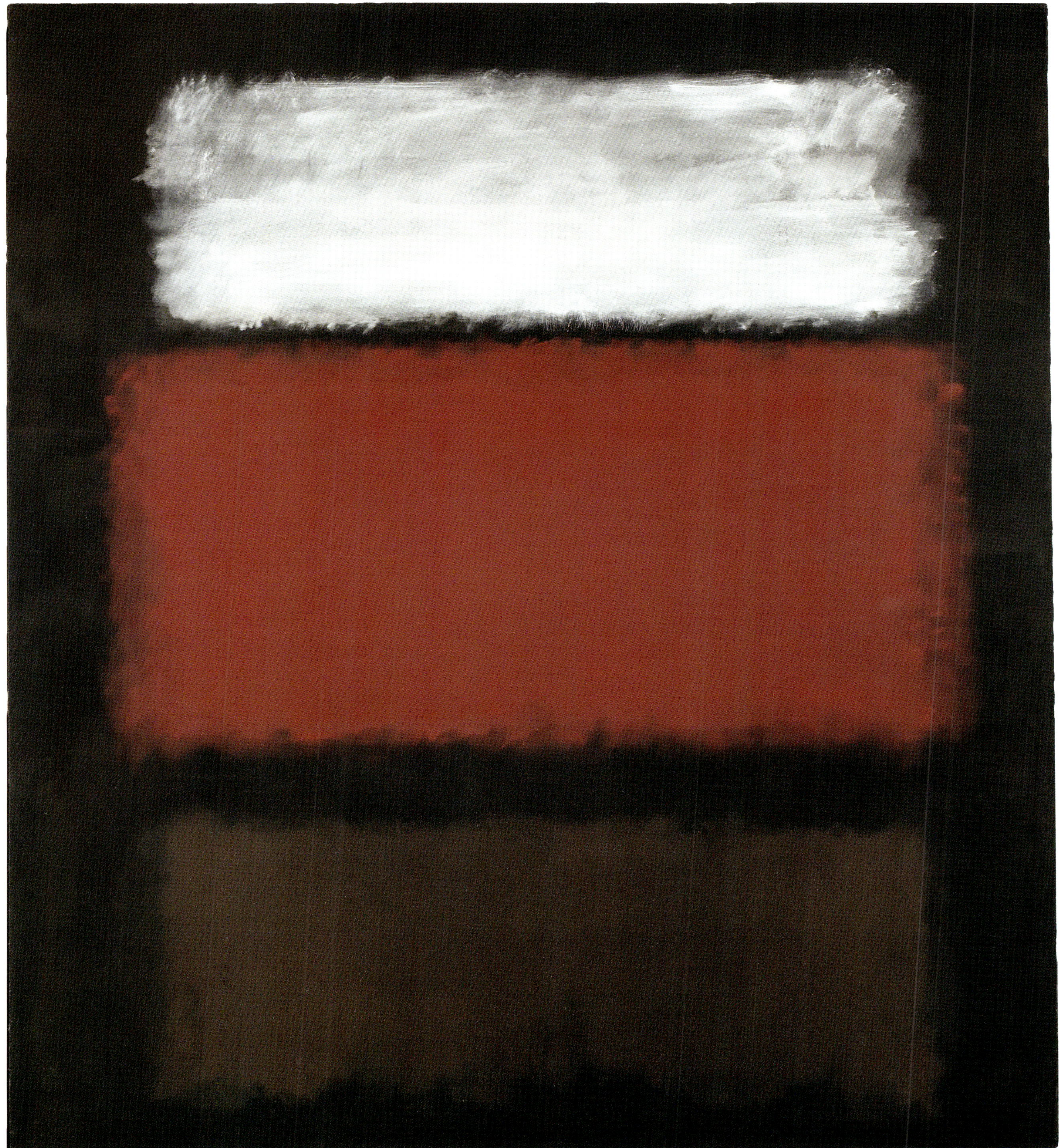

Wraparound Vision

It is not possible to view one painting alone, as another one will always be in the viewer's peripheral vision, creating what Nodelman calls a 'wraparound' effect; the cohesion of the panels as a group is, therefore, not disturbed in any way. He also considers that the deep doorway entrance passages add to the overall effect by creating shadow and depth. Because the viewer is forced to confront the paintings as a group, Nodelman considers that 'the viewer's experience is one of a continually unfolding event', which he explains as follows: as the viewers scan the room, they experience a pulsating effect, which is caused by the variations of the proportions in the central black rectangles that make the dark area look as if it is either expanding or shrinking. Within the classic paintings, Rothko is interested in how the forms grow and vibrate within the canvas. In the Houston chapel works he is experimenting with how his paintings react with each other.

Nodelman also suggests that Rothko is experimenting with spatial effects in the chapel, using a complex system based on perspective. As the actual dimensions of the chapel appear to be affected by the space that each painting creates, the viewer experiences a changing relationship to the space and to the paintings: now close, now distant. This is similar to the effects in the classic paintings, where you will get different readings depending on whether you focus on the central colour area or the surrounding band of colour.

Paint Effects

Rothko used different types of paint for the chapel murals to create effects, using a matt finish for the red and mulberry coloured borders, which makes the dark rectangle recede, while the glossy finish of the black rectangle reflects light so it seems closer to the viewer. As Nodelman points out, this is a contradiction of the standard rules of perspective, which state that dark colours recede. This creates a strange state of ambiguity and an unsettling, even menacing, effect.

Linking it again with possible inspiration from the Torcello Basilica, Clearwater suggests that the west-wall triptych could recall the gaping mouth of hell n the Last Judgment scenes, as the large dark rectangles surrounded by red create a feeling of the depth of the abyss. She suggests that the monochrome paintings without borders give the appearance of expanding outwards and into an infinite realm beyond

In this project, Rothko has been able to control the whole environment to develop his theories about space, form and colour. He was very appreciative to the de Menils for giving him this opportunity, recognizing that it had taxed him up to and beyond what he thought he was capable of. Writing to them on New Year's Day 1966, he states: **'The magnitude, on every level of experience and meaning of the task in which you have involved me, exceeds all of my preconceptions. And it is teaching me to extend myself beyond what I thought was possible for me. For this I thank you.'**

Rothko did not live to see the chapel finished and his paintings installed, but in her inaugural address, Dominque de Menil said: 'We are cluttered with images and only abstract art can bring us to the threshold of the divine ... Rothko was prophetic in leaving us a nocturnal environment. Night is peaceful. Night is pregnant with life.'

Rothko the Man

Rothko appears to have been a person, like most people, with many sides, but with a propensity to swing between being jovial and pleasant and being restless and troubled. He worked for over 20 years at the Brooklyn Jewish Center teaching art to children, and was by all accounts good at the job and well liked.

In a self-portrait of 1936, when he was still an unknown 33-year-old artist, yet known by his friends to be a convivial and open person, his face is expressionless, his eyes are hidden behind dark sunglasses, his body appears stiff and rigid, hands clutched together,

almost as if he is a stranger to himself. The colours in this work, mainly glowing copper and deep brown, have been compared to those of Rembrandt, who created many self-portraits through his life, which give us insight into his character and soul as he grew older.

With Rothko, the expressionless self-portrayal keeps us out, locks us away from him; the contrast between the warm colours and the rigid torso perhaps convey the inner emotional depths that he tries to keep in control. He had many friends, including the poet Stanley Kunitz (1905–2006) who gave us a portrait in words, which reflects some of Rothko's many sides: 'His nearsighted eyes behind the thick glasses are liquid with patriarchal affection and solicitude. His mouth is sensuous, quick to tremble with feeling. "Tovarich," he cries with a huge embrace that locks me in, snug against his baronial frame; safe from everything fretful, anxious, invidious; blessed at least for a moment in the religion of friendship ... Once I told him that he was the last rabbi of Western Art. And that made him smile, which was a relief, since one could never be quite certain when his face would darken.'

Inner Conflict

Rothko was embroiled in conflict most of his life, many times of his own choosing. Perhaps deciding to become an artist was partly a reaction against the family expectations and the society that had expected him to do well in a lucrative profession, but which, particularly through his time at Yale, had at the same time made him feel excluded.

The challenge to society that the life of an artist provided appealed to this side of him, and his participation with his fellow artists in confrontation with the established art world of the time allowed him to assert himself and put forward his ideas with authority, in a way casting himself, perhaps ironically, as the misunderstood hero. However, on the inside, it may have been that this conflict between the artist and society was painful and full of contradictions. The artist's life is full of insecurity and anxiety; he is misunderstood. But on the other hand, this gives him the freedom to explore and innovate – in Rothko's case, to search for the ideal expression of the way to the transcendent experience.

It seems that he spoke little even to his friends about his work, according to Dore Ashton (b. 1928), a close friend, and he preferred to discuss 'life's big issues' and the 'meaning of life'. Perhaps he took after his father, who was the dreamer and the philosophizer rather than the businessman, looking for ways to change the world and make it a better place. This idealism was tempered by lack of concern in other areas. He took little interest it seems about what he ate, was a heavy smoker and, in common with a number of his artist friends, was a heavy drinker. His focus on his 'inner vision', whether he was working in his studio, listening for hours to his beloved music or in discussion with his friends, excluded interest in many of the usual daily occupations of life.

Because of his idealism, he was open to failures and disappointments, and his hopes for the art world to bring about the social change he believed in were consistently punctured by the reality of the business world of art; his aspirations were unattainable and he knew that. This unbridgeable divide between aspiration and reality, and the confrontation between the quest for the ultimate spiritual renewal and the impossibility of ever achieving it, generated an inner conflict all of its own.

Problems of Success

For people like Rothko, whose identity has been forged in taking a contrary stance towards society's values, success can possibly be regarded almost as failure. Although Rothko may seem the heroic figure, standing up for the eternal values of human life and being, there still existed the desire to be recognized, to have success, to have ideas embraced and accepted. For the artist, this means your works reaching a wider audience, having them exhibited, people liking them enough and wanting them enough to buy them.

The paradox is that you then become a part of the system that you have been opposing; you benefit from it financially, you perhaps even gain entry to the 'hall of fame' and become something of a celebrity, all things which Rothko and many of his fellow artists struggled with, even despised and which give rise to new inner conflicts. In his Pratt Institute lecture, Rothko spoke on how he turned

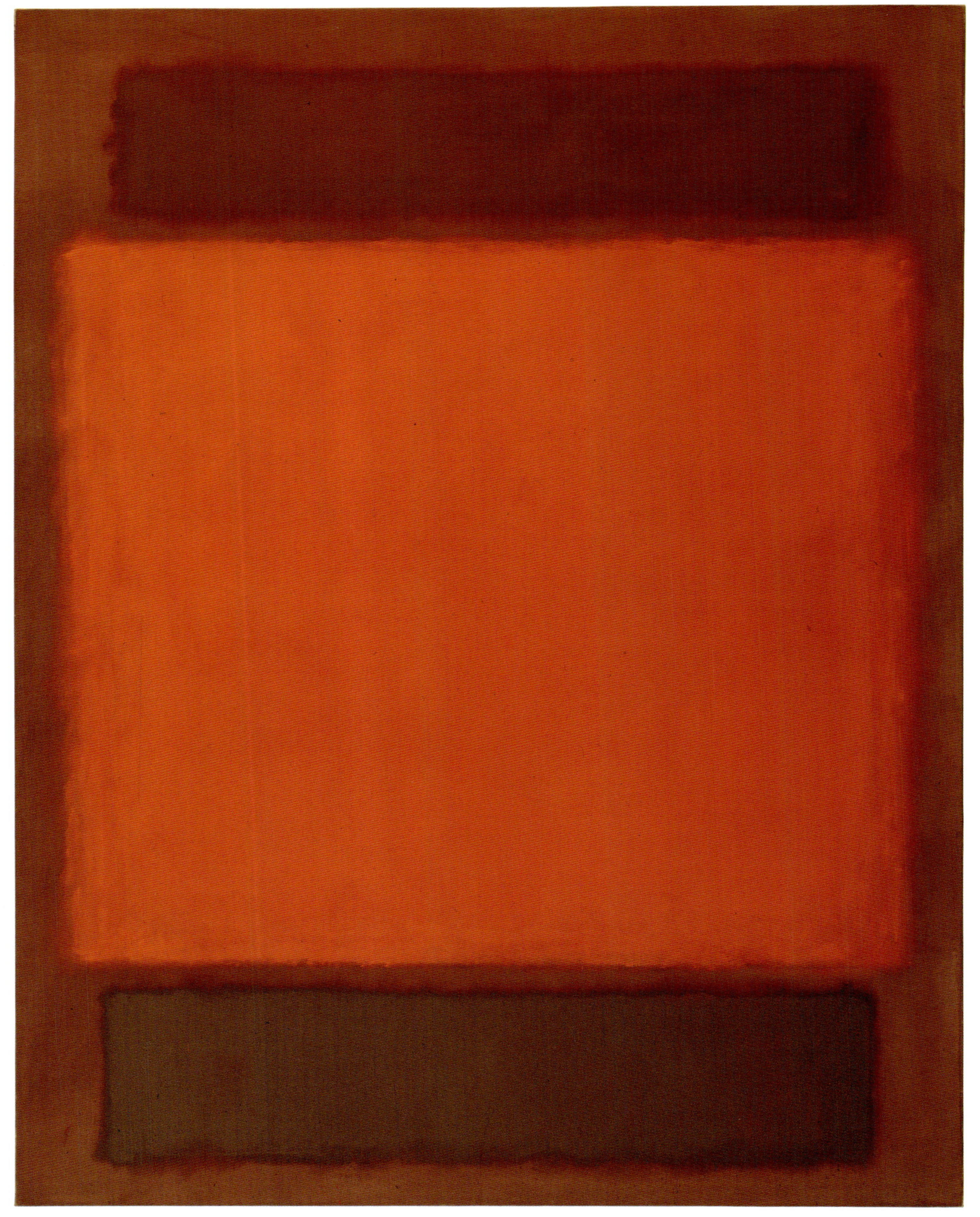

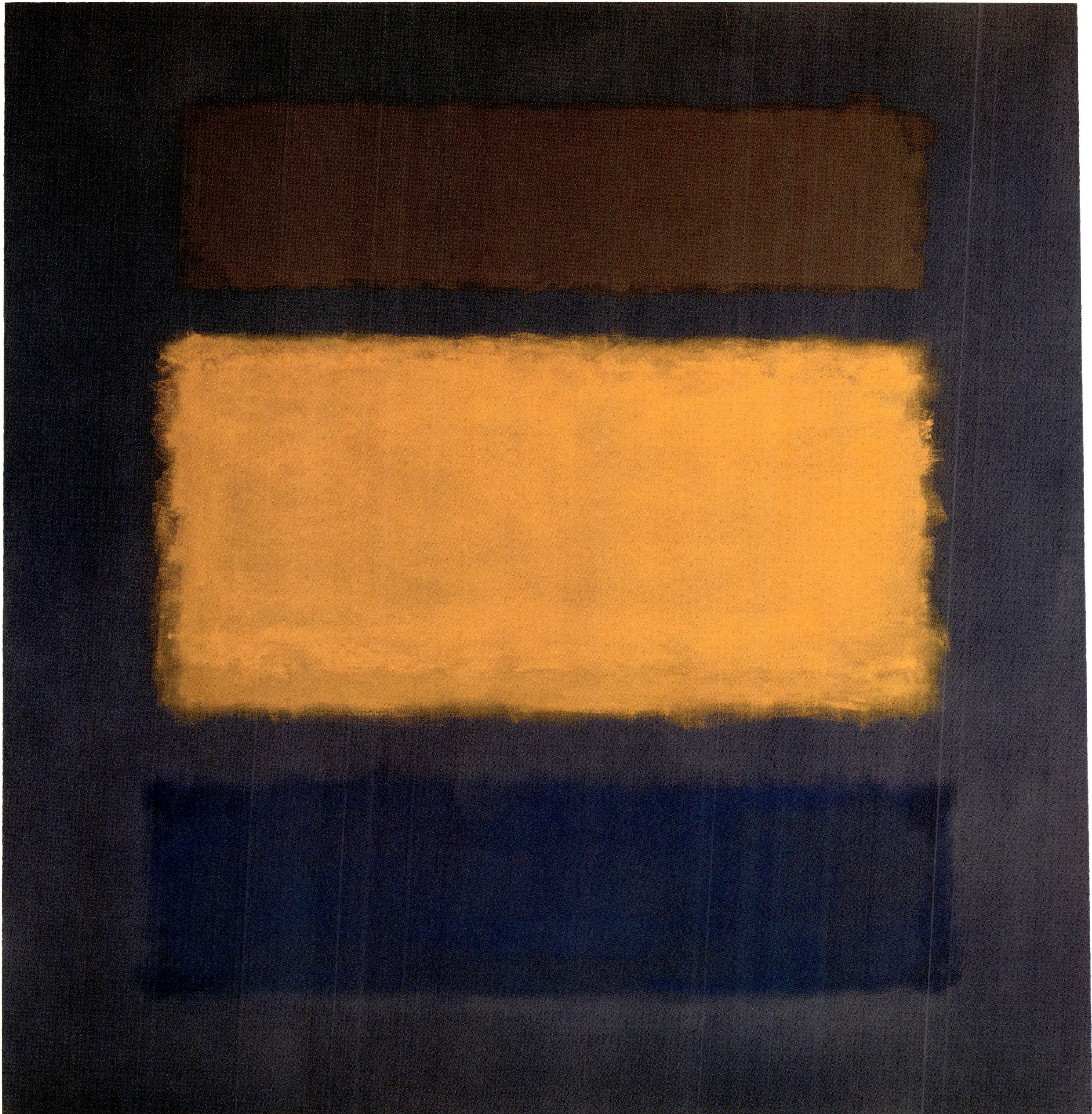

his philosophic thoughts into form in his paintings: 'There must be a clear preoccupation with death – intimations of mortality. Tragic art, romantic art, etc. deals with the knowledge of death.' That a number of the New York school artists were struggling with recognition and success was becoming evident, with early deaths, problems with alcohol, relationship breakdowns. The art that could move you into the transcendent could also ease the pain of that conflict; that plus alcohol and medication.

Personal Issues

Rothko began to experience health problems, and in 1968 had an aneurysm of the aorta, the result of high blood pressure. After a stay in hospital, he recovered, but the doctors insisted he needed to eat a more balanced diet, reduce his alcohol intake and stop smoking, but after a lifetime of habit, he was unable to put these things into practice.

Although his union with Mel had been blessed by the arrival of a son, Christopher, in August 1963, the marriage had been under strain for some time, and pressures came to a head with Rothko moving out to live in his studio at the beginning of 1969. His increasing wealth meant little to him as he was used to living a simple economical lifestyle, another habit that he could not and probably did not want to change. Having money, it seems, was actually a worry to him. It depressed him, and the pressure of what to do with it hung heavy on him. He was becoming more anxious and at times confused, was drinking heavily, smoking and on heavy medication. All through this time, however, he was continuing to work and receive visitors to his studio, who were selected by him as patrons he liked.

Academic Recognition and Departure

In 1969, Rothko was awarded an honorary doctorate from Yale, accompanied by the comments: '... you have made an enduring place for yourself in the art of this century ... your paintings are marked by a simplicity of form and a magnificence of colour. In them you have attained a visual and a spiritual grandeur whose foundation is the tragic vein in all human existence.'

In his acceptance letter, Rothko gives some insight into his thoughts at this time, writing: 'When I was a younger man, art was a lonely thing: no galleries, no collectors, no critics, no money. Yet it was a golden time, for then we had nothing to lose and a vision to gain. Today it is not quite the same. It is a time of verbiage, activity and consumption. Which condition is better for the world at large I will not venture to discuss.' Just 13 months after leaving Mel and moving into his studio, Rothko, now 66 years old, was found dead in his studio by one of his assistants, Oliver Steindecker, when he arrived for work at nine o'clock on the morning of 25 February 1970. There was a razor blade beside the body and the autopsy concluded that Rothko had died of deep incisions and also acute poisoning from anti-depressants. Stanley Kunitz gave the eulogy at the funeral, saying: 'Mark's transcendental quality, his effect of a pulsing spiritual life, of an imminent epiphany, was a secret he did not share with others, and maybe only partly understood himself ... So much of Rothko remains – in a multiplicity of glowing presences, in a glory of transformations. Not all the world's corruption washes high colour away.'

Later Works

That towards the end of his life, Rothko had been working on canvases that were predominantly black and grey confirmed in people's minds that he was becoming increasingly depressed, eventually succumbing to suicide. What they often do not realize was that Rothko was also at the time working on a totally different project. After his aneurysm, his doctors had forbidden him from working on large canvases more than 40 inches high; after three months recuperating, he went on to create over 100 works on paper. Many of these works are only 24 x 18 inches and constitute some of the smallest abstract works Rothko produced.

This prescription by his doctors had led him to begin this new project using fast-drying acrylic paint on paper, on which at times he used gentle tones of pale blue, mauve and yellow, while at other times using brilliant yellow and vibrant orange slashes to create works which dazzle with light. Unlike the large canvases, where Rothko would use layers of thin paint on top of each other, these small works on paper usually have a single colour painted on top of stained paper. Ever probing the use of new techniques, Rothko

also used ink, which lights up the paper's field, so that the works do not have the flicker of the classic paintings but generate more of a glow. Some of the works do use a richer, darker palette such as velvety black and bottle green on a blue background.

Further Experimentation

In the summer of 1968, Rothko used a colour palette of brown and grey acrylic paint on paper, dividing the sheet into two horizontal areas, with the bottom half in various tones of grey. He also used masking tape which, when it was removed, left a white border around the edges, which gives more of a static effect than of movement. Clearwater explains that if the viewer focuses on the top half of the paper, the dark is predominant. If one focuses on the bottom half, then light appears to expand towards the viewer. The viewer's eye is also drawn to the intersection of the two areas of colour, where a kind of horizon is created, so 'the viewer imaginatively travels into infinity'. As the works have a crisp white edge, when displayed against a white wall, the paintings seem to open up to the space beyond, creating something of the effect of a window.

When, after a time, Rothko moved back to work on canvas, he experimented by attempting to transfer the effects of the works on paper on to the canvas, in particular when working on his black and grey canvases. Because of the fact that on white paper, the brown and grey works seemed to glow, in his black and grey canvases he painted on a white surface in order to harness a similar glow effect. Throughout this time, Rothko was also continuing to develop his ideas on space and perception and is considered a pioneer in the perceptual work that has interested artists from the 1960s onwards.

Works on Paper

It was not just during this period of ill health that Rothko turned to working on paper. In fact throughout his career he created many works on paper that are of a high standard, but which for the most part are hidden in store rooms and archives and rarely see the light of day. The majority of these paintings on paper are not preparatory works for other paintings, but intrinsic works of art in their own right.

In the mid 1920s and early 1930s, when he was working on his canvases of urban life, interiors and the human figure, he did few works on paper, but those he did do are watercolours of landscapes, beach scenes, rural views and works in tempera. Such works formed part of his first one-man exhibition in Portland in 1933 and were well received, the reviewer particularly referring to the rich and velvety quality of the temperas. In the 1930s, he did many quickly executed pencil and ink drawings in sketchbooks as he was out and about in the city of New York, sketching the subway, city buildings, and New Yorkers going about their everyday affairs. Some of these he developed later into paintings in tempera on paper, many of which exude mystery and gloom, with people crammed into spaces too small for them in gloomy surroundings. His use of watercolour for landscapes and rural scenes is altogether more delicate and lighter in atmosphere, possibly due partly to the inherent properties of watercolour, which favour a gentle approach.

More Works on Paper

By the mid 1940s, when Rothko was heavily involved in his surrealist-inspired mythological phase, he painted over 200 works on paper, a veritable outpouring of inspiration and effort. The surrealist watercolours exhibit a freedom that probably stemmed from the method of automatic drawing favoured by the surrealists to unlock the unconscious mind.

Experimenting with technique and medium, as always Rothko developed a watercolour style unique to him. He would apply watercolour, gouache and tempera and while they were still wet would draw on them with black ink. Sometimes the black ink would bleed into the surrounding colour, creating something of a black burst. Sometimes he dabbed watercolour on to the surface, at other times he added charcoal to his paint. To finish, he would scrape, gouge and scratch the paint surface to expose areas of the paper beneath.

In 1946, he was given an exhibition of his watercolours at the Mortimer Brandt Gallery in New York. A reviewer commented on the 'byplay of greys and whites and a piercing red accent' in *Omen*. Another commentator said that the watercolours 'recount and

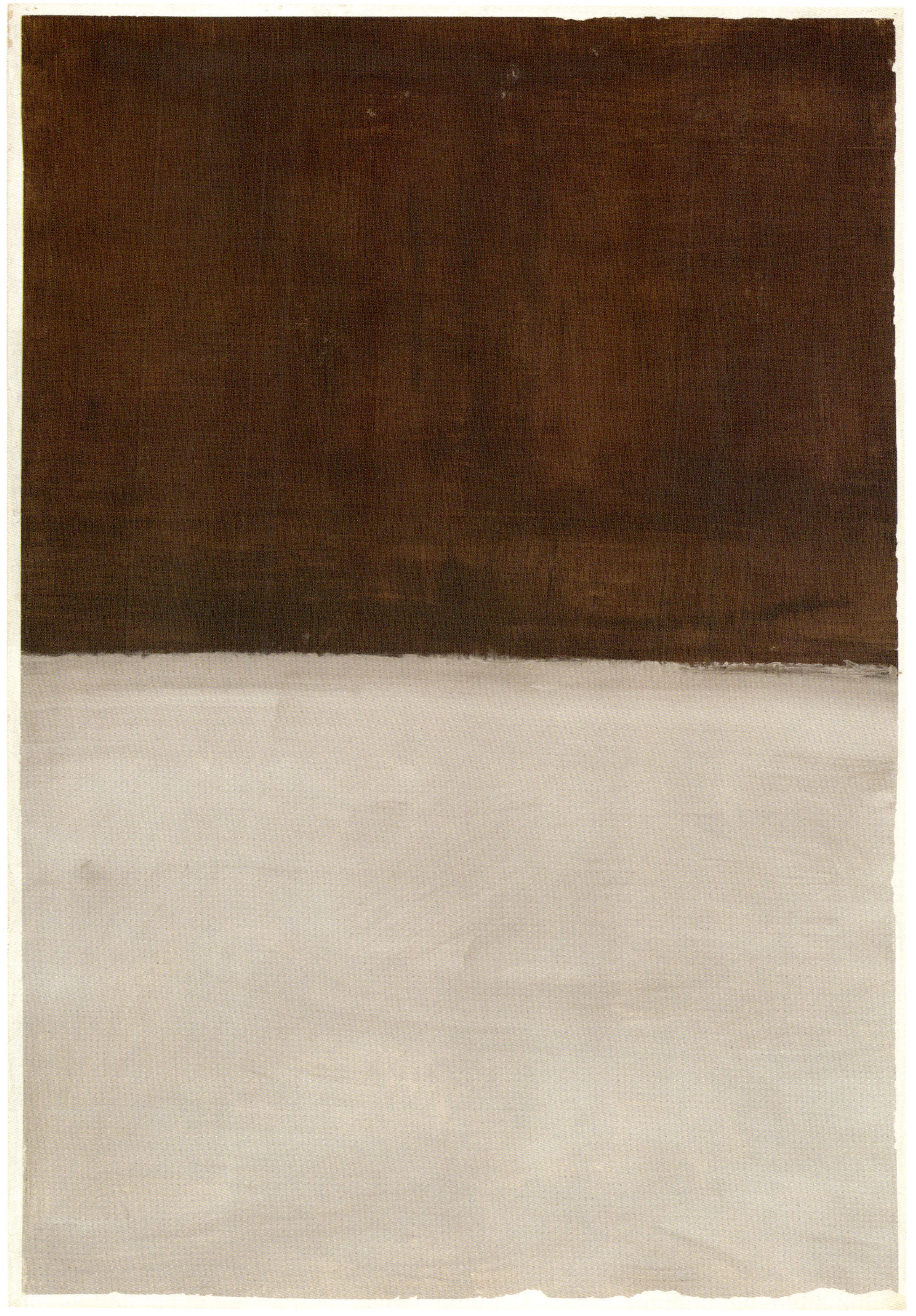

evoke Rothko's lyrical, mythical and metamorphical themes.' One of the works, the mysterious and unsettling *Vessels of Magic* (1946) was bought by the Brooklyn Museum.

These works embrace the same theme as his works on canvas, reaching out to the viewer with the aim of touching the emotions and moving to the economy of the abstract as time progressed. In a number of works, the aquatic theme of amoeba-like forms prevails, indicating a preoccupation with exploring the elemental life force underlying the core of human existence. The mystery of these life forms is created in the delicate brush strokes of watercolour, coupled with the black lines of gestural ink.

Rothko turned again to working on paper in 1959 while involved with his work on the massive murals for the Seagram Building; possibly a smaller sense of scale helped him to refocus and review. He created a series of 17 works on paper, all the same size, 38 inches x 25 inches, using tempera. These works are sombre in tone and dark in colour, reflective and intense, intimate and contemplative, making a personal, more immediate connection with the viewer, with their manageable scale and immediate impact.

Legacy

Rothko's early classic paintings, for which he is most famous, have created a wonderful body of works, which glow with glorious colours and emanate an inner light. Widely accessible to the art connoisseur and the novice alike, they tap into the emotional flow of human existence and possess the ability to move the viewer to a place of reflection where the broader issues of life can be contemplated. They are uplifting and affirming, sweeping viewers into the painting through the powerful use of colour, taking them to a place where they can rest and reflect.

This dynamic and powerful use of colour in abstract works, without any reference to objects or figures, creates a freedom for the viewer to wander at will within the immersive experience. This original approach liberates viewers for a time from an increasingly materialistic and commercially driven society, providing a route to another place where, without any suggested points of reference, they are free to reflect on what is relevant to them.

Rothko's experiments with a darker palette in his later works and his series of murals provide a challenge for the viewer to go deeper, to ponder and contemplate profound issues, to move further into the reflective experience. His amazingly varied body of works on paper reveal even more of his creative efforts to explore the use of shape and colour to draw the viewer into another world and to create that relationship between painting and viewer, in order to facilitate a two-way channel of communication.

His techniques of working using thin layers of colour on top of each other to endow his canvases with an inner glow, his experiments to suggest at times almost uncanny effects of movement between pools of colour and shapes, his exploration of space and rhythm to imitate sensations of pulsation, all bare witness to his creative methods. The body of writings which he has left, and the material gleaned from interviews and conversations, reflect his views on the history of art and the artist's approach, communicating his philosophies of art and demonstrating his incisive mind and powerful, penetrating intellect. His originality of thought and expression make it certain that he will remain celebrated as one of the most innovative and important artists of the twentieth century.

list of works

'CR No.' refers to the catalogue number of the art work as featured in David Anfam's *The Works on Canvas: A Catalogue Raisonné* (Yale University Press, 1998). Titles in round parantheses are those used during Rothko's lifetime but which may not be his own; those in square brackets are purely descriptive; and those in braces ('{...}') are posthumous.

Fig. 1 (page 4, CR Nos. 782–804), **The Rothko Chapel: Interior view of Northwest, North and Northeast Walls**, 1965, oil on canvas, The Rothko Chapel, Houston, Texas

Fig. 2 (page 10, CR No. 6), *Untitled [Still Life with Pitcher]*, *c.* 1926, oil on canvas board, 40.3 x 30.2 cm (15⅞ x 11⅞ in), National Gallery of Art, Washington, D.C.

Fig. 3 (page 11), *Brighton Beach* (recto), *c.* mid 1930s, watercolour, gouache and graphite on paper, 30.4 x 40.3 cm (12 x 15⅗ in), Private Collection

Fig. 4 (page 14 CR No. 47), *Bathers* [or] *Beach Scene*, 1933/34, oil on black canvas, 40.3 x 50.5 cm (15⅞ x 19⅞ in), National Gallery of Art, Washington, D.C.

Fig. 5 (page 15, CR No. 96), *Street Scene*, 1936/37, oil on canvas, 91.5 x 55.8 cm (36 x 22 in), National Gallery of Art, Washington, D.C.

Fig. 6 (page 18, CR No. 135), *Entrance to Subway*, 1938, oil on canvas, 86.4 x 117.5 cm (34 x 46¼ in), Collection of Kate Rothko Prizel

Fig. 7 (page 19, CR No. 179), *Oedipus*, 1940, oil on linen, 91.4 x 61 cm (36 x 24 in), Collection of Christopher Rothko

Fig. 8 (page 22, CR No. 178), *Antigone*, 1940, oil and charcoal on canvas, 86.4 x 116.2 cm (34 x 45¾ in), National Gallery of Art, Washington, D.C.

Fig. 9 (page 23, CR No. 192), *Untitled*, 1941/42, oil on canvas, 91 x 60.6 cm (35⅘ x 23⅞ in), National Gallery of Art, Washington, D.C.

Fig. 10 (page 26, CR No. 206), *The Omen of the Eagle*, 1942, oil and graphite on canvas, 65.4 x 45.1 cm (25¾ x 17¾ in), National Gallery of Art, Washington, D.C.

Fig. 11 (page 27, CR No. 214), *The Syrian Bull*, 1943, oil and pencil on pre-primed canvas, 100.2 x 70.2 cm (39⅖ x 27⅔ in), Allen Memorial Art Museum, Oberlin College, Ohio

Fig. 12 (page 32, CR No. 231), *Birth of Cephalopods*, 1944, oil and charcoal on canvas, 100.3 x 135.9 cm (39½ x 53½ in), National Gallery of Art, Washington, D.C.

Fig. 13 (page 33, CR No. 248), *Slow Swirl at the Edge of the Sea*, 1944, oil on canvas, 191.4 x 215.2 cm (75⅓ x 84¾ in), Museum of Modern Art, New York

Fig. 14 (page 36, CR No. 239), *Hierarchical Birds*, 1944, oil and charcoal on canvas, 100.7 x 80.5 cm (39⅝ x 31⅔ in), National Gallery of Art, Washington, D.C.

Fig. 15 (page 37, CR No. 246), *Vibrations of Aurora*, 1944, oil and chalk on canvas, 69.2 x 99.1 cm (27¼ x 39 in), National Gallery of Art, Washington, D.C.

Fig. 16 (page 40), *Untitled*, 1944–45, watercolour, tempera, graphite and ink on paper, 53.3 x 66.8 cm (21 x 26¼ in), National Gallery of Art, Washington, D.C.

Fig. 17 (page 41), *Untitled*, 1944–45, graphite, brush and black ink and gouache on paper, 66 x 50.8 cm (26 x 20 in), Private Collection

Fig. 18 (page 44, CR No. 278), *Sacrificial Moment*, 1945, oil on canvas, 98 x 70.5 cm (38½ x 27¾ in), National Gallery of Art, Washington, D.C.

Fig. 19 (page 45, CR No. 261), *Phalanx of the Mind*, 1945, oil on canvas, 137.9 x 90.8 cm (54¼ x 27¾ in), National Gallery of Art, Washington, D.C.

Fig. 20 (page 48, CR No. 314), *Untitled*, 1946, oil on canvas, 99.9 x 69 cm (39⅓ x 27½ in), National Gallery of Art, Washington, D.C.

Fig. 21 (page 49, CR No. 319), *No. 18*, 1946, oil on canvas, 155 x 109.8 cm (61 x 43¼ in), National Gallery of Art, Washington, D.C.

Fig. 22 (page 52, CR No. 332), *No. 3*, 1947, oil on canvas, 100.8 x 138.1 cm (39⅔ x 54⅜ in), National Gallery of Art, Washington, D.C.

Fig. 23 (page 53, CR No. 366), *No. 9*, 1947, oil on canvas, 45.1 x 37.5 cm (17¾ x 14¾ in), Private Collection

Fig. 24 (page 56, CR No. 352), *Untitled*, 1947, oil on canvas, 96.2 x 116.4 cm (37⅞ x 45⅕ in), National Gallery of Art, Washington, D.C.

Fig. 25 (page 57, CR No. 336), *No. 26*, 1947, oil on canvas, 99.7 x 137.5 cm (39¼ x 54 in), Dallas Museum of Art, Texas

Fig. 26 (page 60, CR No. 365), *Untitled*, 1947, oil on canvas, 100 x 69.2 cm (39⅜ x 27¼ in), National Gallery of Art, Washington, D.C.

Fig. 27 (page 61, CR No. 359), *Untitled*, 1947, oil on canvas, 96.2 x 53 cm (37⅞ x 20⅞ in), National Gallery of Art, Washington, D.C.

Fig. 28 (page 64, CR No. 382), *Untitled*, 1948, oil on canvas, 126.4 x 111.8 cm (49¾ x 44 in), National Gallery of Art, Washington, D.C.

Fig. 29 (page 65, CR No. 380), *Untitled {Multiform}*, 1948, oil on canvas, 155 x 118.7 cm (61 x 46¾ in), National Gallery of Australia, Canberra

Fig. 30 (page 68, CR No. 389), *Untitled*, 1948, oil on canvas, 108.3 x 111.4 cm (42⅝ x 43⅝ in), National Gallery of Art, Washington, D.C.

Fig. 31 (page 69, CR No. 394), *No. 9 {Multiform/Untitled}*, 1948, oil and mixed media on canvas, 134.7 x 118.4 cm (53 x 46⅝ in), National Gallery of Art, Washington, D.C.

Fig. 32 (page 72, CR No. 415), *No. 8 {Multiform}*, 1949, oil and mixed media on canvas, 228.3 x 167.3 cm (89⅞ x 65⅞ in), National Gallery of Art, Washington, D.C.

Fig. 33 (page 73, CR No. 418), *No. 10 {Multiform}*, 1949, oil on canvas, 141 x 81.4 cm (55½ x 32 in), National Gallery of Art, Washington, D.C.

Fig. 34 (page 76), *Untitled*, 1949, watercolour on paper, 102.1 x 66.2 cm (40 x 26 in), National Gallery of Art, Washington, D.C.

Fig. 35 (page 77, CR No. 401), *Untitled*, 1949, oil on canvas, 131.8 x 74 cm (51⅞ x 29⅓ in), National Gallery of Art, Washington, D.C.

Fig. 36 (page 82, also page 1, CR No. 406), *No. 22/No. 16*, 1949, oil on canvas, 170.9 x 136.9 cm (67¼ x 53⅘ in), Private Collection

Fig. 37 (page 83, CR No. 414), *No. 7/No. 11*, 1949, oil on canvas, 173 x 111 cm (68⅛ x 43¾ in), National Gallery of Art, Washington, D.C.

Fig. 38 (page 86, CR No. 433), *Untitled*, 1949, oil and mixed media on canvas, 228.9 x 112 cm (90⅛ x 44⅛ in), National Gallery of Art, Washington, D.C.

Fig. 39 (page 87, CR No. 425), *Untitled*, 1949, oil on canvas, 206.7 x 168.6 cm (81⅜ x 66⅜ in), National Gallery of Art, Washington, D.C.

Fig. 40 (page 90 & front cover, CR No. 423), *Untitled*, 1949, oil on canvas, 52.4 x 95.3 cm (20⅝ x 37½ in), Collection of Christopher Rothko

further reading

Anfam, David, *Abstract Expressionism*, Thames and Hudson, 1990

Baal-Teshuva, Jacob, *Rothko: Pictures as Drama*, Taschen, 2003

Breslin, James, *Mark Rothko: A Biography*, University of Chicago Press, 1993

Clearwater, Bonnie, *The Rothko Book*, Tate Publishing, 2006

Cohen-Solal, Annie, *Mark Rothko: Toward the Light in the Chapel*, Yale University Press, 2015

Collins, Bradford, R., *Mark Rothko: The Decisive Decade 1940–1950*, Skira Rizzoli Publications, Inc., 2012

Golding, John, *Paths to the Absolute*, Thames and Hudson, 2000

Greenberg, Clement, 'American-Type Painting', *Partisan Review*, no. 22, Spring 1955

Hughes, Robert, *The Shock of the New*, Thames and Hudson, 1980 and 1991

Kuh, Katharine, 'Mark Rothko', *Art Institute of Chicago Quarterly*, vol. 48, no. 4, 15 November, 1954

Messer, Thomas, M., 'Preface', in Diane Waldman, *Mark Rothko*, Thames and Hudson, 1978, reprinted 1986

Nodelman, Sheldon, *The Rothko Chapel Paintings: Origin, Structure, Meaning*, Houston and Austin, 1997

Rosenblum, Robert, *Modern Painting and the Northern Romantic Tradition: Friedrich to Rothko*, 1975, reprinted Thames and Hudson, 1994

Rothko, Christopher, *Mark Rothko: From the Inside Out*, Yale University Press, 2015

Rothko, Mark, *The Artist's Reality*, Yale University Press, 2004

Waldman, Diane, *Mark Rothko*, Thames and Hudson, 1978, reprinted 1986

acknowledgments

Susan Grange (author) is a writer, musician and art historian with a wide range of interests. She holds an MA in Art History and is the author of *L.S. Lowry: Masterpieces of Art*, *Rembrandt van Rijn: Masterpieces of Art* and *Giovanni Bellini: Music, Art and Venice*. She teaches privately and in secondary education and has taught in higher education. She has also reviewed exhibitions and art books for the art journal *Cassone*.

Sincere thanks to Henry Mandell for his help in creating this book; and to all those who supplied images.

Picture Credits

Images courtesy of: **akg-images**/Andrea Jemolo: 153. **Bridgeman Images:** Private Collection / Photo © Christie's Images: 1 & 82, 41, 110, 115, 119, 137, 152, 173; Private Collection: 11; Allen Memorial Art Museum, Oberlin College, Ohio, USA / Gift of Annalee (Mrs. Barnett) Newman / in honor of Ellen Johnson: 27; Private Collection: 53, 103, 107, 140, 156; Dallas Museum of Art, Texas, USA / Gift of the Mark Rothko Foundation: 57, 102; National Gallery of Australia, Canberra / Purchased 1981: 65; Private Collection / Photo © Boltin Picture Library: 99; The Phillips Collection, Washington, D.C., USA / Acquired 1957: 111; Los Angeles County Museum of Art, CA, USA / De Agostini Picture Library: 118; Private Collection / Mayor Gallery, London: 123; Fogg Art Museum, Harvard Art Museums, USA / Gift of Ruth and Frank Stanton: 136; National Gallery of Australia, Canberra / Purchased 1978: 145; Private Collection / James Goodman Gallery, New York, USA: 157; Art Gallery of Ontario, Toronto, Canada / Gift from the Women's Committee Fund, 1962: 165; Saint Louis Art Museum, Missouri, USA / Funds given by the Shoenberg Foundation, Inc.: 168; Detroit Institute of Arts, USA: 172; Empire State Plaza Art Collection, Albany, New York, USA / Photo © Boltin Picture Library: 177. **Estate of Mark Rothko**: Collection of Christopher Rothko: 19, 28–29 & 91, 144; Collection of Kate Rothko Prizel: 18, 90 & front cover; Museum of Modern Art, New York: 33. **Harvard Art Museums**/Fogg Museum, Transfer from Harvard University, Gift of the Artist, 2011.638.1/Imaging Department © President and Fellows of Harvard College: 169. **NGA Images/National Gallery of Art, Washington**: Gift of The Mark Rothko Foundation, Inc.: 3 & 141, 6–7 & 185, 10, 14, 15, 22, 23, 26, 32, 36, 37, 40, 44, 45, 48, 49, 52, 56, 60, 61, 64, 68, 69, 72, 73, 76, 77, 83, 86, 87, 94, 95, 98, 106, 122, 130, 131, 132–33 & 148, 149, 160, 161, 164, 176, 180, 181, 184, 192; Gift of Enid A. Haupt: 78–79 & 114; Collection of Mrs. Paul Mellon, in Honor of the 50th Anniversary of the National Gallery of Art: 126, 127. Rothko Chapel, Houston, Texas/Photo by Hickey-Robertson: 4.

index

Page numbers in *italics* indicate illustrations.

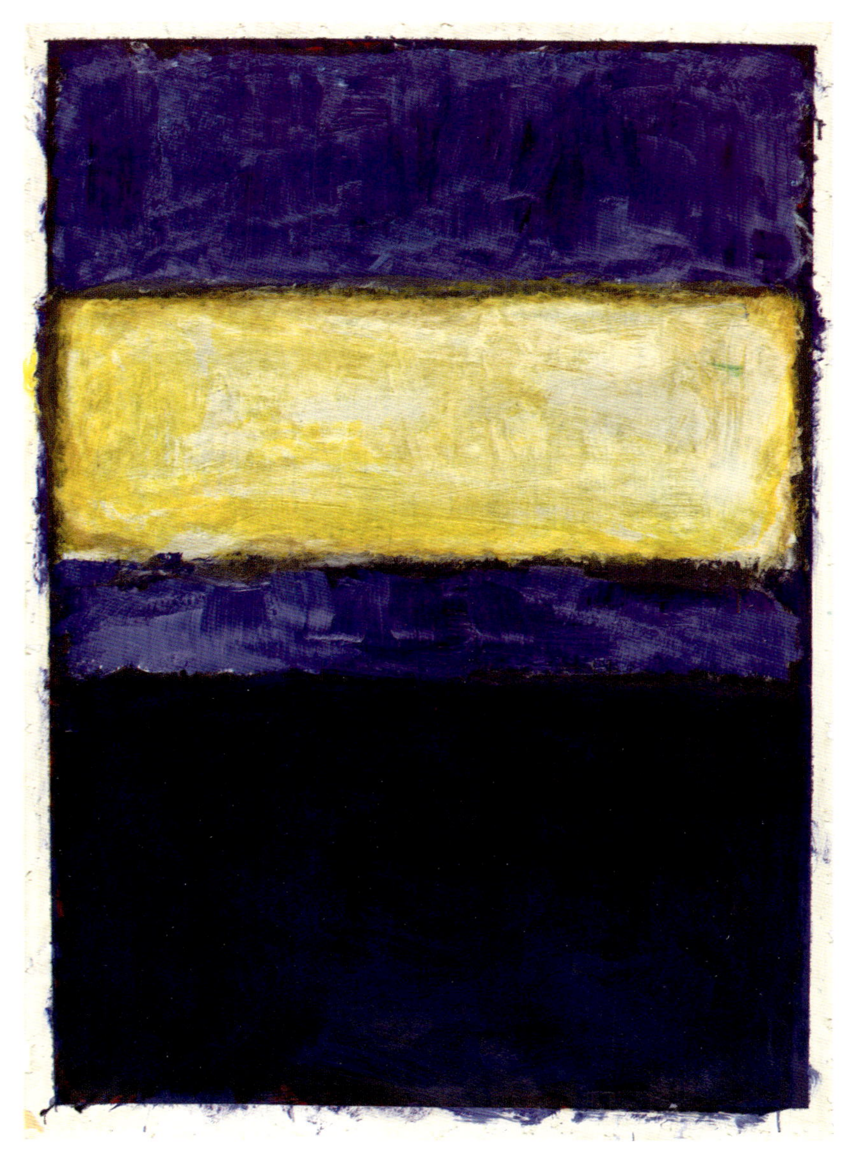

For further illustrated books on a wide range of
art subjects, in various formats, please look at our website:
www.flametreepublishing.com